Postmodern, Feminist and Postcolonial Currents in Contemporary Japanese Culture

This book analyses the fictional and critical work of four contemporary Japanese writers: Murakami Haruki, Yoshimoto Banana, Yoshimoto Takaaki and Karatani Kōjin. Murakami Fuminobu uses the Euro-American theoretical framework of postmodernism, feminism and postcolonialism to examine the work of these writers and also reconsiders postmodern theory itself from the perspective of Japanese literary work.

Murakami Fuminobu is associate professor in the Department of Japanese Studies at the University of Hong Kong. He specialises in Japanese literature and his research interest lies in *monogatari* and *shōsetsu*.

Routledge/Asian Studies Association of Australia (ASAA) East Asia Series

Edited by Tessa Morris-Suzuki and Morris Low

Editorial Board: Dr Gemerie Barmé (Australian National University), Professor Colin Mackerras (Griffith University), Professor Vera Mackie (Curtin University) and Associate Professor Sonia Ryang (John Hopkins University).

This series represents a showcase for the latest cutting-edge research in the field of East Asian studies, from both established scholars and rising academics. It will include studies from every part of the East Asian region (including China, Japan, North and South Korea and Taiwan) as well as comparative studies dealing with more than one country. Topics covered may be contemporary or historical, and relate to any of the humanities or social sciences. The series is an invaluable source of information and challenging perspectives for advanced students and researchers alike.

Routledge is pleased to invite proposals for new books in the series. In the first instance, any interested authors should contact:

Professor Tessa Morris-Suzuki
Division of Pacific and Asian History
Research School of Pacific and Asian Studies
Australian National University
Canberra, ACT0200 Australia

Professor Morris Low
Johns Hopkins University
Department of the History of Science and Technology
3505 N. Charles Street
Baltimore, MD 21218, USA

Postmodern, feminist and postcolonial currents in contemporary Japanese culture

A reading of Murakami Haruki, Yoshimoto Banana, Yoshimoto Takaaki and Karatani Kōjin

Murakami Fuminobu

LONDON AND NEW YORK

First published 2005
by Routledge
2 Park Square, Milton Park, Abingdon, Oxon, OX14 4RN

Simultaneously published in the USA and Canada
by Routledge
270 Madison Ave, New York NY 10016

Routledge is an imprint of the Taylor & Francis Group

Transferred to Digital Printing 2009

© 2005 Murakami Fuminobu

Typeset in Times by
Taylor & Francis Books

British Library Cataloguing in Publication Data
A catalogue record for this book is available from the British Library

Library of Congress Cataloging in Publication Data
A catalog record for this book has been requested

ISBN10: 0–415–35807–8 (hbk)
ISBN10: 0–415–54664–8 (pbk)

ISBN13: 978–0–415–35807–1 (hbk)
ISBN13: 978–0–415–54664–5 (pbk)

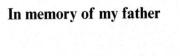
In memory of my father

Contents

Illustrations

Preface

The original manuscript of this book was written in Hong Kong between 1995 and 1998 with financial support from the Committee on Research and Conference Grants, University of Hong Kong, as a publication project for a book entitled *Postmodern Japanese Literature*. The research was completed in June 1999, but the manuscript took two years to find a potential publisher. In late 2001, I sent the publication proposal to the Asian Studies Association of Australia, East Asia Publication Series. The editors of the series, Professor Morris Low and Professor Tessa Morris-Suzuki – and their editor at Routledge, Mr Joe Whiting – suggested that I update the research and resubmit a new manuscript. Following their suggestions, the revised version was completed in March 2003 under the new title of *Postmodern, Feminist and Postcolonial Japanese Literature: Murakami Haruki, Yoshimoto Banana, Yoshimoto Takaaki and Karatani Kōjin*. Furthermore, following one of the reviewer's comments in the process of reviewing, I discussed the title with a new editor at Routledge, Ms Stephanie Rogers, and we finally arrived at the present title of *Postmodern, Feminist and Postcolonial Currents in Contemporary Japanese Culture: A Reading of Murakami Haruki, Yoshimoto Banana, Yoshimoto Takaaki and Karatani Kōjin*. Under this new title I want to indicate that the book's concern is not only Japanese literary criticism and analysis *per se* but more widely the intellectual issues identified therein.

A draft of Chapter 1 was presented, in English, at a seminar organised by the Committee for the Betterment of the Postmodern World at the University of Hong Kong in October 1996, entitled 'Murakami Haruki's Postmodern World'. An abridged version of this chapter was also published in the journal *Japan Forum* (volume 14, no. 1, April 2002, website *www.tandf.co.uk/journals*) under the title 'Murakami Haruki's Postmodern World' (Murakami F. 2002a). The main part of Chapter 2 was presented, in Japanese, at a graduate seminar organised by the Department of Japanese Studies, University of Hong Kong, in November 1997, under the title 'Yoshimoto Banana no kazoku' ('Yoshimoto Banana's Family'). This chapter was also abridged and submitted to the *Romanian Journal of Japanese Studies*, as an article entitled 'Yoshimoto Banana's Feminine Family'. At the time of writing it has not yet appeared. Part of Chapter 3 was presented, in Japanese, at a conference held at the Centre for Japanese Studies, Nankai University, Tianjin, China, in September 2001, entitled 'Yoshimoto Takaaki and Globalisation'. The presented paper was later translated into Chinese and published in the conference proceedings in August 2002 (Murakami F. 2002b). Chapter 4 and the introductory and concluding chapters are presented here for the first time. The parts which originally appeared in *Japan Forum* and the conference proceedings are used with permission.

I would like to thank the Committee on Research and Conference Grants of the University of Hong Kong for financially supporting this project, the organisers of the above seminars and conferences for giving me chances to present my papers, and their participants for their valuable comments. I also thank Marie Lenstrup, Mark McLelland and Chantal Stoughton who helped edit my English in this book. Without their help, this book would never have been published. Thank you indeed. My sincere thanks also go to anonymous referees commissioned by Routledge; the editor of *Japan Forum*; Mark Williams; two editors of the Asian Studies Association of Australia, East Asia Publication Series; Morris Low and Tessa Morris-Suzuki, and Joe Whiting and Stephanie Rogers, editors at Routledge.

I would also like to thank the Centre for Physical Education and Sport, University of Hong Kong, and the Hong Kong Philharmonic Orchestra. These may seem unusual acknowledgements, but both provided me with much-needed relaxation while I was working on this book.

I would also like to thank my friends, colleagues and students for keeping my spirits up, especially Jeremy Tambling for his valuable comments on the book. Needless to say, I am much indebted to the four Japanese writers dealt with in this book – Murakami Haruki, Yoshimoto Banana, Yoshimoto Takaaki and Karatani Kōjin. I know none of them personally, but I hope they will forgive me for taking the liberty of making generalisations about their rich and profound works. Lastly, my family: thanks to my wife Kiyama Tomoko, our daughter Nanako, and our parents, siblings and their families. They warm my heart and cool my brain. I dedicate this book to my late father who passed away before this book was published.

Note: All Japanese names appear in Japanese order, that is, surname first; for instance, Murakami Haruki, instead of Haruki Murakami.

Murakami Fuminobu
Hong Kong, June 2004

Introduction
Western ideologies and Japan

Rationality's dubious legitimacy and its oppressive factor

This book aims to analyse the fictional and critical work of four contemporary Japanese writers, Murakami Haruki, Yoshimoto Banana, Yoshimoto Takaaki and Karatani Kōjin, using the Euro-American theoretical framework of postmodernism, feminism and postcolonialism. In the process of analysis, I will attempt not only to use Euro-American theory to examine the work of the above authors, but also to reconsider this body of theory itself by looking back on it from the perspective of Japanese literary work.

In this introductory chapter first I shall briefly summarise the focal points of modernism and postmodernism discussed in this book and make a short historical survey of the debate on them. I will introduce theories of feminism and postcolonialism in Chapters 3 and 4 respectively, in relation to Yoshimoto Banana's and Yoshimoto Takaaki's works. My understanding is that the conceptual paradigm shift brought about by postmodernist theory contributed in important ways to the feminist and postcolonial movements.

Theoretically, postmodernism in general attacked the legitimacy of the rationalism that underlay the Enlightenment project. Rationality emancipated us from the irrationality and despotism of the pre-Enlightenment period and established individual sovereignty of the mind. Thus, to completely discard rationality is a proposal nobody would support. But at the same time, any accepted mode of thought must be subject to review – and rationality is not an exception. In this book I will focus on two aspects of rationalism that postmodernists reject – rationality's dubious legitimacy and its oppressive factor. These two are key issues that connect postmodernism with feminism and postcolonialism. Until these dubious aspects of rationality became clear, it was considered a universal truth. This realisation opened up the discussion on male-centred and Euro-American-centred rationality, recognising it as oppressing female and non-Euro-American people.

Nietzsche was one of the first to challenge Western understanding of rationality-based morality. His 'genealogy' showed supposedly moral virtues to be rooted in power-relations. Nietzsche revealed that 'good' is nothing other than what is considered 'noble', 'aristocratic' and 'high', while 'bad' is 'common', 'plebeian' and 'low' (Nietzsche 1967: 27–28). We can list many examples of moral judgements that support Nietzsche's insistence. We implicitly approve of the 'strong is good' ideology, because as Nietzsche suggested, the ideology that 'stronger' or 'higher' or, in Nietzsche's terminology, 'will to power', is good underlies all rational moral judgement. However, Nietzsche's conclusions are different from those characteristic of postmodernism, in that Nietzsche approved of power. That is, although he pointed out the arbitrary nature of moral values based as they are on power-relations, he actually justified this kind of morality in terms of the 'will to power' and attacked Christianity for favouring the weak. We will return to this point later.

As often cited, Max Weber has also offered a critique of rationality in his analysis of bureaucracy described below:

> The bureaucratic state apparatus, and the rational *homo politicus* integrated into the state, manage affairs, including the punishment of evil, when they discharge business in the most ideal sense, according to the rational rules of the state order. In this, the political man acts just like the economic man, in a matter-of-fact manner 'without regard to the person', *sine ira et studio*, without hate and therefore without love. By virtue of its depersonalization, the bureaucratic state, in important points, is less accessible to substantive moralization than were the patriarchal orders of the past, however many appearances may point to the contrary.
>
> (Weber 1991: 333–334)

As Best and Kellner point out, Weber argued that 'uncontrolled rationalization could turn into a form of bureaucratic and institutional domination, in which bureaucratic elites and institutions justify their power and authority on the grounds of superior knowledge and by claiming that their power embodies the claims of reason itself' (Best and Kellner 1991: 219). In contrast to Nietzsche who detected the immoral basis of morality, Weber discerned in rationality a sort of depersonalising force being exercised on people. Yet Weber's ideas are even more alien than Nietzsche's to the postmodern ideology, in that he represents humanism; although he pointed out the problems inherent in rationality, he did so from the perspective of humanistic love and respect. Michel Foucault distinguishes humanism from the Enlightenment and inclines to see both of them in a state of tension rather than identity (Foucault 1984: 42–45). However, the concept of 'love' and 'hate' (humanism) described by Weber as being subsumed in state bureaucracy (the Enlightenment) is, as will be discussed later, typically modern.

In 1947, Horkheimer and Adorno published a book called *The Dialectic of Enlightenment* where, following ideas outlined by Weber and Nietzsche, they argued that the logic implicit in Enlightenment rationality was a logic of domination and oppression. According to Horkheimer and Adorno, modern men only wanted to learn about the natural world in order to dominate and manipulate it and other men. The progress of Western society since the Enlightenment has been towards an increasingly totalitarian dictatorship over nature and people (Horkheimer and Adorno 1973: 6–24). Consequently they argued that the lust for domination over nature entailed the domination of human beings, and that could only lead, in the end, to 'a nightmare condition of self-domination' (Bernstein 1985: 6; Harvey 1989: 13).

In a fully rational society, individuals are obliged to conform to the models of that society's leaders who supposedly represent superior rationality and knowledge. The result is domination, oppression, and a totalitarian and authoritarian society in which the rationally weak are suppressed by bureaucratic or economic power which works in the interests of the rationally strong. In this kind of society, rationality or Enlightenment does not automatically embody freedom and progress, but rather something completely opposite (Best and Kellner 1991: 218–219; Young 1990: 7). Hence, postmodern theorists build upon these insights and reject rationalism (the Enlightenment project) not only because of its dubious legitimacy but also because of its inherently oppressive and suppressive factors.

Despite these many critics, rationalism still has its supporters, including, as we will see soon, Habermas and Giddens. One of the basic elements underlying the reliability of rationality is the necessity of evolution. We have long admired rationality because we have considered it as the only way to evolve or progress. Nietzsche's 'will to power' also stems from the longing for evolution. For him, fairness as represented by Christianity is degradation, while the will to power is progress. Nietzsche regards the Christian doctrine valorising the weak and preaching equality to be not only hypocritical but also impossible, for human beings are destined to evolve. Yet, we have a problem: if the idea that 'rationality-is-good' or 'strong-is-good' is closely related to the 'evolution-is-good' ideology, and the driving force behind modernity is this notion of 'evolution-is-good', then, if evolution is discarded, what kind of implications will this have for social advancement?

As early as the beginning of the twentieth century, Henri Bergson cautioned that unless the human race ceaselessly progresses, even courting fatigue, then human evolution will be retarded, stopped, or dragged back by its tendency towards the vegetative life (Bergson 1920: 119). Whether it is possible or not to remain at a certain stage of evolution, or to slow down the speed of evolution, is beyond the scope of this discussion. But it seems clear that one of the main factors preventing the realisation of human freedom, equity, and emancipation is the need for evolution. If we discard evolution, surely a happy society of contented people would be the result. In this realm, disenchantment with rationality, knowledge and power, and at the same time a lack of empathic emotion, in other words apathy, all co-exist: as we will see later, this is the postmodern utopia/dystopia specifically narrated in some of Murakami Haruki's fiction.

As David Harvey laments, the optimism characteristic of modernism has been shattered by the twentieth century with its two world wars, its death camps, the destruction of Hiroshima and Nagasaki and the threat of nuclear annihilation (Harvey 1989: 13). Wars are still being fought between different ethnic and religious groups who label each other terrorists. They are, in a sense, evidence that an all-pervasive dominating force over human beings is still at work. It also shows that the 'strong-is-good' ideology still remains as the foundation of rationalism. But when Horkheimer and Adorno point out the dehumanising aspects of the rational Enlightenment project, what concept of humanity do they see as being dominated by rationality? Max Weber presents a concept of 'ethos' as the opponent of reason. He says:

> The position of all 'democratic' currents, in the sense of currents that would minimize 'authority', is necessarily ambiguous. 'Equality before the law' and the demand for legal guarantees against arbitrariness demand a formal and rational 'objectivity' of administration, as opposed to the personally free discretion flowing from the 'grace' of the old patrimonial domination. If, however, an 'ethos' – not to speak of instincts – takes hold of the masses on some individual question, it postulates *substantive* justice oriented toward some concrete instance and person; and such an 'ethos' will unavoidably collide with the formalism and the rule-bound and cool 'matter-of-factness' of bureaucratic administration. For this reason, the ethos must emotionally reject what reason demands.
>
> (Weber 1991: 220–221)

Perhaps that which is dominated by rationality is a sort of instinctive emotional and libidinal–aesthetic aspect of humanity; as Weber argued the 'ethos' must emotionally reject what reason demands. But if the emotional aspects of our nature drive us, the result seems to be not dissimilar to being driven by rationality – a nightmare condition of self-domination by emotion.

Emotion or desire (which is called 'mind' in Murakami Haruki's *The Hard-Boiled Wonderland and the End of the World*) is certainly one of the main factors leading many people to commit acts of violence. René Girard clarifies the relation between mimetic desire and violence and says: 'Mimetism is a source of continual conflict. By making one man's desire into a replica of another man's desire, it invariably leads to rivalry; and rivalry in turn transforms desire into violence' (Girard 1977: 169). But besides rivalry, we should not neglect the fact that the emotions of love and respect become sources of violence, though they may also derive from mimetism. The idea of rivalry is related to the notion of progress, evolution and the 'strong-is-good' ideology based upon individuality, whereas love and respect are connected to identification and totality. Thus, love and respect for one's own people can be seen as the hidden face behind fascism,

Stalinism and Japanese militarism: when one sees one's beloved people, including oneself, oppressed by outsiders, one resists with violence. Although, obviously, the domination aspect or the 'strong-is-good' ideology of rationalism is also a source of the rivalry supporting nationalism, imperialism and ethnocentrism, we should not overlook the role of love and respect as a source of totalitarian violence.

In the modern period, love and respect have long been considered beautiful emotions. But they have negative aspects, too. If love is a merging which 'breaks down the barriers of the ego, fusing the separate senses of self into a common identity' (Gaylin 1986: 20–21), it must be closely related to the common, social identity that discriminates outsiders from insiders. We love 'inside' people with whom we share a common social identity. To identify with that to which one belongs, however, results not only in love of the same but also in discrimination against the 'Other', thus creating an ideology of 'insiders-are-secure' and 'outsiders-are-dangerous'.[1] Once you identify yourself as a member of your family and love it, you must discriminate against other families; once you belong to your nation-state, you must differentiate other nations; once you attach yourself to your own ethnic group, you must separate from other ethnic groups; once you identify yourself with your own gender, you must distinguish yourself from other genders, and so on. Almost always the latter are constructed as enemies and the former as friends. A deep love for one's own culture often leads to hatred of another culture to which one does not belong.

Andreas Huyssen mentions that 'Auschwitz, after all, did not result from too much enlightened reason – even though it was organised as a perfectly rationalized death factory – but from a violent anti-enlightenment and anti-modernity affect, which exploited modernity ruthlessly for its own purposes' (Huyssen 1990: 255). In contrast, Zygmunt Bauman challenges the view that the Holocaust was a failure, not a product, of modernity. He maintains that the Holocaust was born and executed exactly in our modern rational society, and for this reason, it is a problem of that society, civilisation and culture. As a fundamental purpose of genocide, Bauman pinpoints a grand vision of a perfect society. Consequently, for Bauman, the compelling force of progress in modernity is the major cause of the Holocaust (Bauman 1989: x, 5, 13–14, 76, 91). Introducing Bauman's study, Jim McGuigan claims, probably following Habermas's argument, the importance of separation between the formal and substantive rationality, or instrumental or purposive reason and critical reason or the 'reason' of using the rationality (McGuigan 1999: 45–46).[2]

It seems that for McGuigan, as well as for Huyssen, the fundamental factor that led modern people to genocide is the depersonalised and dehumanised aspect of instrumental or purposive rationality. But, witnessing the subsequent and continuous genocides and terrorisms still occurring at the beginning of the twenty-first century, one cannot but feel difficulty in supporting the idea that the problem of the purposive rationality is only one factor causing all these tragedies. In this regard, I agree with Bauman when he writes that, though the instrumental rationality was the Holocaust's *necessary* condition, it was not its *sufficient* condition (Bauman 1989: 13).

Behind the will to progress pointed out by Bauman, there must be a tendency that strong people attempt to unite with each other, by means of excluding weak people. This is, in a sense, part of the phenomenon of 'homosociality' pointed out by Eve Kosofsky Sedgwick (1985: 1–5; 1991: 87–88). Also, besides the will to progress and homosociality, I would like to pay attention here, as another major factor that leads us to genocide, to the emotion and desire of humanity. If one of the key modern ideologies is 'love-is-beautiful' which implies violence towards others who are considered dangerous to one's beloved, then not only Auschwitz but also many other genocides are certainly products of modernity.[3] In such different levels as individuals, families, nation-states, ethnic groups, etc., we form distinctions between 'inside' and 'outside', or homogeneous and heterogeneous. Insiders are united with the ideology of 'love-is-beautiful' and fight with outsiders on the basis of 'strong-is-good' ideology. Erotic desire and the desire to do violence are certainly closely related to these categories and the problem of discrimination also appears here.

These two ideologies, 'strong-is-good' and 'love-is-beautiful' hidden behind the rational morality and emotion/desire are typically modern ideologies, and it is apparent that the domination of one human being by another can be achieved both through rationality and through emotion/desire. Rationality, in a sense, is formed on the basis of recognition, and thus, as Ferdinand de Saussure has argued, based on differentiation, but at the same time it unavoidably abstracts common features from individual existences, and consequently neglects their uniqueness. In contrast, emotion/desire, as has been mentioned, also plays two roles – identification with the same and discrimination against others. These four ideas are closely related. In a sense it can be said that the modernist is torn between two extremely polarising axes, individual differentiation and totalitarian identification, arising both from rationality and emotion, which as a whole is destined to evolve.

A key figure in considering the relation between rationality and emotion/desire is Michel Foucault whose work analyses the relation between power structures and knowledge. Having pointed out the sterility of focusing solely upon the evident relationship between increasing rationalisation and political power, Foucault attempted to analyse power relations from a new perspective. In order to understand how power relations work, he investigated various forms of resistance to power and attempts made to dislocate power relations (Foucault 1983: 210–211). Foucault examined the ways in which people struggle against power and pointed out that the fundamental struggle was against the 'government of individualisation'. In these conflicts, the right to be different is asserted and everything which makes individuals truly unique is emphasised on the one hand, while everything which separates the individual from the community, everything which breaks the links between individuals, or forces the individual back on himself and ties him to his own identity in a constraining way is simultaneously attacked (Foucault 1983: 211–212). Foucault concludes his essay by saying that:

> Maybe the target nowadays is not to discover what we are, but to refuse what we are. We have to imagine and to build up what we could be to get rid of this kind of political 'double bind', which is the simultaneous individualization and totalization of modern power structures.
>
> The conclusion would be that the political, ethical, social, philosophical problem of our days is not to try to liberate the individual from the state, and from the state's institutions, but to liberate us both from the state and from the type of individualization which is linked to the state. We have to promote new forms of subjectivity through the refusal of this kind of individuality, which has been imposed on us for several centuries.
>
> (Foucault 1983: 216)

In terms of our discussion, the simultaneous individualisation and totalisation of modern power structures outlined by Foucault, can be interpreted as differentiation from and identification with others underlying two modernist ideologies 'strong-is-good' and 'love-is-beautiful'. To put this into our context, Foucault is saying here that we have to try to liberate ourselves from individual differentiation and totalitarian identification, arising both from rationality and emotion. Our essential problem in this book is this modernist dichotomy, which emerges at various levels of society. From Chapters 2 to 4 we will repeatedly discuss this issue by analysing the work of four writers.

In order to overcome the modernist predicament, Deleuze and Guattari advocate schizophrenic infinitesimal lines of escape, instead of the paranoiac fascisizing perspective of the large aggregates (Deleuze and Guattari 1984: 276–280). They recognise that in modern Western capitalist society 'everything moves to the rhythm of one and the same desire, founded *on the differential relation of flows having no assignable exterior limit, and where capitalism reproduces its immanent limits on an ever widening and more comprehensive scale*' (Deleuze and Guattari 1984: 239; emphasis in the original). But there seems to be another way to escape from the paranoiac modern capitalist nightmare, no matter how static, infertile and suicidal it may seem. It is to stop here, go around and eternally repeat the same. Schizophrenic escape seems to be in a sense a modification of the dynamic movements along the lines of Nietzsche's 'will to power', Bergson's '*élan vital*', Marx's 'historical materialism', Freud's 'Oedipal triangle' and so on, although, unlike these, schizophrenic escape is not necessarily oriented in the direction of rivalry and evolution. In contrast to these vital movements, the eternal repetition of the same is a world of sweet slumber and nostalgia.

Murakami Haruki's postmodern world and Yoshimoto Banana's feminine family, as we will see later, exist in the latter paradigm, in which the protagonists feel comfortable in distancing themselves from all extreme rationalisation, emotionality, totalisation, and individualisation, favouring instead indifference and detachment. The waning of affect, which Fredric Jameson has pointed out as one of the features of postmodernism thus, emerges here (Jameson 1991: 10).

What, then, motivates their postmodern heroes and heroines? Free from rationality and emotion, individualism and totalism, what moves them? Probably nothing. As often mentioned in the postmodern discourse, 'nihilism' (Baudrillard 1984; Kellner 1989: 117–121) appears on the surface and 'gaming' (Lyotard 1985) is also one of the main strategies they live by. Perhaps the two most crucial standards informing a postmodern perspective are fairness and justice and these will be discussed later in relation to Murakami Haruki's novel *Norwegian Wood*.

Before we go on, let me briefly define here the concept of modern/modernity/modernism used in this book. Best and Kellner in their earlier book *Postmodern Theory* distinguish between 'modernity' conceptualised as the modern age and 'postmodernity' as an epochal term for describing the period which allegedly follows modernity in the field of social theory. They also highlight the contrast between 'modernism' and 'postmodernism' in the arts in which 'modernism' is used to describe the art movements of the modern age (impressionism, *l'art pour l'art*, expressionism, surrealism, and other avant-garde movements), while 'postmodernism' describes the diverse aesthetic forms and practices which come after and break with modernism (the architecture of Robert Venturi and Philip Johnson, the musical experiments of John Cage, the art of Andy Warhol and Robert Rauschenberg, the novels of Thomas Pynchon and J. G. Ballard, and films like *Blade Runner* or *Blue Velvet*) (Best and Kellner 1991: 2–4).[4]

In contrast to Best and Kellner, Terry Eagleton first introduces the general understanding that 'postmodernity' refers to a style of thought which is suspicious of classical notions of truth, reason, identity and objectivity, of the idea of universal progress or emancipation, of single frameworks, and of grand narratives or ultimate grounds of explanation. It sees the world as contingent, ungrounded, diverse, unstable, indeterminate, a set of disunified cultures or interpretations which breed a degree of scepticism about the objectivity of truth, history and norms, the givenness of natures and the coherence of identities. In contrast, 'postmodernism' is, Eagleton suggests, a style of culture which reflects something of this epochal change, in a depthless, de-centred, ungrounded, self-reflexive, playful, derivative, eclectic, pluralistic art which blurs the boundaries between 'high' and 'popular' culture, as well as between art and everyday experience. Upon introducing this distinction as a general concept, Eagleton however says that he tends to stick to the more familiar term 'postmodernism' to cover both of these things, since they are clearly closely related (Eagleton 1996: vii–viii).

In this book, however, I define the concept of modern/modernity/modernism mainly as an ideology in which the struggle for power is dominant, though these terms are occasionally used spatio-temporally. For the focus of this book will be on the way in which power structures act as a pivot for the two ideologies – modernism and postmodernism. It is possible to argue for instance that the modern in Japan commenced with the Meiji Restoration (1868) and the policy of open trade with the West, or that its seeds were already present in the thought of some Neo-Confucian scholars in the Edo period (1603–1867). It can also be contended that in non-Western cultures modernisation is nothing other than Westernisation. However, I do not use the terms modern/modernity/modernism in this book primarily as spatio-temporal concepts, but as terms which specifically designate an ideology which values power, ideals, enlightenment, the future, development, progress, advancement, evolution, etc., and which has existed throughout history and which still exists in the present globalised world.

My understanding is, however, that this modernist ideology has been gaining in strength throughout human history and was greatly accelerated by the triumph of rationalism in the Enlightenment project of the eighteenth century, finally reaching its zenith in the global capitalist systems of the present period. In contrast, I consider postmodernism to be the tendency to oppose modernism in various ways. Thus, I sometimes use the terms 'modern Western culture' and 'capitalism' not in a spatio-temporal sense, but as indicating modernism, in the sense that they are both representative of modernist ideology.

Debate on modernism and postmodernism from the 1980s

From the early 1980s to the mid-1990s the academic world appeared to be dominated by terminology developed in postmodern discourse. The subversion of subjectivity, anti-totalitarianism, power/knowledge, deconstruction, schizophrenia, pluralism, gaming, difference, etc. were key concepts in a wide variety of fields and they took root in the wider academic world. In the continuous debates concerning modernism and postmodernism in the late 1990s some prominent criticisms against postmodernism appeared. First, from a scientific viewpoint, Alan Sokal and Jean Bricmont's *Fashionable Nonsense: Postmodern Intellectuals' Abuse of Science* (1998) revealed, as its title indicates, the abuse of science by the postmodern philosophers.

Also, from the perspective of other cultures, Denis Ekpo in Nigeria writes that for hungry Africa, the celebrated 'postmodern condition' is 'nothing but the hypocritical self-flattering cry of overfed and spoiled children of hyper-capitalism' and 'the postmaterial disgust and ratiocination of the bored and the overfed' (Ekpo 1995: 122). British–Pakistani writer Ziauddin Sardar also insists that, far from being a new theory of liberation, postmodernism, particularly from the perspective of the non-Western culture, is simply a new wave of domination riding on the crest of colonisation of non-western cultures. For Sardar, by discovering 'Otherness' everywhere and arguing that everything is relative, postmodernism is incapable of suggesting that everything is in some distinctive way itself, and consequently it avoids the politics of non-western marginalisation. He says that the postmodern world of free choices is open only to the individuals in Europe, North America and other rich countries; they do not include those dying of famine in Africa, where at least one billion citizens living in an abject poverty in rural areas cannot choose not to live below the poverty line (Sardar 1998: 13–19).

It seems that both Ekpo and Sardar overemphasise the continuation from modernism to postmodernism, and that they neglect or at least underestimate the anti-modernist aspect of postmodernism which has been discussed in the previous section of this chapter. Nevertheless, it is obvious that, as they insist, we have to seriously consider people in poverty who are struggling for survival, and problematise the theoretical frame that cannot help them.

In contrast to these criticisms of postmodernism, there are studies that support the modernist project. As I have mentioned, Jürgen Habermas and Anthony Giddens are the central figures in this field who see potential in the modernist endeavour or attempt to maintain the view that the project of intellectual modernity is revisable and renewable. Habermas insists that in order to resolve the problems which exist between rationality and power structures, we should give up instrumental or purposive rationality, subject-centred reason, which functions as a dominating force, and rely instead on communicative rationality, reason understood as *communicative* action, as a mode of freedom and progress (Habermas 1984–1987 II: 1; 1993: vii).

Whereas, Ulrich Beck, Anthony Giddens and Scott Lash advocate the 'reflexive modernity' and insist on the possibility of a creative (self-)destruction, in which one kind of modernisation undercuts and changes another modernisation. They assert that, if the orthodox modernisation means the disembedding and re-embedding of traditional social forms by industrial social forms, then the reflexive modernisation means the disembedding and re-embedding of industrial social forms by another modernity. In this sphere modernisation, understanding its own excesses and vicious spiral of destructive subjugation (of inner, outer and social nature), begins to take itself as an object of reflection (Beck *et al.* 1994: 2, 112).[5] What is underlying the reflexive modernisation seems to be the idea of progress. Though it is opposed to the concept of *linear* progress, *reflexive* seems to be an incessant continuation of progress, reflex and new progress (Beck *et al.* 1994: 11–12; Giddens 1990: 36–45; Giddens 1991: 20–21).

In contrast to these criticisms of postmodernism, at the turn of the new century we witnessed some continuous studies of postmodernism appearing. Fredric Jameson, following his *Postmodernism, Or, The Cultural Logic Of Late Capitalism* (1991), presents his general survey on postmodernism and Marxism in his *The Cultural Turn* (1998). Steven Best and Douglas Kellner in their book *The Postmodern Adventure* (2001) consider that the postmodern movement is far from being a fad or momentary fashion and take the view that we are now between the modern and the postmodern, in an interim period between epochs, where we are undergoing spectacular changes in all realms. They compare it with the Renaissance when people were between the premodern and the modern (Best and Kellner 2001: 5, 12).

In *Postmodern Debates* (2001), which contains important works of post-modern theorists, Simon Malpas insists that the postmodern is neither a contemporary fashion nor a unified movement, but it is a space of debate. He also cautions us against the move led by the media frenzy and subsequent fade-away of the interest in postmodernism, because it fails to address the deeper and more radical changes that are taking place in the world today (Malpas 2001: 1–2). Furthermore, in academic fields at least partially derived from or parallel to postmodernism, such as feminism, lesbian and gay studies, postcolonialism and multiculturism, new research is constantly being presented.[6]

Although it is certain that, compared with the theoretical currents of the 1980s and 1990s, the debate on modernism and postmodernism at the beginning of the 2000s appears to have in general subsided, I will insist that postmodernism still deserves discussion, especially at a time when people still tend to be persuaded that strong military power is crucially important. I will argue that postmodernism is one of the ways towards a world without violence. Even if the paradigm shift of postmodernism, together with that of feminism, lesbianism, homosexuality and postcolonialism is over, their movements must continue until a truly egalitarian, violence-free, genderless, homophobia-free and ethnicity-free society appears.

In any case, what modernism and postmodernism achieved, caused and aimed at are increasingly visible now: modernism realised individual freedom from traditional and archaic collective life. It engendered hope and a spirit of endeavour and fostered romantic love. At the same time the competitive element within it provoked wars, coercive totalitarianism and discrimination. Taking these modernist characteristics into consideration, postmodernism and other theories derived from it or that appeared along-side it, insist on a new ideology that attempts to realise a freer, more equal and less violent society. Modernism, postmodernism, reflexive modernism, feminism, homosexuality, postcolonialism or globalisation – whichever camp one chooses, or whether one rejects them all, we are at a momentous stage in the history of thought.

Postmodernism, feminism, postcolonialism and Japan

In this section I shall briefly overview the recent postmodern, feminist and postcolonial studies on and in Japan. One of the epoch-making events in the 1980s and 1990s in the Euro-American studies on Japan based on Western postmodern perspectives was the publication of *Postmodernism and Japan* (1989) edited by Miyoshi Masao and H. D. Harootunian. Besides two editors, prominent figures such as Marilyn Ivy, Isozaki Arata, Sakai Naoki, J. Victor Koschmann, Ōe Kenzaburō, Bett de Bary, Karatani Kōjin and Asada Akira, contributed chapters, and the book initiated the postmodern study on Japan. Two other books, *Japanese Encounters with Postmodernity* and *Multicultural Japan: Palaeolithic to Postmodern* appeared in 1995 and 1996 respectively. In

Japanese Encounters with Postmodernity one of the editors Johann P. Arnason regards the postmodern epoch as 'merely another episode within the unfolding, and open-ended constellation of modernity' (Arnason and Sugimoto 1995: 24). This book is therefore under the influence of the above-mentioned reflexive modernisation advocated by Giddens and others. The second book, *Multicultural Japan*, is characterised by Gavan McCormack as, 'post-modern cultural relativism rather than any sort of hegemonism, European or Japanese' (Denoon *et al.* 1996: 3).[7] With regard to Japanese literature in particular, Toshiko Ellis's chapter contribution to the above-mentioned *Japanese Encounters with Postmodernity* is very helpful in understanding the postmodern features of Murakami Haruki's work (Ellis 1995). John Whittier Treat's study of Yoshimoto Banana is a useful starting point for analysing postmodern trends in Japanese writing (Treat 1993, 1995), as is Susan Jolliffe Napier's book on modern Japanese literature (Napier 1996).

However, other than these studies, as far as I know, no serious attempt has yet been made to use Euro-American theories of postmodernism, feminism and postcolonialism to analyse contemporary Japanese literature in English. Certainly, a direct comparison between Euro-American post-modern, feminist and postcolonial writers and their Japanese counterparts does not seem a promising topic. Also it is doubtful whether Euro-American theory is applicable to the output of other cultures. Since the contemporary situation in Japan has arisen from specific historical factors, it cannot be simplistically related to Western ideas of postmodernism, feminism and postcolonialism. As we will discuss later in this book, together with Ashcroft, Griffiths and Tiffin, Yoshimoto Takaaki suggests that logic or theories derived from Western cultures are not suitable for analysing the situation in Japan (Ashcroft *et al.* 1989: 11; Yoshimoto 1968–1975 XIII: 17).

However, it is also true that there are common currents underlying global modernisation in the form of power cults and postmodern, feminist and postcolonial strategies of resistance to them. Moreover, as we will confirm with Jace Weaver later, any culture needs to change in contact with other cultures (Weaver 2000: 227–228). Also, as we will note when we consider Perry Anderson's study, if we analyse our own culture and society according to our own cultural and social theories, there is the danger of ending up with the ethnocentric enclosure of each culture and no communication between cultures. We should call for feedback and dynamic interaction between different cultures, by looking at our own culture from a shifted perspective. I hope that through this meeting of two distinct different cultures the boundaries that restrict both Japanese and western modes of analysis can be challenged and transcended. Thus, the manner in which Euro-American theory is adopted, consumed and subverted in Japan is a topic that deserves consideration. I will therefore make that attempt in this book in the hope of not only looking at Japanese culture from a different viewpoint, but also presenting a new look at postmodernism, feminism and postcolonialism – theories previously produced and consumed almost exclusively within the Euro-American sphere.

Asada Akira, an economist and sociologist, first introduced postmodern theories to a Japanese audience in the early 1980s. He was a key figure in the so-called *Nyū aka* (new academism) movement. His work focused on Deleuze and Guattari (Asada 1983). But, after a period of two or three years when postmodern ideas were much in vogue in the Japanese academic world, intellectual interest in postmodernism soon faded away. In the 1980s and 1990s much was published outside Japan from the perspective of Euro-American postmodernism – a point of view that, in general, criticises the Enlightenment and rationalism, and takes a generous attitude toward the values of a multicultural society. After the early 1980s postmodernism had little impact in Japan.[8]

It was in this climate that a young philosopher, Azuma Hiroki expressed his interest in postmodernism and published his article 'The Postmodern Reconsidered' ('Posutomodan saikō') and his book *The Animalised Postmodern* (*Dōbutsuka suru posutomodan*) in 2000 and 2001 respectively. Azuma differentiates the postmodernisation of society and the postmodern ideology (postmodernism); the former includes information technology, consumerism, multiculture, subculture, fragmentation, economic globalisation and so on, whereas the latter is a theory originated in the French philosophy. Azuma insists that although the ideology of postmodernism has ended its job of paradigm shift, the postmodernisation of society is still continuing, and that we have to keep on analysing its phenomenon (Azuma 2000).

With regard to Japanese literature in particular, postmodern literary criticism in Japan is generally understood to focus on the collapse of self-identity, along with the death of teleological concepts of history, and structuralist text critique. It is regarded as part of a reaction against the overemphasis on self-identity in modern Japan and consequently the concepts of similarity and lack of uniqueness have been emphasised. Hasumi Shigehiko illustrates this situation when he states that 'if there is a positive significance in postmodernism, it is no more than the methodisation of the awe of similarity' (Hasumi 1994: 94). From a different angle, Takeda Seiji dissolves postmodern literary criticism into the structuralist analysis of system and text critique (Takeda 1996: 3–6).[9] However, other aspects of postmodernism, as have been mentioned, such as its critique of rationalism, power systems, the structure of discrimination, and utopian/dystopian worlds, have not been given sufficient attention in Japanese postmodern literary criticism. These themes will be explored in this book.

Unlike postmodernism, Euro-American feminist thought has been a wide social movement in Japan from the early 1980s onward and has produced many star players in the academic community, although whether the movement resulted in a gender-free egalitarian society in Japan or not is a different issue. Among them, to name only a few, Ueno Chizuko, Ehara

Yumiko and Takemura Kazuko are actively using Euro-American feminist theories to analyse the Japanese situation (Ueno 1990a, 1994, 1998b, 2002; Ueno and Ogura 2002; Ehara 1988, 2001; Takemura 2000). Many of their achievements are compiled in a series of books entitled *Feminism in Japan* (*Nihon no feminizumu*), edited by Inoue Teruko, Ueno Chizuko and Ehara Yumiko, published by Iwanami in 1994–1995.

In the field of English literary study in Japan, Oda Motoko and Watanabe Kazuko introduced feminist literary criticism of English literature and explored their own views on it (Oda 1988; Watanabe 1993). Concerning lesbian/gay studies in Japan, three journals, *Eureka*, *Imago* and *Gendai shisō* (*Contemporary Thought*) featured gay/lesbianism/homosexuality/queer studies several times in the 1990s, and subsequent studies are ongoing.[10]

With regard to Japanese feminist literary criticism, Saegusa Kazuko, Komashaku Kimi and Mizuta Noriko, among others, have been actively working in this field (Saegusa 1991; Komashaku 1984, 1987, 1991, 1992; Mizuta 1982, 1991, 1993, 2003, 2004). Urushida Kazuyo and Kitada Sachie made general surveys of Japanese feminist literary criticism in the fourth volume of *Women's Studies Lecture Series* (*Kōza joseigaku*) in 1987 and in the second volume of *New Feminism Review* in 1991 respectively (Urushida 1987; Kitada 1991). In 1992 Ueno Chizuko, Ogura Chikako and Tomioka Taeko published a book *On Men Writers* (*Danryū bungaku ron*) and criticised six Japanese male writers from the feminist perspective. In the same year Egusa Mitsuko and Urushida Kazuyo edited a book *Readings by Women of Modern Japanese Literature* that compiled various studies of Japanese modern literature from a feminist viewpoint (Egusa and Urushida 1992).

Concerning the female writers, Yonaha Keiko published a book *On Contemporary Women Writers* (*Gendai joryū sakka ron*) in 1986 and Iwabuchi Hiroko, Kitada Sachie and Kōra Rumiko edited a book *Invitation for Feminist Criticism: Reading Modern Female Literature* (*Feminizumu hihyō e no shōtai: Kindai josei bungaku o yomu*) in 1995. The former compiled literary criticism of the work of six contemporary Japanese female writers, and the latter the work of twelve modern Japanese female writers (Yonaha 1986; Iwabuchi *et al.* 1995). With regard to the analysis of Japanese female writers focusing on the sexuality and identity politics from the connecting point of feminism and sexuality, which I attempt to conduct in this book, Ueno Chizuko's and Takemura Kazuko's studies on sexuality are quite useful references (Ueno 1986, 1989, 1998a; Takemura 1996, 2002). Ueno recently also published a book of her writings on Japanese literature previously published on various occasions under the title of *Ueno Chizuko Studies Literature from a Sociological Perspective* (*Ueno Chizuko ga bungaku o shakaigaku suru*) (Ueno 2000).

Postcolonial study is now increasing in importance in Japan. It was however only in 1996 that a round-table discussion between Karatani Kōjin, Sakai Naoki, Murai Osamu and others, entitled 'What is the Postcolonial

Thought?' ('Posutokoroniaru no shisō to wa nani ka'), took place and introduced Euro-American postcolonial thought to Japan.[11] Current postcolonial study in Japan focuses mainly on the issue of the Japanese occupation and colonisation of Korea, Taiwan, Okinawa and so forth. For example, as we will see later, Murai Osamu questions the hidden aim of the research done by Yanagita Kunio (1875–1962). Yanagita was a scholar and poet, and a highly regarded founder of Japanese folklore studies. Murai examines the way in which Yanagita's work relates to the colonisation of Korea (Murai 1995). From the Euro-American perspective, Sakai Naoki in his two books, *Voices of the Past* (1991) and *Nihon shisō to iu mondai: Hon'yaku to shutai* (*The Problem of Japanese Thoughts: Translation and Subjectivity*) (1997) analyses Japanese writing from the position that language is essentially a site of hybridity (Sakai 1991: 19); the unity of language never emerges (Sakai 1991: 218).

With regard to postcolonial literary criticism, Yamagata Kazumi's *Sai to dōitsuka: Posutokoroniaru bungaku ron* (*Difference and Identification: Postcolonial Literary Theory*) and Komori Yōichi's *Posutokoroniaru* (*Postcolonial*) appeared in 1997 and 2001 respectively. This field of study in Japan, as well as that of lesbian/gay/queer studies, promises to yield a great deal of material in the years to come.

Chapter overview and readership of this book

Since postmodernism, feminism and postcolonialism have each various aspects, I shall first of all acknowledge the theorists who have made this study of Japanese literature and culture possible. Postmodernist theorists have influenced this book, especially Chapter 1 which analyses Murakami Haruki's work. These include Michel Foucault, Jean-François Lyotard, Gilles Deleuze and Félix Guattari in France, and Friedrich Nietzsche, Max Weber, Theodor W. Adorno and Max Horkheimer in Germany. With regard to the USA, this book owes a great deal to Fredric Jameson (Jameson 1991, 1998). For the feminist and queer theories used in my analysis of the stories of Yoshimoto Banana, I am much in debt to the work of Gayle Rubin, Eve Kosofsky Sedgwick, Judith Butler and Cheshire Calhoun on sexuality and identity politics (Rubin, G. 1975, 1984; Sedgwick 1985, 1991; Butler 1987, 1990, 1993, 1997a, 1997b, 2000; Calhoun 2000).

Beside Sigmund Freud, the psychoanalytic perspectives of Jacques Lacan and Slavoj Žižek have also been employed with regard to the feminist critique of 'phallocentric' logic (Lacan 1977a, 1977b; Žižek 1989, 1994). Furthermore, with regard to the relationship between Yoshimoto Takaaki and postcolonialism, I should first of all mention the influential and now classic book *The Empire Writes Back* (Ashcroft, Griffiths and Tiffin 1989) and their subsequent work, *The Post-Colonial Studies Reader* and *The Key Concepts in Post-Colonial Studies* (Ashcroft *et al.* 1995, 1998), as well as the work of Gayatri Chakravorty Spivak (1987, 1988, 1990, 1999) and Homi K. Bhabha (1994).

By reviewing postmodern theory in terms of the above understandings, and also by carefully avoiding the abuses of science, this book will look at various criticisms of modernism. It will focus first on rationalism, which includes its relation to power structures, the elite's suppression of subaltern people and a reconsideration of causal and motivational relations. It will then examine human emotion and desire in relation to violence; the value of romantic love; the subversion of erotic desire felt towards strangers, and in terms of the incestuous desire experienced regarding one's family and kin.

When I come to analyse the work of Murakami Haruki in Chapter 1, I argue that he deconstructs two typically modern ideologies: that strong-is-good and that love-is-beautiful, both of which are underpinned by modernist power structures which over-value progress and romantic love. Having renounced both progress and romantic love, do we then revert to some untroubled, pre-rational existence: what would a world bereft of both love and progress be like? Murakami's answer can be found in his vision of *The End of the World*, which will be discussed later.

In Chapter 2, by using analyses deriving from the study of (homo-) sexuality and feminism, I will highlight Yoshimoto Banana's critique of the modernist dialectic which pits the erotically charged desire to do violence against the stranger (as formulated by Georges Bataille) with the friendly, gentle and incestuous desire experienced in relation to the family. Banana is shown to deconstruct the notion of the 'stranger', which derives meaning only from its binary opposition to the notion of the family.

One of the key aspects I have observed in the literary work of both Murakami Haruki and Yoshimoto Banana is their attempt to reformulate the aforementioned binary oppositions between totalitarian identification and individual differentiation, and between self/family and self/stranger which can be otherwise expressed as the relationship between the self and the homogeneous, and the self and the heterogeneous. They do this by subverting the desire for the 'Other' and instead focusing on desire for the 'same': incestuous desire in the family, homosexual desire among the same-sex, and desire for the same within homogeneous groups. This approach must, however, be treated cautiously for it can resemble a retreat from the world just as an autistic child withdraws to a world of its own. Nonetheless, the links here with postmodern theory's attack on binary logic, queer studies' analysis of (homo-) sexual desire and feminism's call for women's emancipation, seem clear. Furthermore, the narratives of both authors depict a sort of static or cyclic postmodern world in which the progressive, evolutionary 'masculine' linear time gives way to the so-called 'feminine' cyclic time suggested by Julia Kristeva (1991: 445).[12] This is a further link between postmodernism and feminism, particularly apparent in the work of Yoshimoto Banana.

With regard to Banana's father, Yoshimoto Takaaki, modernist power systems surface in his work as the elite's suppression of the subaltern in the name of the Enlightenment project. In considering Yoshimoto Takaaki's theory of collective fantasy (*kyōdō gensō*), one of the key issues I draw attention to is his distinction between violence (power relations) and eros; he attributes the former to the field of social and cultural relations, and the latter to the realm of the family. That is to say, he regards extra-family social relations as rooted in power structures predicated on violence, whereas he understands the family as a utopian sphere in which people can engage in erotic relations without the desire to do violence.

Yet Yoshimoto Takaaki's ideas must also be treated with caution for, in attempting to confine the integrative eros to the inside (family) and cast the disruptive violence on to the outside (society), there is the danger of falling into ethnocentrism. It must also be questioned whether eros without violence is indeed possible in the family, and if it can be shown to be so, whether there is potential here to transcend male and female sexualities, which are supposedly constructed in terms of desire to do violence to, or unite with, the 'Other'. I think that despite the tendency to fall into ethnocentrism and/or male-centredness, Yoshimoto Takaaki's ideas are worthy of further attention.

Finally, when I come to analyse Karatani Kōjin's critical work in Chapter 4, I will focus on his concept of 'intercourse with the Other (exteriority)'. For Karatani, since human relations with the 'same' (interiority) result in either violent discrimination or fascistic identification, we need to have 'intercourse with the Other (exteriority)'. But how? In the first place, in order to engage with the 'Other', he attempts to subvert formality (interiority), since the concept of interiority itself, Karatani argues, hinders people from getting in touch with the 'Other' (exteriority). The 'Other' looked at from the perspective of formality (interiority) is generated by a discourse which prioritises relationships grounded in formality (interiority). Hence Karatani first tries to subvert the notion of interiority in order to encounter exteriority. But, finding this approach to be futile, he then attempts to establish direct contact with the 'Other' as represented by foreigners and children in situations that involve teaching–learning and/or selling–buying.

Furthermore he tries to express the concept of the 'Other' using Saul Kripke's idea of 'proper name'. Kripke argues that the proper name designates that which cannot be substituted in an imaginary world (Kripke 1972: 49). For instance, another pet dog can replace a pet dog; but any other dog cannot replace 'this' pet dog. When regarding the common features of this dog (common name) which it shares with other dogs, it can be replaced by any other dog, but if attention is paid to the singularity of this dog (proper name), it cannot be replaced by any other dog. For Karatani the relationship between people who share common features in a community (interiority) is analogous to the common name, whereas the relationship between people who do not share anything in common (exteriority) is analogous to the proper name.

While maintaining relations between common names in a community, we cannot escape from power systems. But how can we approach the 'Other' as represented by the proper name? What are relations between proper names like? Furthermore, how can we rid ourselves of power systems while at the same time preserving the energy that sustains them? Is it possible to simultaneously repudiate both violent discrimination and fascistic identification, while also maintaining progress? I may not be able to answer these questions directly, but I hope that I will be able to outline the various conditions that have produced these problems in their present form today.

In the last part of this introductory Chapter I shall mention readership. This book is addressed to a wide audience and is not confined to specialists in Japanese literature and culture. Since most of the literary works I deal with in this study, except those of Yoshimoto Takaaki, are available in English translation, it is possible for English-speaking readers to refer to them. The methodology employed derives from techniques pioneered during the transition from structuralism, to post-structuralism, postmodernism, feminism, lesbianism and gay studies, and postcolonialism. To this extent, I attempt to analyse Japanese literature using perspectives deriving from Western logic, although in the process I have also introduced criticisms of Western logic from non-Western sources. So far, there has been little theorisation of the relationship between Japanese critics studying literature and Western writers who have been interested in Japanese literary works. That is, although these two groups have been studying similar objects (literary works), they have been doing so independently and from their own point of view, with only a slight common theoretical basis – although there has, of course, been a certain amount of mutual interest and stimulation. I hope this book, by analysing Japanese literary works through Euro-American methods, will, to some extent, provide a new theoretical perspective that will bridge the gap.

In Chapter 1, postmodern specialists will discover how postmodern analysis can be utilised in understanding a contemporary Japanese writer, Murakami Haruki. In Chapter 2, feminists and queer theorists will be interested to see how these theories can be used to analyse a female Japanese writer, Yoshimoto Banana. In Chapter 3, postcolonial specialists will find a comrade in the figure of the Japanese critic, Yoshimoto Takaaki. For those researchers with an interest in Japanese literature and culture, this chapter will also provide a useful introduction to the critical work of this writer, which is still rarely available in English.[13] Finally, anyone working in the humanities should be interested in the introduction and analysis of the work of one of Japan's leading philosophical and literary critics, Karatani Kōjin, in Chapter 4. I hope that even specialists in Japanese literature and culture will discover in this book how perspectives deriving from postmodernism, feminism, queer theory, and postcolonial studies can be used to facilitate further textual criticism. At the same time, I also hope that the scholars who have generated postmodern, feminist, queer and postcolonial theories in a Euro-American context will discover new aspects of their theories in the light of an analysis of contemporary Japanese writers.

This work follows on from my previous book *Ideology and Narrative in Modern Japanese Literature* (Murakami F. 1996), which analysed modern Japanese literary works from philosophical and linguistic perspectives. The present book attempts to proceed in the same direction, this time analysing Japanese literature from postmodern philosophical perspectives. While the first book took as its approach Marxism, existentialism and phenomenology in an analysis of four modern Japanese writers, Kitamura Tōkoku, Arishima Takeo, Akutagawa Ryūnosuke and Abe Kōbō, this work utilises postmodernism, feminism, queer theory and postcolonial criticism, in an attempt to re-read Murakami Haruki, Yoshimoto Banana, Yoshimoto Takaaki and Karatani Kōjin.

1   Murakami Haruki's postmodern world

The end of modernity: *A Wild Sheep Chase*

The first of Murakami Haruki's novels I shall deal with is *A Wild Sheep Chase* (*Hitsuji o meguru bōken*, 1982).[1] It will be read in terms of the crisis of the legitimacy of rationality and the attack on the modernist 'grand narrative' (Lyotard 1979) together with its obsession with progress. The latter is a common postmodern theme and, I believe, is also inscribed as a main theme in this story. The hero of the novel, 'I', is a copywriter who is blackmailed by a dying right-wing Boss' secretary into going to Japan's northern-most island, Hokkaido, to find a sheep with a star-shaped birthmark. The sheep has the demonic ability to possess and manipulate people, and the hero finally discovers that his friend, Rat, had been possessed by this sheep and committed suicide in order to kill it. Most readers probably wonder what the sheep symbolises.[2]

Kawamoto Saburō believes that the sheep stands for the idea of revolution and self-denial pervasive in Japan from the 1960s to the 1970s (Kawamoto 1988: 113–114). For him, the image of the sheep represents the students' movement of that period. Introducing Kawamoto's interpretation, Fukami Haruka construes the sheep as a sort of symbol of the absolute idea in modern Japan.

> What is the sheep with the star-shaped birthmark?...If we follow the trajectory of the story of the town of Junitaki-cho and the Sheep Professor's and the Boss' lives, the answer appears before our eyes. The Japanese invasion and suppression of the Ainu; the conscription of the son of an Ainu shepherd and his death in China; the birth of the Sheep Professor in the same year; Japan's aggressive expansion on the Chinese continent; the woollen and worsted industry as one of the developments of industrialism; and the Boss' claim to the whole underside of post-war politics, economics and media. As the sheep thrives, Japan starts the climb out of poverty and the oppression of the Ainu begins. Japan invades the Chinese continent and, when this venture fails, the sheep turns to the search for a total conceptual realm. Behind these movements,

the contamination of hometown rivers and the seas, and the people's outrage at this, are quietly growing. It seems that the sheep symbolises the modernist, which includes the anti-modernist, idea; in other words, the absoluteness of ideas.

(Fukami 1990: 36; my translation)

Karatani Kōjin presents a different interpretation. He extracts from the secretary's words an idea of 'the sheep' that resists the 'Western humanism, individual cognition and evolutionary continuity' (Murakami 1982 I: 189)[3] from which nothing but a 'world of uniformity and certainty' (I: 187) and 'what can be counted in numbers' (I: 192) survives. The notion of 'the sheep', for Karatani, is a symbol that represents the negation of thought as it is understood in terms deriving from Western individualism and humanism; a symbol which attempts to maintain people's uniqueness and unpredictability in contrast to a world of uniformity and certainty. He also finds a connecting link between the idea of the sheep and the ideas of Mishima Yukio (1925–1970) who killed himself in imitation of the patriot soldiers in the 26 February incident in 1936[4] (Karatani 1995a: 121–124). Mishima had opposed the 1960s students' movement because he saw it as based upon individualism, and instead advocated the 'cultural defence' of Japan.

What Karatani sensed in the image of the sheep was the Japanese uniqueness in the context of Asia; the significance of this uniqueness was articulated by Okakura Tenshin (1862–1913) and Yasuda Yojūrō (1910–1981) and carefully analysed by Takeuchi Yoshimi (1910–1977) but has now been lost through Euro-American influence. The disappearance of this uniqueness was symbolically enacted in 1970 by two suicides: Mishima Yukio's own suicide and the suicide of the fictional character, Takashi, in Ōe Kenzaburō's *The Silent Cry* (*Man'en gannen no futtobōru*). This uniqueness is something like the 'ethos' described in minute detail in Oketani Hideaki's two books *A Spiritual History of Shōwa* (*Shōwa seishin shi*, 1992) and *A Spiritual History of Shōwa: Postwar Period* (*Shōwa seishin shi: Sengo hen*, 2000) as a spirit that died out with Japan's defeat in the Pacific War in 1945 (Oketani 1992: 654).

It seems that in contrast to Fukami, who focuses on the dark side of Westernised modern Japan – its aggressive expansion including the invasion and suppression of other Asian countries, and its industrial development at the cost of the natural environment – Karatani lamented the loss of the Japanese people's uniqueness. In other words, while Fukami sees in the sheep Murakami's attack on modern Japan, Karatani finds a sort of mourning for something lost during the modernisation of Japan. It seems reasonable to suppose that the sheep is related to both these opposing sides of Japanese modernism at the same time.

Referring to Imai Kiyoto's detailed examination of the concept of the sheep,[5] let me first review here briefly how the sheep is described in *Wild Sheep Chase*. The sheep in this story possesses (in the demonic sense) three people. The first is the Sheep Professor who was born in Sendai in 1905, graduated from the Agricultural Faculty of Tokyo Imperial University, and entered the Ministry of Agriculture and Forestry as one of the elite. He was dispatched by the Ministry to the Korean peninsula to establish a self-sufficiency programme based on sheep for the imminent, large-scale North China campaign. In July 1935, during an observation tour of Manchuria, the sheep with the star-shaped birthmark entered his body (Murakami 1982 II: 40–56).

The second person the sheep possesses is a major right-wing Boss. He was born as the third son of a poor farming household in Hokkaido. His father's generation, though poor, was the one that invaded Hokkaido and suppressed the indigenous Ainu people who were living there. When he was twelve, he left home for Korea, and upon his return to Japan, joined a right-wing group (Murakami 1982 I: 184). Soon afterwards, in 1932 (the year of the 15 May incident),[6] he was imprisoned on charges of complicity in a plot to assassinate a key political figure, and his imprisonment lasted until June 1936 (the year of the 26 February incident), when the sheep entered his body from that of the Sheep Professor (I: 182). Released from prison, he became a major right-wing Boss, and headed over to mainland China where he built up an intelligence network and a personal fortune in the process. After the end of the war, utilising the fortune he brought back from China, he became a key figure in the whole underside world of post-war politics, economics and media. (II: 57–58).

The story of *A Wild Sheep Chase* begins when the sheep possesses its third victim, Rat, a friend of the copywriter, the hero of the novel. Rat's father has already been introduced in another of Murakami's works, *Hear the Wind Sing* (*Kaze no uta o kike*, 1979). He was one of a number of Japanese businessmen who became affluent through taking advantage of the Sino-Japanese, Pacific and Korean wars (Murakami 1979: 86). As the story unfolds, the lives of the Sheep Professor and the major right-wing Boss are gradually revealed to both the protagonist and the reader, and finally the copywriter meets the ghost of his dead friend, Rat, in his vacation villa in Hokkaido. Rat explains how the sheep used the Boss to build up a supreme power base, then earmarked Rat for possession in an attempt to create a realm of total conceptual unity in which consciousness, values, emotions, pain, everything would disappear and all opposites would be resolved, with Rat and the sheep at the centre of this world (Murakami 1982 II: 204–205). Rat killed himself with the sheep in his body, because he valued the things that would have been lost had the sheep won.

If we consider the careers of the characters in the story, it seems clear that the history of modern Japan unfolds around the sheep. These characters are, in a sense, representative of common types found in Japan since the Meiji Restoration (1868). The Sheep Professor is a highly ambitious man with outstanding intellectual abilities, who has a mission to unite east Asia; the major right-wing Boss was born in poverty to the son of an invader of the Ainu's land, made his fortune on the back of Japan's aggressive expansion policy in mainland China, and surreptitiously manipulated post-war Japan's politics, economics and media; and Rat is the son of a merchant who became rich by taking advantage of the wars.[7]

A secretary to the major right-wing Boss tells the hero about the sheep which were introduced into Japan during the Ansei era (1854–1859), just prior to the Meiji period. Up until then, few Japanese had ever seen a sheep or understood what one was. They were imported at the state level from America, and sheep husbandry enjoyed a brief boom. After the war, when the import of wool and mutton from Australia and New Zealand was liberalised, there was no reason to continue raising sheep in Japan and sheep again became scarce. Talking to the hero, the secretary describes sheep as tragic animals that embody the very image of modern Japan (Murakami 1982 I: 172–173).

Though it now appears clear that the sheep is indeed related to modern Japan, we should also investigate the sheep's hopes for the future: the prospect of a total conceptual realm in which consciousness, values, emotions, pain, everything would disappear and all opposites would be resolved, with Rat and the sheep at the centre of this world (Murakami 1982 II: 204–205). The text tells us that Rat is possessed by the sheep because of his weakness in the areas of morality, consciousness, and existence itself (II: 202), but he summons up all his strength and kills the sheep, for he has realised that he is attached to his weakness, his pain and suffering, as well as to summer light, the smell of a breeze, the sound of cicadas, and having a beer with his friend (II: 205). We can see here the sheep's intention to progress, following the line of the modernist endeavour, and Rat's final decision to go against this, instead revaluing his weakness, pain, suffering, and his indulgence in supposed meaningless trifles.

It would seem, therefore, more pertinent to argue that what the sheep symbolises is not simply confined to modernist endeavours and their ethos, but also includes the idea of an evolutional current of time which underlies the modernist way of thinking. The sheep in this story follows the trajectory of modern Japanese society – the unification and oppression of Asian people (Sheep Professor), the consolidation of Japanese people and defence of their culture (right-wing Boss) – and a vision of the future resulting in total conceptual unity (Japanese businessman's son, Rat) – as inevitable stages of evolution.

A Wild Sheep Chase can be interpreted as a work which describes modernist ideology in Japan: its cult of the intellectual, its pursuit of knowledge and rationality; development of political and economic power; its suppression of the 'Other', its deep love and identification with ideological constructions of Japanese tradition, and its future unity. This is contrasted with Rat's rejection of the above and the prospect of an anti-modernist, I would like to call it postmodern, society.[8] The story of *A Wild Sheep Chase* moves away from the modernist ideology, which believes that the strong, powerful, intellectual, and hardworking are good for evolution and which approves of the suppression of the weak, to a postmodern world in which people are attached to their weakness, their pain and suffering, as well as 'to summer light, the smell of a breeze, the sound of cicadas, beers with (their) friend(s)'.

Imai Kiyoto points out Rat's intersubjectivity shared with people, and consequently he regards the sheep as the symbol of this intersubjectivity (Imai 1999: 111–114). But I would like to argue that the intersubjectivity is found in the Rat's preference for identifying with nature, rather than with people. In this sense I agree with Kasai Kiyoshi who sees in the Rat's preference for/identification with nature a Baudelairian sense of 'correspondence' (Kasai 1999: 231–232). The point that I would like to raise here is that, if we compare the identification with nature and the desire to conquer nature, we find in the former postmodernist and in the latter modernist characteristics. We can therefore suppose that Rat intends to prefer the unspoiled, uncontaminated countryside to the modernist evolutional development.[9] In this novel, Rat declares that we should not support the modernist attempt to promote, develop, cultivate, learn, and achieve a higher stage of evolution, and should instead move on to a postmodern world which in this story is symbolised by the countryside that has escaped the modernisation and industrial development of cities.

Reading the narrative in this way is, however, problematic in that the arguments for and against modernism and postmodernism are developed in suggestive and abstract ways through the lives and opinions of the characters, particularly the Boss' secretary and Rat. The secretary tries to help the sheep achieve its aim, no matter what that may be, whereas Rat attempts to thwart it. While the former approves of whatever is evolutionary, even though it may result in losing something dear to him, the latter ventures to stop it, even at the cost of his own life, no matter how beautiful the promised future life may be.

The meaning of the story, however, seems to lie not in their arguments, but rather in the attitude of the protagonist 'I' towards them. The copywriter almost never engages in discussion with either the secretary or Rat. Rather, he problematises the secretary's questions, enquiring whether they make sense (Murakami 1982 I: 187), or responds to Rat's individual questions with generalities (Murakami 1982 II: 202). He remains outside the argument or at least plays with the terms of discussion. 'Do you believe the world is getting better?' Rat asks and the copywriter answers: 'Better or worse, who can tell?' This attitude is of crucial importance to this story, for no matter how categorically the postmodernist rejects ideas of aim, purpose and improvement through evolution, if this rejection itself becomes an aim, then a paradox results. In order to escape this paradox, the copywriter queries whether the questions posed to him themselves make sense by using self-reflexive language[10] that deconstructs the two opposites. In so doing, he can distance himself from the surrounding situation and subvert it. If we regard deconstruction or indifferentiation as tactics characteristic of postmodernism, then there is no one more postmodern than the copywriter in this story.

Murakami Haruki's fundamental detachment from the modernist ideology of aim and purpose is also evident in many of his other characters, who live in their own aimless and lacklustre worlds. The protagonist of *Pinball, 1973* (*1973-nen no pinbōru*) opens a small translation service with one of his friends. Their working style is presented as being very laid-back and comfortable (Murakami 1980: 31–32). Every day the translator arrives at the office at ten, carefully sharpens his six pencils, and then, while listening to music, slowly gets down to business until noon. During the lunch break he plays with some Abyssinian cats at a nearby pet shop. Back at the office, after resharpening his six pencils, he starts his afternoon session. At four he leaves the office and on the way home shops for dinner at the supermarket (75–77). They lead comfortable lives not because they are men of wealth, but because they are free from ambition.

In *Dance Dance Dance* (*Dansu dansu dansu*, 1988), a later novel, the protagonist, a writer, describes his attitude to work as follows:

> I was never choosy about the jobs I did. I was willing to do anything, I met my deadlines, I never complained, I wrote legibly. And I was thorough. Where others slacked off, I did an honest write. I was never snide, even when the pay was low…
>
> And with not one speck of ambition, not one iota of expectation. My only concern was to do things systematically, from one end to the other. I sometimes wonder if this might not prove to be the bane of my life. After wasting so much pulp and ink myself, who was I to complain about waste? We live in an advanced capitalist society, after all. Waste is the name of the game, its greatest virtue. Politicians call it 'refinements in domestic consumption'. I call it meaningless waste. A difference of opinion. Which doesn't change the way we live.
>
> (Murakami 1988: 12)

For these characters, life is meaningless. But, they are not existentialists who agonise over the meaninglessness of life; rather they enjoy playing with it. Complaining and being snide is pointless, for their jobs are from the very beginning pointless. But they still work honestly and systematically, and find satisfaction in doing so. Such postmodern labour is well symbolised by the old men digging a large hole in the town of *The End of the World* (Murakami 1985: 313–317). This hole, which has no special function or meaning, does not transport them anywhere. They have nothing to achieve by their labours, nowhere to get to, no victory, and no defeat. But then again, they enjoy digging the meaningless hole. This lifestyle is typical of Murakami's postmodern characters.

In *Pinball, 1973*, Rat says to J: 'Say…J…here I've lived twenty-five years, and it seems to me I haven't really learned a thing'. J answers: 'Me, I've seen forty-five years, and I've only figured out one thing. That's this: if a person would just make the effort, there's something to be learned from everything. From even the most ordinary, commonplace things, there's always something you can learn' (Murakami 1980: 95–96).

Rat nods and starts thinking; 'I think I see what you're getting at, but...', and swallows the thought. 'But – what? Once the word was on his lips, there wasn't anything more he could say'. Rat's hesitation to approve of the idea that there is something to be learned from everything again indicates a sort of collapse of the modern ideology of instrumental and meritocratic learning. Further, the translator in *Pinball, 1973* says:

> 'I was born under a strange sign. You see, whatever I've wanted I've always been able to get. But whenever I get that something, I manage to spoil something else. You know what I mean?'
>
> 'Kind of'.
>
> 'Nobody believes me, but it's true. I only realized it myself three years ago. That's when I thought, better just not want anything any more'.
>
> She nodded. 'And so that's how you plan to spend the rest of your life?'
>
> 'Probably. At least I won't be bothering anybody'.
>
> 'If you really feel that way', she said, 'why not live in a shoe box?'
>
> A charming idea.
>
> (Murakami 1980: 108–109)

Whenever you get one thing, you manage to spoil something else, so better just not want anything any more. This is diametrically opposed to modernist ways of thinking. Modernists want to reach the goal – a better life. To set oneself a goal and to work hard to achieve it is considered laudable in modern society. But this also requires that we push others aside, and that human relations, including our relationship to ourselves, be characterised by struggle.

These characters indicate a society in which the idea of development or evolution on the basis of rationality – a main cause of domination and suppression of people – does not exist. The lack of ambition and competitiveness displayed by Murakami's characters reflects an antithetical attitude to modernist ideals that force people to progress in order to reach an aim based on rationality. Once we discard the desire to evolve, rationality no longer functions as a driving force for people in society. Freedom and fairness would find their proper places in human relations. But we must keep in mind that in such a world, as Rat says, we would have to lose the beauty of modernity.

Lack of mind: *The Hard-Boiled Wonderland* and *The End of the World*

The Town in *The End of the World* is an imaginary world created by the protagonist, a Calcutec from *The Hard-Boiled Wonderland*, and is completely surrounded by walls. The two stories, *The End of the World* and *The Hard-Boiled Wonderland*, simultaneously unfold chapter by chapter, like Faulkner's

The Wild Palm. The difference is that in Murakami's novel the two are chronologically linked; the story of *The End of the World* starts at the end of *The Hard-Boiled Wonderland*.

In order to prevent information from leaking out, a professor at the 'Central Research System' invented a way of fixing, through brain surgery, a circuit that can hold information in a person's core subconscious. Important information is kept in the subconscious of twenty-six specially trained men, called Calcutecs. The operators in the research organisation can call up information whenever necessary by a method called 'shuffling'. As the next step, the Professor succeeded in visualising the subconscious as a sort of story. By installing another separate circuit into the junction boxes in the Calcutecs's brains, namely by creating a three-way cognitive circuitry, he loaded the visualised core subconscious into the third circuit. As a consequence, the Calcutecs have three different subconscious minds: the normal, frozen and visualised. The title of the visualised story of the protagonist in *The Hard-Boiled Wonderland* is *The End of the World*.

In the plot of this novel, an accident causes him to become stuck inside the third circuit, his own imaginary town in *The End of the World*, with no hope of return. *The Hard-Boiled Wonderland* narrates the hero's everyday life until he becomes trapped in his own imaginary world, and *The End of the World* unfolds that world. Since the latter is created by the imagination of the protagonist of the former world, the two worlds are naturally affected by each other and linked through many commonalties, such as paperclips, the song *Danny Boy*, a young female librarian, and a unicorn's skull which glows when the characters' hearts are in correspondence. With regard to the narrative time of the two stories, the former is gradually approaching the beginning of the latter, and the latter evolves with the expectation of returning to the former, a chronology that is ultimately rejected by the hero.

In the Town in *The End of the World* people have no minds. When newcomers enter the Town, they must strip away the 'shadows' that are the groundings of the self, and let them die. The 'minds' that rise each day are collected and then taken outside the Wall by quiet, calm unicorns. These animals wander around the Town absorbing traces of mind, then ferry them to the outside world where they die in the winter with the residue of people's selves inside them. The Gatekeeper cuts off the heads from the bodies. The skulls are then scraped clean and buried for a full year in the ground to allow their energy to disperse, then they are taken to the Library stacks where they sit until the Dreamreader's hands can release the last glimmers of mind into the air (Murakami 1985: 335–336). 'Mind' in this work is depicted as a sort of desire encompassing love, hatred, longing, etc., in other words the irrational, affective and passionate aspects of human nature. The Colonel in *The End of the World* says to the Dreamreader (who is the Calcutec in *The Hard-Boiled Wonderland*) when he questions whether kindness is the sign of a caring mind: 'No. Kindness and a caring mind are two separate qualities. Kindness is manners. It is superficial custom, an acquired practice. Not so the mind. The mind is deeper, stronger, and, I believe, it is far more inconstant' (Murakami 1985: 170).

According to the Professor in *The Hard-Boiled Wonderland*, the mind forms an identity of self:

> Each individual behaves on the basis of his individual mnemonic makeup. No two human beings are alike; it's a question of identity. And what is identity? The cognitive system arising from the aggregate memories of that individual's past experiences. The layman's word for this is the mind.
>
> (Murakami 1985: 255)

People in *The End of the World* lack this mind. What is it like in a world in which people have no minds? It is calm and peaceful. The Colonel says, 'You are fearful now of losing your mind, as I once feared it myself. Let me say, however, that to relinquish your self carries no shame....Lay down your mind and peace will come. A peace deeper than anything you have known' (Murakami 1985: 318). Little by little the Dreamreader has come to appreciate the Town and the people who live there. He describes the selfless world:

> No one hurts each other here, no one fights. Life is uneventful, but full enough in its way. Everyone is equal. No one speaks ill of anyone else, no one steals. They work, but they enjoy their work. It's work purely for the sake of work, not forced labor. No one is jealous of anyone. There are no complaints, no worries.
>
> (Murakami 1985: 333)

It is easy to understand that if we were to lose our minds or self-identities, we would gain instead a peaceful society in which people are equal and there is no competition. This is precisely Murakami Haruki's postmodern utopia. But it is realised only through the sacrifice of love and respect that have long been considered positive values. No matter how deeply the Dreamreader, who still has a trace of a mind, loves the librarian, his love can never be requited, because she has no mind (Murakami 1985: 169).

The End of the World describes a postmodern utopia, whereas *The Hard-Boiled Wonderland* represents modern society. In the latter people are always rushing about, either chasing after something or fleeing from something else; they must compete in order to achieve. People live their lives in haste because it is necessary to strictly organise time in order to achieve their goals sooner. They also love and hate each other. In the postmodern utopia, however, people do not run. Time stops because once life becomes aimless, time no longer linearly connects the present to the future; it just eternally revolves. People live happily there, but they do not have strong attachments to others, nor do they have music to listen to. They do not hate, but at the same time they cannot love deeply. *The End of the World* is established through the realisation that in order to avoid the failure of modernism, its individualisation of power structures, totalitarian militarism, two world wars, and discrimination, it is necessary to lose, or at least diminish, the functions of the mind, including both love and respect.

Murakami's characters often refer to wars, and the author's emotionally detached attitude is particularly clear here. For instance, in *Pinball, 1973*, the hero talks with twins named 208 and 209 about the Vietnam War.

> 'They're fighting because they think different, right?' 208 pursued the question.
>
> 'You could say that'.
>
> 'So there's two opposite ways of thinking, am I correct?' 208 continued.
>
> 'Yes, but…there's got to be a million opposing schools of thought in the world. No, probably even more than that'.
>
> 'So hardly anybody's friends with anybody?' puzzled 209.
>
> 'I guess not', said I. 'Almost no one's friends with anyone else'.
>
> Dostoyevsky had prophesied it; I lived it out. That was my lifestyle in the 1970s.
>
> (Murakami 1980: 39–40)

People fight because there are always two opposite ways of approaching any problem. In order to establish these opposite poles, people must take sides: insiders become friends and outsiders, enemies. Friends are united by love, respect, a sense of belonging and mutual benefit, and they regard their enemies with hatred. This is the typical pattern of war. Deleuze and Guattari trace the process whereby an extrinsic or Nomad war machine was appropriated by the State (Deleuze and Guattari 1988: 418). What motivated the appropriation was certainly the desire to protect 'our State' for the benefit of 'our people'. Wars are undertaken not by crazed individuals completely different from us, but rather they are the inevitable consequence of the paranoid modern ideology of identification and differentiation, individualisation and totalisation. The lifestyle of Murakami's main postmodern characters is, however, different – almost no one is friends with anyone else. They hardly ever fight, and they scarcely bother other people.

Georges Bataille remarks on war from a different perspective, saying that 'The origins of war, sacrifice and orgy are identical; they spring from the existence of taboos set up to counter liberty in murder or sexual violence' (Bataille 1986: 116). Taboos come from a strong diametrical antinomy between desire and prohibition. Yet once again Murakami's characters have no need of taboos, because they do not experience strong desires. Miyoshi Masao comments on this point rather negatively remarking that 'even his [Murakami's] sex scenes are stylish; their copulating couples remain collected, observant, and uninvolved as they pace themselves through orgasms' (Miyoshi 1991: 234). Though I do not agree with Miyoshi's negative evaluation, it is true that many of Murakami's narrators certainly give the impression that they are almost always cool and detached, both from themselves and from the events taking place before their eyes.

This striking emotional and rational detachment is also evident in Murakami's narrative style. One of the characteristics of early modern narrative style in the Japanese novel is the ubiquitous presence of an introspective narrator's self-consciousness, as can be seen in the character of Bunzō in *The Drifting Clouds* (*Ukigumo*, 1886–1889), in many of Sōseki's heroes, and in the narrative voice of the I-novel (*shishōsetsu*). *Shishōsetsu*, in particular, are characterised by this kind of reflexive self-consciousness. As Suzuki Tomi has remarked on Tayama Katai's *The Quilt* (*Futon*, 1907), which is often regarded as the first I-novel, what is significant in the Japanese I-novel is the problem of self-consciousness – the critical distance between the 'objectified self' and the 'objectifying self', and not the tacitly accepted single-voiced, direct monologue by the author/protagonist (Suzuki 1996: 70–71).

One of the differences in narrative style between Murakami Haruki and the writers of the I-novel, therefore, lies not in the difference between the single-voiced monologue and the dual-voice of evident self-consciousness, but in the stance or the psychological distance between the 'objectifying self' and the 'objectified self'. This narrative style significantly corresponds with the attitude of many of Murakami's protagonists who attempt to deconstruct two opposites and distance themselves from the surrounding situations and subvert them.

If we look at the grammar, on the sentence level it cannot be said that Murakami's narrators' narrative distance is wide, for in most cases he uses the first person and does not alter the narrative distance with frequent changes of narrative perspective and voice. In general, Murakami's stories are consistently narrated by the first person narrator–hero's voice and from his perspective, except in the characters' letters. Characteristic elements of his narrative style include his use of conversation rather than monologue (Ueno *et al.* 1992: 261, 269, 274) in order to avoid introspection. Also, he never forgets irony, a sure sign of detachment. When he narrates a serious topic, as he does in *Norwegian Wood* (*Noruwei no mori*, 1987), he does so retrospectively, thus achieving temporal distance. These narrative characteristics result in a psychologically wider distance, not between the narrator and protagonist, but between the narrator–protagonist's own self and self-consciousness, as well as between the self and its surroundings. The narrator looks at himself as he would look at others. That is to say, he avoids discriminating between self and others, as well as being torn between polarised binary oppositions of rationality and emotion/desire or individualisation and totalisation.

This stance, as has often been remarked, is evident in the frequent use of phrases which indicate a withdrawal from reality, such as '*yare yare*' which cannot be translated into English; its usage is somewhat like the expletives that people murmur to themselves when they step outside a traumatic occasion in which they have been deeply involved (Katō N. 1988: 104–128; Ueno *et al.* 1992: 274). Other phrases include '*sō iu koto da*' (that's the way it is/so it goes) or '*sore dake da*' (that's all), both of which express a sense of resignation towards reality (Katō K. 1983: 210; Miura 1997: 44), '*bengiteki*' (for convenience's sake) which indicates a lack of serious commitment, and '*betsu ni kamawa nai*' (it's no big deal/I don't care/I don't mind), which also reveals the narrator–character's indifference to the events he is confronted with. The regular occurrence of these phrases illustrates the sense of dissociation felt by the narrator towards that which he is narrating. At the same time they are spoken in recognition of the fact that there is nothing in this world worth pursuing, for, as David Harvey puts it (Harvey 1989: 27–28), the idea that there is only one possible mode of representation has already collapsed.

In the last scene of *The Hard-Boiled Wonderland and the End of the World*, the hero, Dreamreader, is tempted by his shadow (self) to go back to the former world of the modernists. But he rejects the temptation and decides to stay in the Town of the postmodern utopia/dystopia.[11] Though he understands that it makes perfect sense to return to his former world together with his shadow, once he discovers that he is the one who has created the Town, he cannot bring himself to leave. 'I have responsibilities', he says, 'I cannot forsake the people and places and things I have created…I must see out the consequences of my own doings. This is my world. The Wall is here to hold *me* in, the River flows through *me*, the smoke is *me* burning. I must know why' (Murakami 1985: 399).

In interpreting this incident, Susan Napier says that '[i]n this late-twentieth-century world the protagonist feels that his responsibilities are to himself, not to a wider society or history' (Napier 1996: 5). Though elsewhere in the same book she mentions that the Dreamreader's concern with responsibilities 'might be seen as in some ways admirable, rather than only self-serving, emblematic of a generation which realizes that to change the world one must start with oneself' (Napier 1996: 214), it seems clear that she interprets the Dreamreader's decision to remain inside his own postmodern consciousness as an abandonment or at least a deferral of his responsibilities in real life. Karatani Kōjin more severely attacks the Dreamreader's final decision by saying that 'the responsibility for people, places and things one has created by one's own discretion is another name for irresponsibility. To emphasise the responsibility for meaningless things is to make the responsibility worthless' (Karatani 1995a: 127; my translation).

Yet I still sense in this last scene the author's own strong determination. Though we should not read too much about the author's intention into the story, in this case it seems that the voice of Murakami, the author, can be discerned in the Dreamreader's words. He tries to stay in the postmodern world to see what will happen there. Murakami himself says in an interview with Kawamoto Saburō that if it is he who has created the fictional 'end of the world' then it would be, in a sense, a sort of [irresponsible] escape to flee from there (Murakami and Kawamoto 1985: 79). He declares that he will take responsibility as author along with the character Dreamreader, for having created the postmodern world, and by remaining there see out the consequences of his own actions.

A love story between postmodern people: *Norwegian Wood*

Norwegian Wood (*Noruwei no mori*, 1987) opens with thirty-seven-year-old Watanabe Toru seated in a Boeing 747, about to land at Hamburg Airport. The background music in the passenger cabin is some orchestra's muzak rendition of the Beatles's *Norwegian Wood*. The melody reminds Watanabe of a meadow in the suburbs of Kyoto where he walked with his girlfriend who was fond of the song, some eighteen years before. At the time, he was thinking about himself and the beautiful woman walking besides him, feeling confident that he was in love with her. *Norwegian Wood*, as opposed to Murakami's other novels, is a realistic and haunting story of love, youth, and tragedy (or, so says the advertisement for the book), which is 'uncharacteristically (for Murakami) devoid of fantasy elements' (Rubin, J. 1992: 492). But it is misleading to read this novel as a love story, because Watanabe and Naoko, two of the major characters in the novel, do not love each other. Ueno Chizuko interprets this story as depicting discommunication. 'If love is a human relation', she says, 'this novel does not describe any love, but instead it follows the process in which people fail to communicate' (Ueno *et al.* 1992: 274, 308).[12]

When Watanabe asks Naoko if they can live together, she rejects his proposal. Naoko explains herself by saying:

> But it's impossible....Because it can't be. It's just no good. It...wouldn't be the right thing to do. Not for you, not for me...it's just impossible, the idea of somebody watching over someone else for ever and ever....That just wouldn't be a fair arrangement. You couldn't call that a relationship, could you?
>
> (Murakami 1987 I: 15–16)

Naoko's perspective is based on the idea that people are independent, different and alienated. The story unfolds around the relationship between this alienated couple who can never love each other, no matter how hard they try. Eventually, Naoko kills herself, and Watanabe loses his sense of identity as formed by modern human relations.

Marx considered capitalist society to be a major cause of alienation, and he advocated its elimination in order to re-establish human bonds in a communist society. But there is no absolute reason why the kind of human relations proposed by Marx should be considered ideal. It is possible, after all, to create comfortable relationships between people even in an alienated society. It is not impossible to suppose that the Marxian ideal of an egalitarian society is only realisable at the expense of the ideal of human unification. As we have seen in the previous section, in order to avoid hatred and discrimination, Murakami's postmodern characters advocate discarding love, unity and social identity. Though they subscribe to Marx's ideal of an egalitarian society, they attempt to realise it not through a sense of community, but in a society of alienated people. To this extent, according to a postmodern understanding, that which is lost is not just the contents of experiences, which can be shared, but also the very notion of sharing itself. When the ties that bind people together, rooted in rationality, morality and affection, are lost – the result is schizophrenia, in Fredric Jameson's sense.

Jameson, using Lacan's account of schizophrenia and Saussurean structuralism, defines schizophrenia in a slightly different way from Deleuze and Guattari (Deleuze and Guattari 1984). He explains that meaning is not a one-to-one relationship between signifier and signified, but is generated by the movement from signifier to signifier. Thus, when the relationship among signifiers breaks down, that is, when the links in the signifying chain snap, schizophrenia results 'in the form of a rubble of distinct and unrelated signifiers' (Jameson 1991: 25–31; Harvey 1989: 53–54). Though Jameson focused on the temporal unification of personal identity and on schizophrenia as its result, his ideas are also applicable to the inter-human unification of personal identity, since the relationship between signifiers and the links of the signifying chain are formed *a priori* in inter-human communication as *langue*, and presented to newcomers in a language culture.

Schizophrenics apprehend the relation between signifiers differently from others and, as their ways of categorising phenomena are disparate, we cannot understand them nor they us. The concept of alienation presupposes a self-identity (particular) that is alienated from a social identity (universal). But if a common sense of social identity is missing in society, then the concept of alienation is clearly inapplicable. From this perspective, schizophrenia can be read as a symbol for how an individual's identity, forged through both temporal and inter-human unification, is now in the process of transformation; the individual prefers a fragmented sense of self rather than a perceived unity with others. A lack of social identity results in the collapse of self-identity, too, for the latter is necessarily formed reflexively through distancing itself from the former.

In *Norwegian Wood*, Naoko's mental disease is supposedly a type of symbolic schizophrenia in Jameson's sense. She has trouble writing letters to Watanabe. Reiko, Naoko's roommate in a convalescence home, says in a letter to Watanabe: 'The more I think about it, the first sign was that she couldn't write letters...Whenever she started to write a letter, all sorts of voices would talk to her and interfere. They'd prevent her from choosing her words' (Murakami 1987 II: 176). Naoko explains her own illness in the following terms:

> I'm not good at talking,...Haven't been for the longest while. I start to
> say something and the wrong words come out. Wrong or sometimes

completely backward. I try to go back and correct it, but things get even more complicated and confused, so that I don't even remember what I started to say in the first place. Like I was split in two or something, one half chasing the other. And there's this big pillar in the middle and they go chasing each other around and around it. The other me always latches on to the right word and this me absolutely never catches up.

(Murakami 1987 I: 41)

When Watanabe answers her: 'That happens more or less to everyone, ... Everybody goes through times when they want to say something, but they can't and they get upset', Naoko seems almost disappointed at his answer and says: 'That's something else'. Watanabe's response presupposes that people have a message they want to convey, but Naoko's trouble is that her self has been split.

If Naoko were completely schizophrenic then she would not suffer from mental anguish. Her problem is that she is split into two schizophrenic and paranoid selves, and in order to cure herself, she must choose one or the other. Reiko explains the characteristics of their (Naoko's and her own) illness:

You know, the most important thing for us who have these problems is reliability. Knowing that I could leave things up to him and if my condition took the slightest turn for the worse, if the screw started to come loose, he'd notice and carefully, patiently, fix me back up – tighten the screw, unravel the ball of yarn. Just knowing we can rely on someone is enough to keep our problems at bay. As long as there's that sense of reliance, it's pretty much no more *sproing*!

(Murakami 1987 I: 225)

The most important component of their problem is their need for someone on whom they can rely. This, however, leads them to establish paranoid modernist human relations.

Naoko probably lost her paranoid relations with others when her boyfriend, Kizuki, committed suicide. They had grown up hand in hand loving each other, as an inseparable unit. They had retreated from outside society into their own world. Their only friend had been Watanabe (Murakami 1987 I: 240–241). Consequently, when Kizuki killed himself, Naoko could not establish deep human relations with anyone else in the outside world. Neither Kizuki nor Naoko could bear their paranoid human relations, but at the same time they could not be contented among schizophrenic people either. They are in this regard neither complete modernists nor perfect postmodernists. They are doomed to exile from modern society, and yet are unable to find their own postmodern world.

In *Norwegian Wood* there is a character called Nagasawa who is an elite student at Tokyo University. At first sight, he is very different from the other postmodern characters in the story, but he does share certain features with them in that he is a complete schizophrenic. While talking to Watanabe, Nagasawa emphasises the importance of effort, which is typically modern.

> 'How come these simpletons don't make an effort? They don't make an effort and they complain that things are unfair!'
>
> I shot Nagasawa a surprised look. 'Correct me if I'm wrong, but from where I sit I sure get the impression that people are grinding away like mad. Am I wrong?'
>
> 'That's not effort, that's just labor', Nagasawa spat out. 'Not the effort I'm talking about. The effort I'm talking about is to go about things with will and purpose.'
>
> 'Like taking up Spanish once you've landed a job, when everybody else would just lie back?'
>
> 'Precisely. I'm going to master Spanish by spring. To add to my English and German and French, plus passable Italian. Can you get this far without making an effort?'
>
> (Murakami 1987 II: 103)

It is typically modern to make an effort through willpower and purpose. Ueno Chizuko finds something of the spirit of the 1960s in Nagasawa, probably deriving from this type of passage (Ueno *et al.* 1992: 269). But Nagasawa's effort is fundamentally opposed to the modernist effort. When the second part of the Foreign Ministry exam that Nagasawa is taking has finished, Watanabe asks him why he wants to enter the Ministry. Nagasawa answers:

> 'I want to test my mettle in the biggest pool around, the state. Just to see how far I can rise in this vast bureaucracy, how far I can go on my own talents. You follow?'
>
> 'It all sounds like a game.'
>
> 'Exactly...I don't have any of this lust for wealth or power – well, hardly any...I'm your selfless, emotionless, detached man. What I do have is curiosity. That and a will to try my stuff in the tough, wide world.'
>
> 'Which leaves no room for ideals, I take it?'
>
> 'Of course not...What's needed isn't ideals but role models.'
>
> ....
>
> 'So tell me, Nagasawa, what the hell kind of role model do you have?' I thought to ask.
>
> 'You'd laugh, I know', he said.
>
> 'Laugh? Not me', I said.

'A gentleman, that is what I aspire to be.'

...

'And just what does this being a gentleman entail?...'

'A gentleman is he who does not what he wants to do but what he ought to do.'

(Murakami 1987 I: 105–107)

Nagasawa has no lust for wealth or power; he is a selfless, emotionless, detached man. He has nothing but curiosity and a will to try, surely not a will to power. What he needs is not an ideal but a role model, the gentleman – a person who does not do what he wants to do, but what he ought to do. Everything is a game for Nagasawa and in this respect he is a quintessentially postmodern character.

Nagasawa's remark that he and Watanabe are alike is interesting. When Watanabe, Nagasawa and his girlfriend, Hatsumi, are having dinner together to celebrate Nagasawa's success in the examination, Nagasawa mentions several times that both he and Watanabe have certain things in common. Nagasawa says that they are basically alike in that they are really only interested in themselves. Neither is interested in being understood by other people and they are both incapable of loving. The only difference between them is that Watanabe does not yet quite recognise this side of his personality, and that is why his feelings are capable of being hurt (Murakami 1987 II: 113–117). Nagasawa declares that Watanabe is a postmodernist, and that he cannot love anyone.

Watanabe, like many other characters in Murakami's novels, is primarily concerned with not being disturbed by others. When Kizuki, his intimate friend in Kobe, committed suicide, he made up his mind to no longer take things too seriously and not to let things get too close (Murakami 1987 I: 48). Though in this story the reader is given the impression that Watanabe is deeply and desperately in love with Naoko, through his relationship with Midori he gradually realises that he cannot love Naoko. Schizophrenic postmodernists are incapable of loving each other.

Another of Nagasawa's characteristics is his fairness and honesty; he never lies, and always admits his own errors and faults. Nor does he hide things that are not to his advantage (Murakami 1987 I: 62–63). As mentioned before, fairness and justice are crucial values in a postmodern society. After deconstructing idealistic truth, morality and aims founded on rationality which used to provide links between people, a pragmatic fairness and justice still remain for postmodernists; these do not serve to unite people emotionally or rationally, but simply to prevent society from falling apart. In modern society, people devalue fairness in favour of love and progress: for the sake of loved ones and for the sake of progress, people sacrifice fairness and justice. Max Weber illustrates this when he points out that:

Whenever the external order of the social community has turned into the culture community of the state it obviously could be maintained only by brutal force, which was concerned with justice only nominally and occasionally and in any case only so far as reasons of state have permitted. This force has inevitably bred new deeds of violence against external and internal enemies; in addition, it has bred dishonest pretexts for such deeds. Hence it has signified an overt, or what must appear worse, a pharisaically veiled, absence of love.

(Weber 1991: 355)

Two points in Weber's analysis are pertinent here: the absence of justice and of love for maintaining cultural community. Justice in the modern period must be subordinate to reason, and we now know that reason is founded on evolution. In this sense, Nagasawa can only be fair to the extent that he has no strong desire for progress to the idealistic aim. As for the absence of love that Weber diagnosed as a consequence of reason, post-modern thought approves of this because it is a safeguard against discrimination. Thus Nagasawa is able to be fair because he loves no one deeply.

Concerning beauty, happiness and fairness, Naoko, on her part, writes in a letter to Watanabe:

Over these four months I've done a lot of thinking about you. And the more thinking I do, the more I've come to realize that I wasn't fair to you. Couldn't I have acted more like a responsible human being?

But maybe this line of thought isn't quite normal. For one thing, girls my age would never use the word 'fair'. Basically, what does the average girl care whether something is fair or not? The really typical thing for girls is not whether something is fair or not, but whether it's beautiful or if it can make her happy, and that's the heart of it. 'Fairness' just seems to be one of these words that males use. Even so, I can't help feeling there is something perfectly apt about this word 'fairness'.

(Murakami 1987 I: 163–164)

Disregarding Murakami's assumptions about female/male discrimination, it is possible to see that Naoko is here arguing for a shift from beauty and happiness towards common fairness: the former being characteristic of modernist and the latter postmodernist positions.

Lyotard also argues for justice, saying that '[c]onsensus has become an outmoded and suspect value. But justice as a value is neither outmoded nor suspect. We must thus arrive at an idea and practice of justice that is not linked to that of consensus' (Lyotard 1979: 66). But what is justice without consensus? Without consensus, it would surely invite nothing but turmoil. Watanabe talks with Midori's father on his deathbed about the *deus ex machina* in Euripides' plays.

All sorts of people appear, each of whom has their say about their circumstances and reasons, each seeking justice and happiness in their own way. Which throws everything into one fine mess. Predictably. Even in principle it would be impossible for everyone to receive justice or for everyone to achieve happiness. What you get is chaos. So what do you think happens? It's really very simple. In the end, the gods come out. To kind' of conduct traffic. You come here, you go there, you two get together, you stay right there a while, like that. A regular fixer. That's the way everything falls into place, nice and neat. It's called *deus ex machina*.

(Murakami 1987 II: 82–83)

As Watanabe predicted, if we were to lose the consensus underlying justice, it would result in chaos. Furthermore, it should not be forgotten that ideas of justice, equity, fairness or morality are forged on the basis of rationality. For postmodernists who doubt the legitimacy of rationality, the concept of a unitary justice, equity, fairness or morality is nothing but an illusion. As Watanabe tells Midori's father, there seem to be multiple justices, fairnesses, etc., each demanding its own legitimacy.

The rationality versus emotion/desire issue, which is problematised by postmodernists, can be subsumed, to a certain extent, in the wider category of universality/generality versus originality/particularity[13] – since both rationality and emotion/desire are factors that serve to unite and differentiate between people. It seems pertinent to understand this conflict between universality/generality and originality/particularity, not as something outside the individual (universal/general) as opposed to something inside (original/particular), but as two sides confronting each other within an individual. In this paradigm justice, equity, fairness and morality are not construed as something external to individuality. As Richard Rorty and John McGowan insist, we should think of morality 'as the voice of ourselves as members of a community, speakers of a common language' (Rorty 1989: 59; McGowan 1991: 194). If we take this dichotomy of universality and particularity that exists within ourselves into consideration, we can replace the notion of normative justice, fairness and morality with our own voices as members of a community, speakers of a common language in Rorty's sense.

We have to be careful here. As Lyotard noted, without a single rule of judgement, we cannot communicate with each other, but a single universal norm tends to get caught up in totalitarianism. We have to avoid both extremes. I can see the possibility in Stanley Raffel's suggestion that justice without consensus in Lyotard's sense resides in 'something like being as certain as possible that no one is forcing anyone else to do anything against their will' (Raffel 1992: 60). In this respect, the concept of postmodern justice and fairness reminds us of the notion of kindness mentioned by the Colonel in *The End of the World*, as well as the role models suggested by Nagasawa.

Compared with the mind, which is deeper, stronger, and far more inconsistent, kindness is a manner, a superficial custom, and an acquired practice.

The mind produces profound love and hate relationships, but kindness results in a shallow etiquette which helps reduce friction. In contrast to ideals for which people must strive at the cost of their dignity and for whose sake they must disadvantage others, resulting in anxiety and paranoia, the gentleman simply follows by etiquette. One of the significant characteristics of the paradigm shift from modernism to postmodernism is the change from abstract ideals to practical etiquette and from deep love to shallow kindness. When ideals are invoked, people struggle and swing from one extreme to another – from disappointment to fulfilment, from alienation to unification; and they necessarily coerce others to follow them. In this paradigm, an externally enforced norm is necessary in order to keep society on course. In contrast, in the postmodern paradigm, morality and justice as normative forces have been replaced with kindness and etiquette. Justice in Lyotard and Raffel's sense appears only in the latter paradigm.

As has often been mentioned, it is paradoxical to say that 'there is no truth in this world' or 'nothing in this world is universal'.[14] What is involved then, in making this statement, is not so much the collapse of universality in favour of fragmentation, but to effect a paradigm shift from modern to postmodern ideology. For modernism, as we have noted, the main ideologies are evolution-is-good and love-is-beautiful, which are underpinned by notions of justice and morality that serve to maintain the status quo.

In contrast, in the postmodern paradigm evolution is understood as the cause of suppression and oppression of the weak, love (totalitarianism/consensus) is construed as a factor producing discrimination against and hatred of others, and justice and morality are seen as normative, external forces that restrain people. Regarding the above negative aspects of modernism, the postmodernists favour egalitarianism, schizophrenic fragmentation, and the waning of affection. The rule of the game is fairness or justice without force. The postmodern endeavour can be conceived, from this perspective, simply as valuing fairness and justice over evolution and love.

Though Watanabe is an unwitting postmodernist, he also exhibits modern characteristics. Nagasawa's talent amazes him, but he also harbours a sort of longing for his late friend Kizuki whose minor talents were used to help both Naoko and himself. Nagasawa however, dispenses his overwhelming mastery in all directions, as if it were all a game (Murakami 1987 I: 66). This kind of longing for Kizuki is typical of modernity. Watanabe also feels more comfortable with Midori's father than with Nagasawa, because the former cares too much for his family and his daughter to consider the difference between effort and labour which Nagasawa mentions (Murakami 1987 II: 103–104). Watanabe is here rather sentimental about modernist human relations.

Nagasawa's girlfriend Hatsumi is depicted as a symbol of empathy since she wants to be understood by others. As Nagasawa points out, normal people call it love when one individual wants to understand another (Murakami 1987 II: 115–116). Some twelve or thirteen years later, when Watanabe is in Santa Fe, New Mexico, he sees a miraculously beautiful sunset and, suddenly, in the face of that overwhelming view, he is reminded of Hatsumi, understanding that what she evoked in him was an unfulfilled – and eternally unfulfillable – adolescent infatuation; an infatuation which was pure, unblemished, and unremitting, and which had long been set aside inside him, its very existence erased from memory (Murakami 1987 II: 117–119). Hatsumi is a compassionate figure who seeks empathic love, and who possesses romantic characteristics.

In her study of relations between Japanese romantic and realist traditions, Susan Napier, with reference to Jameson, finds in the works of Mishima Yukio and Ōe Kenzaburō several anti-mimetic elements. She points out that their use of romance or fantasy offers means of escape from the suffocatingly bleak realism of the Naturalists in Japan of the 1960s and 1970s (Napier 1991: 8–9). As Napier points out, Fredric Jameson also argued that the role of romance in the nineteenth century was part of the gradual reification of realism in late capitalism wherein romance came to be seen as the place of narrative heterogeneity and of freedom from that reality principle to which an oppressive realistic representation was hostage (Jameson 1981: 104).

We should first clarify the meaning of romance. Napier focuses on romance as 'an extraordinary and improbable tale of adventure' (Napier 1991: 228), while for Jameson, romance is something which offers the possibility of sensing other historical rhythms and of demonic or Utopian transformations of a real world (Jameson 1981: 104); yet there is at least one more side to romance, what Northrop Frye calls the idyllic world. Frye presents two worlds of romance:

> There is, first, a world associated with happiness, security, and peace; the emphasis is often thrown on childhood or on an 'innocent' or pre-genital period of youth, and the images are those of spring and summer, flowers and sunshine. I shall call this world the idyllic world. The other is a world of exciting adventures, but adventures that involve separation, loneliness, humiliation, pain, and the threat of more pain. I shall call this world the demonic or night world. Because of the powerful polarizing tendency in romance, we are usually carried directly from one to the other.
>
> (Frye 1976: 53)

In contrast to Napier and Jameson who focus on the second of Frye's two worlds of romance, I want to highlight the tension between the worlds. Gerald N. Izenberg characterises romanticism by saying that:

> in Romantic imagery and concept, whether it be that of humankind's relationship with nature or with the state, whether it be the artist's rela-

tion to the work of art or the lover's relation to the beloved, the Romantic idea of infinite individuality is always linked with the notion of an all-inclusive totality other and greater than the self, in a relationship not of reciprocity but of dependency. The Romantic contradiction is that the individuated self's dependency on, even fusion with, this totality, invariably figured in maternal terms, is the very condition of absolute free individuality; or to reverse the terms, the absolute, ungrounded agency of the self is seen to derive from the dissolution of the self into a larger whole.

(Izenberg 1992: 8)

This quotation shows how most romantics oscillate between infinity of self (individuality/differentiation) and belonging to others (totality/identification). They are pulled in both directions by these two contradictory yearnings. In most romantic works, individual freedom is usually reconciled in a happy unification and can be understood as the unfulfillable adolescent desire to reunite with the mother. That is the reason why modernists in their adolescence, when they are forming their self-identities, fall desperately in love with others.[15]

In contrast to romance, fantasy has its own features. As Tzvetan Todorov points out, fantasy also, as a literary text, creates a situation in which the reader identifies with the character (Todorov 1973: 33). But compared with romance, fantasy is too far from verisimilitude to ensure empathic identification between reader and character. Further, as Marshall Tymn defines it, fantasy goes beyond rational consideration and opens doors to other worlds and other peoples (Tymn *et al.* 1979: 3–4, 37–38). This analysis is reminiscent of the characteristics of postmodernism.[16] I shall define as 'fantasy' works that overly stress the role of the imagination in either or both of these two worlds of romance, to the extent that they lose close correspondence to the ordinary world of experience. If we accept this distinction between romance and fantasy, Jameson's and Napier's definition of 'romance' as something which offers the possibility of flight from the reality principle and of sensing other historical rhythms seems to be more applicable to fantasy than to romance. Predictably, paranoid romance will disappear in postmodernism as a result of the schizophrenic lack of empathy.

In *Norwegian Wood*, Hatsumi is depicted as a symbol of romance searching for empathic love with Nagasawa. That is why she evokes in Watanabe an eternal and unfulfillable adolescent infatuation; a romantic unification of two people in the throes of a love that has been set aside and long disregarded, its very existence erased from memory. This means that when Watanabe remembers Hatsumi in Mexico, he has long since given up the paranoid ways of modernist life.

The relation between Hatsumi's romantic, paranoid and modern love, depicted as beautiful and priceless, and Nagasawa's apathetic, schizophrenic and postmodern tendencies is complex. Though it is certain that Hatsumi's love is depicted as an elegy for something that is disappearing, something which has faded, whether the narrative leads the reader to attempt to recover or discard this is ambiguous. Also, as Katō Kōichi mentioned, we should pay attention to Nagasawa's mistreatment of a drunken woman (Murakami 1987 I: 63; Katō Kōichi 1999: 114–115). His nasty character is a result of a lack of empathy – a facet of the apathy typical of postmodernists. At this point, a certain amount of clarification is necessary.

It seems that what underlies postmodernism is a political, economic and social egalitarianism in which each schizophrenic individual approves of the differences displayed by every other individual. But, as has been seen, in order to achieve this, two basic desires – evolution and romantic empathic love must be discarded. Is the narrative of this novel suggesting that we should go on living without evolution and love? Here, I should mention that the author Murakami himself, not only later but even when he wrote this novel, seems reluctant to go on living without at least attachment (love). The evidence abounds: at the beginning of this story, thirty-seven-year-old Watanabe apparently regrets and misses what he has lost; the narrator's attitude towards Nagasawa is indifferent, whereas towards Hatsumi he is, as mentioned before, compassionate. Also Murakami has remarked in an interview with Shibata Motoyuki that he regards Nagasawa as a morally fallen man, whereas Watanabe is free from that defect (Murakami and Shibata 1989: 20–21). Furthermore, as I will mention in the following sections, in *The Wind-Up Bird Chronicle* (*Nejimakidori kuronikuru*, 1994–1995) Murakami later deals with violence which is closely related to compassionate love.

To go back to *Norwegian Wood*, Murakami mentions in the interview with Shibata Motoyuki cited above that he is split into two people: Murakami the writer and Murakami the man. He is a different person when he is writing a novel and when he is not; when writing, a sort of 'demonic' force controls him. Hence, it is possible to suggest that while Murakami Haruki the man, during an interview for instance, is attached to the idea of empathic love, his hidden 'demonic' side, which appears only when he is writing a novel, is indifferent. Also, I believe that this story awoke this 'demonic' element that lay dominant in its more than 3.5 million readers in late 1980s Japan[17].

In the last scene of *Norwegian Wood*, Watanabe, having lost Naoko, decides to live with Midori and calls her.

> I called Midori and told her I simply had to talk to her. I had loads to tell her. Things I had to get off my chest. There was nothing else I wanted in this world but her. Let's meet and talk, I said, everything depends on that.
>
> Midori stayed silent on the other end of the line the whole while. Silent as all the rain in the world falling over all the grass of the world, on and

on. I pressed my forehead against the windowpane and shut my eyes. And finally Midori spoke to me. 'Where are you now?' she calmly asked.

Where was I now?

I looked up, receiver in hand, and spun around in the phone booth, taking in my surroundings. Where the hell was I? I couldn't tell. Not a clue. All I could see about me were people, scores of people, all tired of walking about aimlessly. I held on to the line to Midori from there in the middle of nowhere.

(Murakami 1987 II: 255–256)

Ueno Chizuko focuses on Midori's psychology in this last scene and mentions that Midori rejects Watanabe because she senses that he is not calling out of concern for her (Ueno *et al.* 1992: 289). But if we pay attention to the trajectory of Watanabe's life, we can interpret the last scene to mean that when he decides to live with Midori and calls her, he loses his place. Because of Naoko's influence, and also because of his own inclination, Watanabe has unconsciously transformed himself from a modernist to a postmodernist. But, he is still drawn towards the empathic and romantic love of the modernists, embodied in his love for Midori. Once he decides to act on that empathic love, he unavoidably loses his place in modern society because of his postmodern characteristics. This never happens when modernists establish relations with each other.

This last scene highlights the influence of post-war Japanese literature on Murakami's work. Although Ōe Kenzaburō believes that there is nothing directly linking Murakami with the postwar Japanese literature of the 1946–1970 period, Murakami's deliberate dissociation from Mishima Yukio and Ōe himself has been noticed by Karatani Kōjin (Ōe 1989: 200; Karatani 1995a). In this final scene from *Norwegian Wood* we can also see Abe Kōbō's influence. In the last scene of *The Ruined Map* (*Moetsukita chizu*, 1970; original 1967) Abe's protagonist detective calls a woman from a telephone booth.

I dialed, and this time the line was free and I could hear the bell ringing…

It was a woman's voice…At once a glib lie came mechanically to my lips.

'Excuse me, but I've found a purse. There was a piece of paper in it with this number on it. I called, thinking it might by chance be yours…'

The response was more than I expected. Suddenly the woman broke out laughing.

'What? It's you, isn't it?' she said guilelessly and smoothly in a low, throaty voice. 'What were you saying?'

'Do you know me...who I am...? Someone...'

'Don't go on with that ridiculous joke.'

'I want you to help me...I'm in the telephone booth at the foot of the slope that leads to High Town. Please. Come and get me here.'

'You're terrible...at this hour! Are you tight?'

'Please! I'm sick. Please. Won't you do something?'

'You're impossible. Well...wait there where you are. Don't move. I'll be right down.'

(Abe 1970: 295–296)

Replacing the receiver, however, Abe's hero makes a dash for the other side of the street, directly opposite the telephone booth, and conceals himself in an alley there. The woman appears and searches the booth and the area around it. But the detective continues to hide himself in the narrow, dark crevice, choking back his screams behind clenched teeth, until she is gone. Abe's protagonist is deeply attached to others and looks for their help, and at the same time he ceaselessly attempts to escape from them. In contrast, Murakami's hero simply rejects them and is rejected by them. We can see here a significant shift from the late modernist to the early postmodernist.

A new switch-panel in a death chamber: *Dance Dance Dance*

Dance Dance Dance (*Dansu dansu dansu*, 1988) is the sequel to *A Wild Sheep Chase*. The copywriter in the latter work has now become a freelance writer. He often dreams about the Dolphin Hotel where he stayed in *A Wild Sheep Chase*, and feels he belongs to the hotel – he is part of it. He hears someone softly, almost imperceptibly, weeping for him there. Supposing that Kiki, his girlfriend in the previous novel, is seeking him once more and that only by becoming part of the Dolphin Hotel will he ever see her again, he once again journeys to Hokkaido. Once there, he finds that the old five-story Dolphin Hotel has been completely rebuilt and transformed into a gleaming twenty-six-story Bauhaus Art-Deco symphony of glass and steel, with the flags of various nations waving along the driveway, smartly uniformed doormen hailing taxis and a glass elevator shooting up to a penthouse restaurant. With the hotel as the connecting link, a new story unfolds around the writer, the hotel receptionist Yumiyoshi, Yuki, the daughter of a famous photographer called Amé, and an old friend of the writer, now a movie star, called Gotanda.

The other worlds appear more clearly here than in Murakami's other novels, namely in the Sheep Man's room at the Dolphin Hotel and in the death chamber in downtown Honolulu. The author himself refers to these different worlds in an interview with Shibata Motoyuki.

Most novels I have written include two worlds; in short, this world and that world. *Norwegian Wood* is no exception. Simply speaking, the world of the convalescence home in Kyoto where Naoko stays is that world, while the world in Tokyo in which Midori lives is this world. Apart from them, in my consciousness, there are two kinds of time concepts, this time and that time. Specifically these are the limited realistic time of the 60s, 70s and 80s that is the stage of my novels, and an unrealistic time beyond that.

(Murakami and Shibata 1989: 18–19; my translation)

This unrealistic time flows in the Sheep Man's room at the Dolphin Hotel and in the death chamber in downtown Honolulu.

This kind of pluralism is one of the key characteristics of postmodern fiction. Discussing Italo Calvino's *Invisible Cities*, Brian McHale draws our attention to the space that is capable of accommodating incommensurable and mutually exclusive worlds. He explains that this space juxtaposes, like Michel Foucault's concept of a *heterotopia*, worlds of incompatible structure (McHale 1987: 43–44). Quoting a passage from Borges, Foucault means by *heterotopia* a world that is organised by epistemological categories quite other than our own. In such a world (described by Borges), animals are categorised as (1) property of the Emperor, (2) embalmed, (3) tame, (4) having just broken the water pitcher, etc. In Foucault's *heterotopia* they 'make it impossible to name this *and* that, because they shatter or tangle common names, because they destroy "syntax" in advance, and not only the syntax with which we construct sentences but also that less apparent syntax which causes words and things (next to and also opposite one another) to "hold together"' (Foucault 1994: xviii). Foucault here is describing precisely the breakdown of the relationship of signifiers among themselves, what Jameson refers to as snaps in the links of the signifying chain. As we have noted, it results in a world of schizophrenics who lose their grasp on common prevailing relations between signifiers.

The pluralism of *utopias* and *heterotopias* suggests the collapse of a single correct mode of representation. As David Harvey also mentions, this is 'co-existence' in 'an impossible space' of a 'large number of fragmentary possible worlds' or, more simply, incommensurable spaces juxtaposed or superimposed upon each other. Characters no longer contemplate how they can unravel or unmask a central mystery, but are forced instead to ask, 'Which world is this? What is to be done in it? Which of myselves is to do it?' (Harvey 1989: 48). The pluralism of different, co-existing worlds can also be found in *A Wild Sheep Chase*.

Turning all this over in my mind, I started to imagine another me somewhere, sitting in a bar, nursing a whiskey, without a care in the world. The more I thought about it, the more that other me became the real me, making this me here not real at all.

(Murakami 1982 II: 144)

I wasn't seeing my mirror-flat mirror-image. It wasn't myself I was seeing; on the contrary, it was as if I were the reflection of the mirror and this flat-me-of-an-image were seeing the real me. I brought my right hand up in front of my face and wiped my mouth. The me through the looking glass went through the same motions. But maybe it was only me copying what the me in the mirror had done. I couldn't be certain I'd wiped my mouth out of my own free will.

I filed the word 'free will' away in my head and pinched my ear with my left hand. The me in the mirror did exactly the same. Apparently he had filed the word 'free will' away in his head the same as I had.

I gave up and left the mirror. He also left the mirror.

(Murakami 1982 II: 182–183)

These feelings must be related to losing one's place in the real world, as Watanabe does in the last scene of *Norwegian Wood*. The mirror-image, which reflects reality, becomes more real because he has lost his place in this real world. One can identify one's place by confirming the location of the fabric knot of relations with others. Lack or change of the location of that knot results in losing one's place in this real world.

Again, we find Abe Kōbō's hero in *The Ruined Map* expressing himself in similar terms almost twenty years previously:

No, perhaps I was not the one who had lost himself but the one who had been lost. I had experienced a moment's pain as if I had been thrown off the bus when it had started off a while ago. If that were true, the I here was not the lost I but the I that had suffered the loss.

(Abe 1970: 286)

Both have lost their places in this real world. The difference is that while Abe's detective is suffering, Murakami's copywriter is rather playing with his alter ego.

In *Dance Dance Dance*, the room at the Dolphin Hotel on the 15th, 16th or 17th floor (the first time the hero discovers it, it is on the 15th floor, the second and third times on the 16th and 17th respectively), which varies in dimensional space, and the death chamber in downtown Honolulu are supposed to be set in a different reality in which a different order prevails. According to the Sheep Man, the room at the Dolphin Hotel (*this world*) works like a switchboard through which people are connected (Murakami 1988: 84). The room is the freelance writer's own place, where he can put himself in relation to others.

He tells the Sheep Man about his life: how he has managed to support himself, yet never managed to go anywhere, but aged all the same; how he lost track of what mattered; how he worked like a fool; how it didn't make a difference either way; how he was losing form, the tissues hardening, stiffening from within, terrifying him; how he barely made the connection to this place

(Murakami 1988: 82–83). The Sheep Man says that what he must do is to dance as long as the music plays. Once his feet stop, he must stay in *this world*. He is going to be dragged from *that world* to *this world*. The writer wonders what *this world* is about, because it is meant to help him connect with others; it must exist for him. The Sheep Man's answer is simply that the writer is not ready for this place, not yet. It is too dark, too big, and too cold, there is nothing to eat. Though this is not the world of death, it is a different reality from the writer's world. The reason the Sheep Man chose this one is that he dislikes war and has nothing to lose. But since the writer has still got warmth, the Sheep Man advises that he should stay in *that world* (Murakami 1988: 86).

At the end of *A Wild Sheep Chase*, Rat commits suicide in order to stop the modern ideology of progress and to subvert the concept of human unification. That is why the writer tries to forget about Rat in *Dance Dance Dance* (Murakami 1988: 82). He wants a life completely dissociated from *this place* of connecting people. But he cannot have that, so he comes back to *this place*. He cannot get *this place* out of his mind. No matter how hard he tries to forget things, and regardless of whether he likes it or not, he realises that he belongs to *this place*. In his dreams about *this place*, he is part of everything; someone is crying for him here, someone wants him (Murakami 1988: 82). The Sheep Man's room and the death chamber (*this world*) are doubtless places in which people are connected. But it is hard to imagine the story going back to the modern human relations of the 1960s, when people were united by rationality and emotional love. These rooms must be different other worlds in which schizophrenics are to be connected, and so must have the same qualities as the world in *The End of the World*.

Led there by Kiki, in Honolulu the writer discovers a downtown death chamber, which contains six human skeletons.

> Two human skeletons were seated side by side on the sofa. Two complete skeletons, one larger, one smaller, sitting exactly as they might have when they were alive. The larger skeleton rested one arm on the back of the sofa. The smaller one had both hands placed neatly on its lap …
>
> I walked slowly around the room. There were six skeletons in all. Except for one, all were whole. All sat in natural positions. One man (at least from the size, I imagined it was a man) had his line of vision fixed on a television. Another was bent over a table still set with dishes, the food now dust. Yet another, the only skeleton in an imperfect state, lay in bed. Its left arm was missing from the shoulder.
>
> (Murakami 1988: 271)

All together six skeletons. The one whose left arm is missing from the shoulder must be Dick North, Amé's boyfriend who lost his left arm in Vietnam and was later killed in a traffic accident in Japan (Murakami 1988: 309), and the one with his line of vision fixed on a television must be Gotanda. The writer supposes that the others must be Rat, Kiki and Mei

(360). And when Yuki says that, 'You were such a good guy. I never met anyone like you', the writer wonders *'Why the past tense?'* (345), so we may perhaps suppose the last skeleton to be that of the writer himself. But we are not quite ready to reach this conclusion yet.[18]

It is apparent that *Dance Dance Dance* is a sequel to *A Wild Sheep Chase*. The Dolphin Hotel is the hub between the two works. But connections with *The Hard-Boiled Wonderland and the End of the World* can also be detected. The writer thinks of the coldness of the Sheep Man's room: 'The temperature was falling. I suddenly seemed to remember this chill. A bone-piercing, damp chill. Long ago and far away. But where? My mind was paralyzed. Fixed and rigid' (Murakami 1988: 87).

The coldness reminds us of that in *The End of the World*. Most readers will vividly recall the coldness there. The writer in *Dance Dance Dance* is trying to remember the chill of *The End of the World*.[19] Further, Gotanda talks about his shadow when he says that he has killed Kiki:

'I strangled her. But I wasn't strangling *her*, I was strangling my *shadow*. I remember thinking, if only I could choke my shadow off, I'd get some health. Except it wasn't my shadow. It was Kiki.'

'*It all took place in that dark world.* You know what I'm talking about? Not here in this one.'

(Murakami 1988: 356)

Gotanda has attempted to lose his mind in the other world by killing the shadow that carries his ego. This feature is also from the story of *The End of the World*; a different world of imagination in which people must strip away the shadows.

It is mentioned several times that in the room at the Dolphin Hotel, or in the death chamber in Honolulu, someone is weeping for the writer: 'I listen carefully. That's when I hear someone softly, almost imperceptibly, weeping. A sobbing from somewhere in the darkness. Someone is crying for me' (Murakami 1988: 2), and 'After all, that whole place is for you. Everyone there cries for you' (371). On the other hand, when the hero of *The End of the World* plays *Danny Boy* on the accordion, the librarian girl weeps.

Long after I set down the instrument, she clings to me with both hands, eyes closed. Tears run down her cheeks. I put my arm around her shoulder and touch my lips to her eyelids. The tears give her a moist, gentle heat.

(Murakami 1985: 369)

The weeping librarian girl in *The End of the World* is narrated as a duplication of the librarian girl in *The Hard-Boiled Wonderland* who suffers from gastric dilation. The skeleton bent over a table set with dishes might be the librarian girl. She is weeping and calling for him to connect with her in the world without mind.

The small skeleton seated on the sofa with both hands placed neatly in its lap reminds us of the Sheep Man in *A Wild Sheep Chase* who, when he came to visit Rat's vacation villa in Junitaki-cho, placed both hands on his knees when he sat down on the sofa (Murakami 1982 II: 154). So there is a possibility that the two human skeletons seated side by side on the sofa are Rat and the Sheep Man. Rat killed the sheep, the symbol of modernism, and further, as Murakami revealed, Rat is the alter ego of the protagonist (Murakami and Shibata 1989: 21). In this sense Yuki's prophecy came true. The writer left his alter ego in the chamber.

They are the ones who have lost their minds. The Sheep Man's room and the death chamber are conceived as places in which postmodern people who have lost their minds are connected. Yumiyoshi and the writer's self in the real world can have no place there for themselves, because at the very end of the story they have passed through the wall to the other world (*that world*) from *this world*. In the last scene, back in the Sheep Man's room at the Dolphin Hotel, the writer carelessly lets go of Yumiyoshi's hand.

At the very moment I extended my hand, her body was absorbed into the wall. Just like Kiki had passed through the wall of the death chamber. Just like quicksand. She was gone, she had disappeared, together with the glow of the penlight.

'Yumiyoshi!' I yelled.

No one answered. Silence and cold reigned, the darkness deepened.

'Yumiyoshi!' I yelled again.

'Hey, it's simple', came Yumiyoshi's voice from beyond the wall. 'Really simple. You can pass right through the wall.'

'No!' I screamed. 'Don't be tricked. You think it's simple, but you'll never get back. It's different over there. That's the otherworld. It's not like here.'

No answer came from her. Silence filled the room, pressing down as if I were on the ocean floor.

I was overwhelmed by my helplessness, despairing. Yumiyoshi was gone. After all this, I would never be able to reach her again. She was gone.

There was no time to think. What was there to do? I loved her, I couldn't lose her. I followed her into the wall. I found myself passing through a transparent pocket of air.

(Murakami 1988: 390–391)

Then he wakes up and finds himself lying on the bed. Yumiyoshi smiles as she sits on the sofa besides the bed. They have returned from the postmodern world without mind to the modernist world of love and progress, becuase he loves her.

In *Dance Dance Dance*, the hero has returned from the world of *The End of the World*. If the Sheep Man's room is a place where postmodern schizophrenics can be connected, the last scene where the writer escapes from there to the room where Yumiyoshi is waiting for him indicates that this is a move from the postmodern to the modern world. Is this based on the realisation that we cannot live in the world of *The End of the World*? Did Murakami resign his responsibility for having created that postmodern world? Is it because, as the Sheep Man says, the writer is not ready, not yet? Has the writer still got warmth? Is it too dark and too cold in the postmodern world?

It seems to me that Murakami Haruki finished his postmodern adventure with *Dance Dance Dance*. He concludes his later essay on the translation by saying:

> The most necessary thing for translation is probably language ability, but no less important than that, I think, especially in the case of fiction, is love full of personal prejudice....The love full of prejudice is one of the things in this unstable world that I love most – prejudiced though it is.
>
> (Murakami 1996a: 69; my translation)

The love full of personal prejudice is far removed from the postmodern world. Kimata Satoshi compares Murakami's *The Blind Willow and the Sleeping Woman* (*Mekura yanagi to nemuru onna*) in its original version from 1983 and its revised one in 1995 and points out that a sort of morality has appeared in the latter. Kimata also mentions that in Murakami's later work *The Wind-Up Bird Chronicle* (*Nejimakidori kuronikuru*, 1994–1995), the author has shifted his moral consciousness from leaving the moral void as it is in his early novels to fighting it in this novel (Kimata 1995: 4).

Murakami's *South of the Border, West of the Sun* (*Kokkyō no minami, taiyō no nishi*, 1992), published between *Dance Dance Dance* (1988) and *The Wind-Up Bird Chronicle* (1994–1995), is criticised by Mukai Satoshi who labels it a 'failed work' (Mukai 1993: 300–303). At first sight, the novel certainly appears to lack the tension between the modern and postmodern worlds familiar in Murakami's other works. Instead, it can be read in the tradition of Abe Kōbō's heroes' escape from communal relations with neighbours (*rinjin*) to relations with strangers (*tanin*). In his three novels from the 1960s, Abe's heroes start from a neighbours' (*rinjin*) relationship in the sand-hole, representative of peaceful communal life (*The Woman in the Dunes*, 1967a; original 1962); experience alienation as strangers (*tanin*) in neighbour's (*rinjin*) society, with a face disfigured by a laboratory explosion (*The Face of Another*, 1967b; original 1964); and attempt to discover self-identity through anonymous collectivity or inter-subjectivity in *tanin* society (*The Ruined Map*, 1970; original 1967) (Murakami F. 1996: 50–61). These heroes either attempt to escape from their families or try regaining them, and consequently find a new relation with other alienated people. In contrast, Hajime in *South of the Border,*

West of the Sun knows full well that we must hurt each other in this world, but nevertheless finally decides to stay with his family.

In this novel we find two important metaphors: the desert (Kobayashi 1995: 85) and the lack of facial expression, both of which are found in Abe's *The Woman in the Dunes* and *The Face of Another* respectively, and both of which seem to represent the lack of human relations. In this reading, as Mukai has pointed out, *South of the Border, West of the Sun* appears to lose its tension and we cannot help but read the novel as no more than an illicit love story with a happy ending, illustrating a decline in Abe's fiction. But probably, the directions and the meanings of this and that world are reversed here. As Yokoo Kazuhiro (1994) and Saitō Eiji (1993) have suggested, Shimamoto, heroine of this story, may have come as a spirit from a different world to seduce and lead the hero Hajime there.[20] That different world is probably somewhere like room 208 of the hotel in *The Wind-Up Bird Chronicle*: a place for complete mutual understanding and violence. In this reading, though he is strongly attracted by that world, Hajime is somehow released from there through Shimamoto's mercy and returns to this world without the deep love of identification. That is, this real world of the story-now is already postmodern for Murakami, and that other world is imagined as the modern world with love, hate and violence.

Concerning this change in the meaning of the other world, two reasons can be put forward. First, it seems to be based on Murakami's realisation of the futility of his static postmodern world in *The Hard-Boiled Wonderland and the End of the World*. And second, it might correspond with changes in his understanding of the present situation: from solidarity experienced between people in the 1960s and 1970s to their indifference in the 1980s and 1990s. Murakami himself mentions that he changed his position from one of 'detachment' to one of 'commitment' after staying in the USA in 1991 (Murakami and Kawai 1996: 9–18), or from 'individuality' to 'something beyond individuality' (Murakami 1995: 276). In an interview with Ian Buruma, Murakami also mentions that before going to the USA, he had wanted personal independence and individual freedom, whereas in America he felt that the question was where to go from there (Buruma 1996: 70). That is, the transformation of the author's recognition of this world underlies the exchange of the two other worlds in his stories. For Murakami, this world has already lost human empathy, but is still not entirely indifferent to human relations. We are now at a turning point from deep dark empathy to mindless indifference. In his early novels, Murakami attempted a release from the former power, but now he seems to have realised that he is already in the latter world and is trying instead to find something to cure the wounds inflicted there.[21]

Violence and empathy: *The Wind-Up Bird Chronicle* and beyond

Many would agree that one of the unique points of *The Wind-Up Bird Chronicle* (*Nejimakidori kuronikuru*, 1994–1995) is that it narrates the violent action that has been rarely depicted in Murakami's previous novels.[22] The hero of the story, Okada Toru describes himself, like other Murakami's heroes, as a detached man. He says that he can distinguish between himself and another as beings of two different realms, and claims that it is a kind of talent or a special power, because it is not an easy thing to do (Murakami 1994–1995: 78). But in the process of the story he gradually realises two important points. One is that he can use violent action in order to save his beloved, and the other is that he shares something with others as human beings. That is, in this new approach to the modern world, Toru, as well as the author Murakami, seems to notice the two different typically modern ideologies we have been considering in this chapter: strong-is-good and love-is-beautiful. The former is mentioned in a description of a character, Toru's wife Kumiko's father, in *The Wind-Up Bird Chronicle*.

> The father was convinced that the only way to live a full life in Japanese society was to earn the highest possible marks and to shove aside anyone and everyone standing in your path to the top. He believed this with utter conviction.
>
> It was shortly after I had married his daughter that I heard these very words from the man himself. All men are *not* created equal, he said. That was just some righteous-sounding nonsense they taught you in school. Japan might have the political structure of a democratic nation, but it was at the same time a fiercely carnivorous class society in which the weak were devoured by the strong, and unless you became one of the elite, there was no point in living in this country. You'd just be ground to dust. You had to fight your way up every rung of the ladder. This kind of ambition was entirely healthy. If people lost that ambition, Japan would perish.
>
> (Murakami 1994–1995: 72–73; emphasis in the original)

Toru counters this argument by saying that it exhibits a terribly shallow, one-sided and arrogant philosophy; it does not pay attention to nameless people who are supporting the society at its base; it does not allow for intro-spection into man's inner world and the significance of life; and it lacks imagination and scepticism.[23] In spite of this criticism of the idea of strong-is-good, Toru is, if unconsciously, affected by the same idea when he is forced by Wataya Noboru, Kumiko's brother, to divorce his wife Kumiko. He says to Noboru: 'I may be a nobody, but at least I'm not a sandbag. I'm a living, breathing human being. If somebody hits me, I hit back' (Murakami 1994–1995: 203). He calls it *Wild Kingdom* (204). This is the understanding of the world governed by efficiency and the law of the jungle exactly described by Kumiko's father (560).

Toru's violent actions also derive from the idea of love-is-beautiful. It is significant that the two people against whom Toru uses violence are 1) a guitar player who calls for the audience's empathy by burning his palm in an after-concert trick show and 2) Wataya Noboru who has the ability to draw from others the power of empathy and violence by means of symbolic incest.[24] Thus, the relationship between empathy – or feeling of sharing – and violence is apparent.

This feeling of sharing is described by Lieutenant Mamiya, a character in this story, in his experience in the midst of the Mongolian steppe where the surrounding space is so vast that it becomes more and more difficult to keep a balanced grip on his being. He feels that his self, as an individual human being, is slowly unravelling in the landscape. The mind expands to fill the entire landscape, becoming so diffuse in the process that one loses the ability to keep it fastened to the physical self (Murakami 1994–1995: 139). In this isolated region, a Russian officer catches Mamiya and compels him to jump into a well, where he is left to die. Then, when a blinding flood of sunlight pours straight down the well at high noon, Mamiya experiences a wonderful sense of 'oneness', an overflowing sense of 'unity' (166). Later he calls it the very core of his own consciousness (208). He felt he ought to die right then and there (166). But he could not die there, and after coming back to Japan he lived like an empty shell (171).

This understanding of Mamiya corresponds with Rat's insistence on killing the sheep in *A Wild Sheep Chase*. As we have seen, Rat killed himself with the sheep in his body in order to stop the sheep's attempt to create a realm of total conceptual unity in which consciousness, values, emotions, pain, everything would disappear and all opposites would be resolved, because he has realised that he is attached to his weakness, his pain and suffering (Murakami 1982 II: 204–205). Thus, the violence and love, the feeling of sharing, the wonderful sense of oneness Mamiya experiences at the bottom of the well are exactly what Rat attempted to stop at the cost of his own life in *A Wild Sheep Chase*. It is the modernist ideal world of total conceptual unity between people by the power of deep love.

In *The Wind-Up Bird Chronicle*, room 208 at the hotel in the other world is also depicted as a place for mutual understanding, sex, incestuous empathy and violence. The empathy and violence are depicted here as interrelated and strongly connected through the hero's conduct. They lie at the centre of man's mind and the sharing of these desires is confirmed by repeatedly emphasising the lack of free will of human beings (Murakami 1994–1995: 261–262, 510, 525). The story narrates the process whereby Toru frees his wife Kumiko from the hotel room, because he loves her (577). Though Katō Norihiro sees a continuity of the theme of a different world in all of Murakami's stories and calls it an 'autistic world' (*naihei*)[25] (Katō N. 1996: 205), it seems to me that in this novel, the meaning of that world has thoroughly changed from a cold, dry end of the world (*The Hard-Boiled Wonderland and the End of the World* and *Dance Dance Dance*) to the hotel's dark bedroom smelling of flowers, with air dense as mud (*The Wind-Up Bird Chronicle*).

If we dig deep in the well, the very core of one's own consciousness, we will find something human beings have in common.[26] Underlying room 208 is the very core of one's own consciousness shared with others. It is the bottom of the well in the vacant house where Miyawaki was living, and, as we have seen, also the bottom of Mamiya's well in the Mongolian steppe. There must be a deep sexual desire and the desire for violence in the total unity between people. *The Wind-Up Bird Chronicle* narrates the protagonist's attempts to save his wife Kumiko from room 208, but this is a symbolic action. As Kasahara May says, Toru is fighting for a lot of other people at the same time he is fighting for his wife (Murakami 1994–1995: 325). Toru's mission in this novel is most probably to distil love and discard violence from the depths of human consciousness.

In Murakami's later novel *Sputnik Sweetheart* (*Supūtoniku no koibito*, 1999; English translation 2001) a female character Miu took piano lessons in Paris when she was 25. One summer she stayed alone in a small town in Switzerland. One day in the town she was stuck inside a Ferris wheel overnight in an amusement park. Looking through binoculars at her own apartment room, she saw a naked man, Ferdinando, whom she suspected of following her. He was there making love with her second self, her Doppelgänger. Later she recalls the event and says: 'It was all meaningless and obscene, with only one goal in mind – to make me thoroughly polluted' (Murakami 1999: 170).

As Tsuge Teruhiko points out (1999: 17–18), this corresponds with the incident in which Wataya Noboru defiled Kano Creta in *The Wind-Up Bird Chronicle* (Murakami 1994–1995: 211). Both actions must be symbolic of mutual understanding, sexual desire, incestuous empathy and polluted violence. Miu says that her other self took her black hair, her sexual desire, her periods and her ovulation, and part of her will to live (172). By the symbolic action of looking at her own desires in her own apartment room from the little gondola of a Ferris wheel, and feeling them to be horrible, she left another 'her' in the room together with her desire to live. That is why her hair turned white in this world.

As has been repeatedly mentioned, there are two sides of human nature; detachment and attachment; differentiation and identification; individuality and empathy. Miu in *Sputnik Sweetheart* explains that she lacked the latter sides when she was young. While she was studying music in France, she noticed that pianists whose technique was worse than hers – and who did not practise nearly half as much as she did – were able to move their audiences more than she ever could. Something was missing from her. Something absolutely critical, the kind of depth of emotion a person needs to make music that will inspire others (Murakami 1999: 173).

Music is here again used as a metaphor of mutual empathy as in *The End of the World*, in which postmodern people do not have music to listen to, and in which the tears of the girl librarian as she listens to *Danny Boy* on the accordion suggest a trace of a 'mind' (Murakami 1985: 369). Miu says:

> Being tough isn't of itself a bad thing. Looking back on it, though, I can see I was too used to being strong, and never tried to understand

those who were weak. I was too used to being fortunate, and didn't try to understand those less fortunate. Too used to being healthy, and didn't try to understand the pain of those who weren't.

(Murakami 1999: 174)

Miu lacks empathy.

Therefore, it is certain that in *Sputnik Sweetheart* Miu is divided into two, one half is the one who has the flair of mutual understanding, sexual desire, incestuous empathy, and the desire of violence symbolised by her Doppelgänger who is making love with Ferdinando in the *other* world. Meanwhile the half in *this* world lacks empathy (Murakami 1999: 51, 230). The *other* world in this novel, the apartment room where Miu's Doppelgänger is making love with Ferdinando, is therefore, like room 208 of the hotel in *The Wind-Up Bird Chronicle*, and unlike the Sheep Man's room at the Dolphin Hotel in *Dance Dance Dance*, set as a world for mutual understanding, sex, incestuous empathy, and violence.

A lot of the relating metaphors, which describe the other world and this world, are used in *Sputnik Sweetheart*, too. Later when the protagonist teacher is seduced to go into the *other* world, the things that invite him are music and moonlight (Murakami 1999: 184–185). In order to flee from there the teacher retreats to his usual place of refuge. It is the very bottom of the freezing, dark, sea of consciousness, which reminds us once again of the town of *The End of the World* (186). *This* world is narrated as a lonely place. Though people here are yearning for others to satisfy them they are, nevertheless, isolating themselves. They are like

the descendants of Sputnik, even now circling the Earth, gravity their only tie to the planet. Lonely metal souls in the unimpeded darkness of space, they meet, pass each other, and part, never to meet again. No words passing between them. No promises to keep.

(Murakami 1999: 196)

Although the *other* world is narrated as a dark and polluted place, if we compare the two worlds in the following passage, we recognise that the *other* world for Murakami is also imagined as an ideal world. In the penultimate chapter of the novel the teacher tells one of his pupils, called Carrot, a story of his own childhood days.

I feel like I've been alone ever since I was a child. I had parents and an older sister at home, but I didn't get along with them. I couldn't communicate with anyone in my family. So I often imagined I was adopted...I imagined a town far away. There was a house there, where my real family lived. Just a modest little house, but warm and inviting. Everyone there can understand one another, they say whatever they feel like. In the evening you can hear Mum bustling around in the kitchen getting dinner ready, and there's a warm, delicious fragrance. *That's* where I belong. I was always picturing this place in my mind, with me as a part of the picture.

(Murakami 1999: 212; emphasis in the original)

Would it be possible to realise his imagined world, excluding Miu's *other* world of polluted sexual desire and violence?

In Murakami's more recent novel *Kafka on the Shore* (*Umibe no Kafuka*, 2002) the relation between incestuous sexual desire and violence is succinctly narrated as Oedipal desire (Murakami 2002 II: 348).[27] The story's young hero Tamura Kafka killed his father and committed incest with his mother and sister (as in many cases of Murakami's works, whether the murder of the father and incest with the mother and sister are conducted in reality or in an imaginary world is ambiguous). For Murakami's reader, this story contains a lot of nostalgically familiar elements. At the beginning of the story Kafka says that in order to reduce the baggage for travel, he would better not go to a cold place. This implies that the destination, Shikoku, is in this story regarded not as the postmodern world of the cold town in *The End of the World*, but again as a place of violence and incestuous sexual desire (Murakami 2002 I: 12).

In contrast, the wood Kafka enters and comes back from in the latter half of the story is considered a place without violence like *The End of the World*. A tall soldier says 'There is nothing to hurt you in the woods....Poisonous snakes, spiders, insects and mushrooms, even the Other will not hurt you here'. (Murakami 2002 II: 332; my translation). There are two persons in this story, Nakata and Saeki, whose shadows are dimmer than those of others (I: 87; I: 368; II: 138–139; II: 289). Like Miu in *Sputnik Sweetheart*, they have lost their sexual desire and the desire to do violence.

Significant in this novel is that violence, power and strength, which have been seamlessly united in Murakami's previous stories, are now clarified. The ideal strength is clearly stated by the protagonist Kafka who says:

What I want, the strength I want is not the strength with which people win or lose. Nor do I want walls to push back the power from the outside. What I want is the strength to grasp the outside power and endure it. It is the strength with which we can quietly bear the unfairness, misfortune, sorrow, misunderstanding and lack of perception.

(Murakami 2002 II: 155; my translation)

We may now be able to say that *Sputnik Sweetheart* and *Kafka on the Shore* go some steps further in the direction of understanding violence. What Murakami's stories aim to overcome is the Oedipal desire of modernity, the desire to grasp the outside power and endure it, and to go back to one's imagined nostalgic family with oneself as a part of it.

Though the last scene of *Dance Dance Dance* appears to be a turning point in the return to the modernist world, and *South of the Border, West of the Sun, The Wind-Up Bird Chronicle, Sputnik Sweetheart* and *Kafka on the Shore*, all seem to take steps towards a new understanding of empathy and violence, Murakami Haruki's early works in general allow the reader a glimpse of a postmodern world: a comfortable and cosy, yet mindless and anti-evolutionary world. At the same time, they also make us realise the features of modernity, its progress and beautiful love and its discrimination and suppression of others. We can see the two polarised forces of individualisation and totalisation, or identification and differentiation, underlying these features of modernity. It is in any case worth remembering that in the late 1970s and the early 1980s, the Japanese people, the younger generation in particular, enthusiastically welcomed Murakami's static and futile postmodern world, to such an extent as to create a noteworthy social phenomenon. Also, following the postmodern world depicted in his early works and the subsequent space for mutual understanding, sex, incestuous empathy and the desire for violence narrated in his later novels, which is the future direction of Murakami's narrative that is worth paying attention to.

2   Yoshimoto Banana's feminine family

Food versus sex or kitchen versus bedroom

> I think it is very, very interesting to see the move, the very slow move, from the privileging of food, which was overwhelming in Greece, to interest in sex. Food was still much more important during the early Christian days than sex. For instance, in the rules for monks, the problem was food, food, and food. Then you can see a very slow shift during the middle Ages, when they were in a kind of equilibrium...and after the seventeenth century it was sex.
> (Foucault, 'On the Genealogy of Ethics: An Overview of Work in Progress', in Foucault 1984: 340)

Many would agree that both Yoshimoto Banana and Murakami Haruki are major Japanese novelists whose work is tinged with postmodern ideas. Both writers have published internationally acclaimed novels that have been translated into many languages and found a wide audience particularly among young people. This chapter analyses Yoshimoto Banana's literary works from the perspectives of postmodernism, feminism and queer theory.[1] I discuss how these theories can highlight and explain certain themes in Banana's work that she shares with other contemporary writers. However, I also consider whether her work simply follows Euro-American trends or whether she adds a different perspective. From the perspective of continuation of the previous chapter about Murakami Haruki, we will find in Banana's work significant common features with Murakami's. As we have seen, he is attempting to deconstruct the polarised oppositions between individual differentiation and totalitarian identification, arising both from rationality and emotion, which as a whole supports the ideologies of strong-is-good and love-is-beautiful. His early works try to keep a sense of detachment from others, whereas his later works change the stance from detachment to commitment and directly face the binary desire by dealing with the deep love and the desire to do violence. In contrast, Yoshimoto Banana's work attempts to discover difference in totality or commonness in individuality by changing the form of desire. In what follows we will see how she is attempting to achieve this.

Before going on to discuss Banana's stories, let me first introduce the terminology and methodology of postmodern criticism by considering

Banana's metaphor of the 'kitchen'. There is an actual well-known post-modern kitchen in a postmodern house created by a Canadian–American architect, Frank O. Gehry who bought an old house in Santa Monica, California, in mid-1977, and rebuilt it for his own family (Marder 1985: 100–112). One of the most remarkable features of the house is its kitchen, which is located in the former driveway and yard, outside the frame of the main house. In an interview with Barbaralee Diamonstein, Gehry confesses that he was fascinated with the tension between the old and the new components of the house. Diamonstein also mentions that the kitchen/dining room relates to the inside versus the outside – the former driveway is now the existing dining room in between the first structure and its wrapper (Diamonstein 1980: 43–45).

Charles Jencks categorises the Gehry House in his book *Architecture Today* (1988), as postmodern. He illustrates its postmodern characteristics by pointing out that all the boundaries of the house have been broken, as can be seen in its kitchen, and its traditional borderlines have literally been transgressed (Jencks 1988: 216). For Jencks, this transgression, where new frames erode old; high collides with low; the outside destabilises the inside – or vice-versa – is one way in which postmodern space relates to religious and mystical space.

Fredric Jameson also classifies the Gehry House as postmodern, and remarks on the 'effacement of the categories of inside/outside, or a rearrangement of them' in its dining area and kitchen. He says:

> In a more articulated way it confronts us with the paradoxical impossibilities (not least the impossibilities of representation) which are inherent in this latest evolutionary mutation of late capitalism toward 'something else' which is no longer family or neighbourhood, city or state, nor even nation, but as abstract and nonsituated as the placelessness of a room in an international chain of motels or the anonymous space of airport terminals that all run together in your mind'.
>
> (Jameson 1991: 112–116)

Unlike structuralists who take dialectic as a primary method of analysis, post-structuralists and postmodernists attempt to break down fundamental boundaries and borderlines or to subvert categories, such as inside/outside, interiority/exteriority or up/down. They do this, not by making the inside into the outside, or up into down, but by deconstructing these dualistic concepts themselves. Thus, as Jencks and Jameson have pointed out, breaking down boundaries and borderlines, and subverting categories by deconstructing the dualistic concepts themselves has become a major post-modern strategy. By locating new and old, inside and outside, or high and low in the same place, or by exchanging them, the Gehry House subverts these modernist concepts. This is symbolically represented by the kitchen, which is located in between the old and the new structures.

However, unlike the Gehry House, the kitchen in Banana's novel *Kitchen* is not placed outside the frame of the house, but instead, its function in the story deconstructs, subverts, and effaces the traditional cultural ideology in a different manner. Just as the people in Murakami Haruki's early works stop moving or eternally move around in a circle through the postmodern deconstruction of modern cultural ideologies, Banana's stories also narrate a quiet world in which the characters eternally move around in cyclic time. Let me first analyse how and what Banana's fiction appears to be deconstructing.

'The place I like best in this world is the kitchen'. This is the opening sentence of Banana's *Kitchen* (*Kitchin*, 1988a). The heroine, Mikage, is a university student who appears in the story as an orphan. Her parents both died when she was young and her grandfather passed away when Mikage entered junior high school. The story starts with her grandmother's death leaving Mikage sleepless and alone. One morning at dawn she trundles out of her room in search of comfort and finds that the one place she can sleep is beside the refrigerator in the kitchen (4).[2] Later in the story when she moves into her boyfriend Yuichi's apartment, Mikage sleeps on the enormous sofa in the living room against the backdrop of the large kitchen (8).

Sone Hiroyoshi, a professor at Nihon University who taught Banana the methodology of novel writing when she was an undergraduate, mentions in his commentary notes to *Kitchen* that the sexual desire in this story is submerged in the desire for food (Sone 1991: 233–235). Ueno Chizuko also argues that in this novella the 'bed scene' is substituted by the 'table scene' and criticises Banana for failing to openly deal with sexual desire within the family (Ueno 1990b: 28–32).

There are clearly elements in the story that support Sone's and Ueno's interpretations. For instance, after the death of Eriko, Yuichi's transsexual father/mother, Mikage and Yuichi are left alone. But unlike in a modernist narrative in which the lovers would most probably go to bed, Mikage instead cooks a huge meal and they cheerfully enjoy an extravagant dinner. As the narrative unfolds, Yuichi becomes aware that he loves Mikage, and Mikage also decides to love Yuichi. But yet again, sexual desire is subsumed by food desire. Instead of a sexual unification between the two lovers, after deliberation, Mikage gets a take-out package of incredibly good *katsudon* (deep-fried pork in broth over rice) from a restaurant where she is staying in Izu and takes it by taxi all the way to Isehara to have Yuichi eat it.[3] In these scenes the common appetite for food is used to connect the two characters' hearts and the reader witnesses a transformation of sexual desire into food desire, and feels reassured to see them beautifully, cheerfully and openly satisfying their hunger. Banana's postmodern characters eat together where modernists would sleep together.

However, although Sone and Ueno consider that the sexual desire in this story is hidden behind or substituted for the desire for food, it seems to me that in Banana's *Kitchen* the concepts structuring the sexual and food desires are subverted or deconstructed. That is, though both Sone and Ueno seem to presuppose the unaltered existence of sexual desire and see it with its affiliated cultural meaning behind the desire for food in this story, it is more pertinent to argue that the borderline between the sexual and food desires has been broken down. For, even if we see the desire for food as a sort of metaphor for the sexual desire, once it is narrated in this manner, the latter interpretation cannot remain without drastic modification.

Further, what is apparent in Banana's *Kitchen* is not a metaphor in the traditional sense, but an infringement of the desire for food upon the sphere of sexual desire. If this is a matter of metaphor, it is a metaphor of restructuring the current existing discourse and creating something new: namely, the cultural meaning so far associated with sexual desire is, in this story, associated with the desire for food. In doing this, Banana's story subverts the borderline between sexual and food desires and consequently brings out 'something else' which is neither sexual desire nor food desire. What then does the deconstruction of the boundary between sexual and food desires indicate in the current cultural discourse?

It is not difficult to find here a transfiguration of the negative images associated with sexual desire into the opposite impressions connoted in the desire for food. Erotic desire has been treated ambivalently not only in modern Japanese literature, but literature worldwide. It has commonly been regarded as a low passion or an evil desire inherent in the animal side of people. Yet sex has also been represented as a creative activity or connecting link between self and others. Many modern writers have struggled to reconcile the tension between these opposing views, or openly acclaimed the positive side of the erotic desire. But in *Kitchen* Mikage and Yuichi are united not by erotic lust but by hunger. Furthermore, as Yuichi says of Mikage, cooking is an art for her (Yoshimoto Banana 1988a: 61), thus the desire for food and skills necessary to satisfy it are described as artistic and creative activities, replacing sexual desire. That is, the negative aspects of sexual desire are discarded, and its creative and unifying aspects are united in the desire for food.

We may also notice, following Fredric Jameson, that the waning of affect, which is one of the characteristic features of postmodernism, can be found here, too (Jameson 1991: 10). But more relevant to our discussion is that, by means of deconstructing the sexual and food desires and depicting the latter as a creative and unifying force, the structure of this story results in an effacement of the boundaries within human desire, and diffuses the energy that has been overly represented by sexual desire in the modern period. The transfiguration of sexual into food desire implies the emancipation of a desire, which has so far been subsumed by sex. This is, however, still not the whole story. Let me explore this contrast a little further.

It is natural to assume a relationship between the desire for food and the kitchen on the one hand, and the sexual desire and the bedroom on the other; moreover, as John Whittier Treat mentions, in Banana's *Kitchen* 'even the least attentive reader will conclude that the kitchen is a metonym for the family'

(Treat 1995: 288). The kitchen (dining room) is not only the place for cooking food and satisfying one's appetite, but also the room in which the whole family gathers. The relation between the desire for food and family is also discerned in 'the rite of eating together' (*kyōshoku girei*) (Ueno 1990b: 29).

There are many stories in world mythology such as that of Persephone in Greece or Izanami in Japan, where to eat food in hell requires that one stay there, because to eat food prepared by a society means to become a part of the society (Matsumura 1954–1958 II: 425–439). And furthermore, as P. J. Hamilton-Grierson writes in the *Encyclopædia of Religion and Ethics*, along with the intermingling of blood, as seen among the Reschiât of Lake Rudolph and the Karens of Burma, pseudo-brotherhood is often established with strangers through a ritual meal (Hastings 1909: 861–862). As Edward Westermarck has put it, it is natural to suppose that to eat food together establishes a bond between two heterogeneous people or groups (Westermarck 1968: 188–190). The use of the desire for food as a method for uniting people in a family is not an idea unfamiliar to us.

In this sense, as I mentioned at the beginning of this chapter, it is interesting to note that both for the architect Frank O. Gehry, and for the novelist Yoshimoto Banana, the function of the kitchen seems to be to connect the inside (family) and the outside (strangers). By situating the eating-place outside the frame of the house, the Gehry house provides his family with a refreshing, open experience when eating together, as if they were friends gathering at a picnic. Likewise, Banana's story invites outsiders into her dining room, as if they were eating together everyday like family. For these two artists eating together is a very significant activity in (re)constructing human relations.

In contrast to the close relations established between the desire for food/kitchen and family, what kind of relations are established by erotic sexual desire? The sexual desire is, to be sure, generally directed at non-family-members because of the incest taboo. The incest taboo has been well documented and there is no reason here to go into the arguments about its origin presented by Freud, Lévi-Strauss, Robin Fox, and W. Arens among others. However, with regard to the relation between incest and gender identity, I will later refer to Gayle Rubin's pioneering work (Rubin, G. 1975, 1984) as well as Judith Butler's subsequent analysis (Butler 1990). Furthermore, I will also deal with the Oedipal triangle and incest taboo, referring to the ideas of Deleuze and Guattari, René Girard and others.

The important point for the current discussion is neither the origin nor the cause of the incest taboo nor the exogamous system, but the emotional interrelation between two or more phenomena that take place concurrently within the institution of the incest taboo. Bronislaw Malinowski suggests that the prohibition of incest resulted from an internal contradiction within the biological family, between mutually incompatible feelings, such as the emotions attached to sexual relationships and parental love, or the sentiments which form naturally between brothers and sisters (Malinowski 1961:

251). Edward Westermarck, from a slightly different perspective, points out the relation between the absence of erotic feelings among family members and the prohibition of incest, and takes the former to be the fundamental cause of the latter (Westermarck 1968: 80).

Disregarding arguments over its origin, it seems clear that the emotional distinction between the family and the stranger is closely related to the incest taboo. We can distinguish the calm and tender feelings one holds for one's family and relatives, and the strong but ambivalent feelings of attraction and fear one feels towards outsiders. At the same time, we prohibit ourselves from expressing sexual desire for our family members and yet direct it at strangers. We can argue that these two processes occur simultaneously. As W. Arens remarks on Malinowski's study, 'the prohibition [of incest] and the family are coterminous, rather than one having precedence over the other' (Arens 1986: 50). Hence, the 'beloved' or the object of one's sexual desire is someone who is not a family member, that is someone who embodies the concept of the stranger or the 'Other'. Consequently having projected sexual desire outside of the family and on to strangers, we have established two worlds: the safe, calm homogeneous family, and the attractive but ambivalent heterogeneous stranger.[4]

The above argument reminds us of the opening scene of *Kitchen*, in which the kitchen is depicted in contrast to the bedroom. Mikage's preference for sleeping in the kitchen shows that she prefers to do in that room what people normally do in the bedroom. The fact that Mikage prefers the kitchen indicates that she feels relaxed with her family, or to put it in another way, she feels uneasy when she looks at or is looked at by her lover, who is an outsider. Lying on the big sofa in Yuichi's apartment, Mikage thinks:

> I was too sad to be able to sleep in the same bed with anyone; that would only make the sadness worse. But here was a kitchen, some plants, someone sleeping in the next room, perfect quiet...this was the best. This place was...the best.
>
> (Yoshimoto Banana 1988a: 16)

The sexual act is completely erased in this story, and even Mikage sleeping alone in the bedroom is rarely depicted. She sleeps in the kitchen in her old house, and in the living room (also a family place) in Eriko and Yuichi's apartment. The heavy and deep sexual desire felt towards one's lover in the dark bedroom is transformed here into the light and shallow desire for food experienced in the kitchen with one's family members.

It is important to emphasise at this point that there can be an erotic power structure of violence felt even within the family, and also that it is possible to establish warm and tender empathic relations with strangers. But, the issue here is not so much everyday experience as a symbolic formation of human desire. It seems clear that the ideological distinction between the emotions felt for one's family and the desire felt for the stranger is more or less universal. In some cultures the bond between the emotions felt for one's family and the family itself and/or erotic and violent desire and strangers may be stronger than in other cultures. In some cultures the relations between them appear in situations different from other cultures. But still we can argue that as long as incest is prohibited, the family/strangers distinction must exist.

Concerning the relation between family and sexuality, Michel Foucault in his *The History of Sexuality* says:

> The family, in its contemporary form, must not be understood as a social, economic, and political structure of alliance that excludes or at least restrains sexuality, that diminishes it as much as possible, preserving only its useful functions. On the contrary, its role is to anchor sexuality and provide it with a permanent support....The family is the inter-change of sexuality and alliance: it conveys the law and the juridical dimension in the deployment of sexuality; and it conveys the economy of pleasure and the intensity of sensations in the regime of alliance.
>
> (Foucault 1978–1986 I: 108)

Besides the family's role to anchor sexuality and provide it with a permanent support, it is also necessary to mention that by anchoring sexuality and providing it with a permanent support, the family plays another role – to supply the desire with the site of its transformation. In the course of family formation, especially taking the modern Japanese marriage system as an example, most husbands and wives shift their emotions from 'stranger' (sexual desire) to 'family' (desire for food).

The conjugal relation is in this sense ambiguous in that the marriage relationship is one between heterogeneous strangers within the homogeneous biological family; that is, the husband and wife are the only ones who are neither related by blood nor have the experience of living together from childhood. If they can express their familial friendship in a sexual act that originally served to satisfy the ambivalent libidinal erotic and violent desire towards strangers, then, as we will see later, this may be one of the ways to deconstruct the distinction between family and strangers, or homogeneity and heterogeneity. And furthermore, if it is true that women can more easily find friendship in sexual conduct, they should have greater potential to break through the modernist binary oppositions than men. In any period the socially lower classed or weak people have greater opportunities to change society than the socially higher classed or stronger people.

By erotic sexual desire, I refer to human desire as a cultural heritage that has been produced and constructed throughout time, in terms of the Lacanian formula that our desire is the desire of the Other (Lacan 1977a), and also in terms of Michel Foucault's and Gayle Rubin's assertion that desire is not a pre-existing naturally given biological entity, but rather a historically constructed social practice (Foucault 1978–1986 I: 105; Rubin, G. 1984: 276). As the desire for food has at least two functions – to preserve the individual body and to reaffirm human unity within the family, the sexual desire also has at least two meanings – to maintain the species and to unite with the stranger. It is astonishing to notice how we have skilfully utilised our two basic instincts – to preserve the individual (to eat food) and to maintain the species (to have sex) – and articulated our contingent desires according to these instincts. We eat with homogeneous familiar persons and have sex with heterogeneous strangers.

Furthermore, if we look carefully at our sexual desire, we can find at least two typical ways of interacting with strangers – a power struggle and a beautiful and strong emotion which occurs when we unite with strangers. We have a desire to do violence as well as to communicate and unite deeply, not with our family members, but with strangers. In essence, here we can confirm that, as Georges Bataille states, 'the domain of eroticism is the domain of violence, of violation' (Bataille 1986: 16). Freud was probably right when he suggested that the connection between sexual desire (incest) and murder (patricide) was essential for understanding modern human culture. In a sense, as I mentioned earlier, we have yet to discover how best to negotiate our relationships with strangers except through violence or sexual union, and, as we have seen in the previous chapter, this is also the question Murakami Haruki identifies. In any case, the incest taboo, self-identity, sexual desire, desire to do violence, familial love, friendship and the stranger – these institutions and desires are closely interrelated.

In modern Japanese literature many characters confront two ideas: sexual desire as a relation between self and stranger, and self-identity as a relation between the self and self-consciousness which results in more or less excluding or avoiding family relations. This is probably one of the reactions against the Neo-Confucian literature in the Edo period (1603–1867), which emphasised family relations. We can argue that the relation between self and self-consciousness, or self and strangers has formed modern Japanese writers' self-identities. It would not be an exaggeration to say that modern Japanese literature started with Utsumi Bunzō's self-consciousness in his private room in *The Drifting Clouds* (*Ukigumo*, 1886–89), and the I-novel (*shishōsetsu*) began with Tayama Katai's sexual desire in his own study room in *The Quilt* (*Futon*, 1907). One of the significant points of Yoshimoto Banana's fiction is that she has introduced the concept of the family in its new form to the modern Japanese literary scene that almost entirely consists of the relations between self and self-consciousness, and self and strangers.

We should now add the contrast 'family' versus 'stranger' and 'homogeneity' versus 'heterogeneity' to the original formula 'kitchen (dining room)/desire for food' versus 'bedroom/sexual desire'.

bedroom		kitchen (dining room)
sexual desire	vs	food desire
stranger		family
heterogeneity		homogeneity

Concerning the binary opposition of homogeneity and heterogeneity, from a multicultural studies' perspective, David Theo Goldberg points out the significance of the concept of heterogeneity for a radically multicultural state and regards the notion of homogeneity as underlying the standpoints of the monoculturalists. He claims that historically, especially throughout modernity, heterogeneity is the representative and prevailing condition, because movement and migration are the defining socio-historical conditions of humanity (Goldberg 1994: 20–24; 2000: 73). Ali Rattansi criticises Goldberg's distinction as creating a binary opposition between homogeneity and heterogeneity and argues that it is to reify and essentialise in an unhelpful manner. Instead of the unnecessary and unviable binary opposition of *either/or*, Rattansi proposes the concept of *both/and* as a central plank of deconstructive reflexivity (Rattansi 1999: 104). Even if we grant that the binary opposition between homogeneity and heterogeneity is static and modernistic, however, what Rattansi means by being *both* homogeneous *and* heterogeneous at the same time to one object is still not clear enough to grasp. How can one regard one object as having *both* homogeneity *and* heterogeneity? I would like therefore to understand what Rattansi means by incessantly transgressing the borderline of homogeneity and heterogeneity.

Thus, according to my interpretation, by deconstructing the sexual and food desires, and the bedroom and the kitchen, the structure of Banana's *Kitchen* subverts the modernist binary oppositions of the self–stranger, self–family, and heterogeneity and homogeneity ideologies. The significance of this subversion of binary formulation is that, in Banana's fiction, it neither transfers the former items to the latter sphere, nor does it suggest conflict between them but, instead, it incessantly keeps on reconfiguring the borderlines of these binaries and ceaselessly makes something new appear. To substitute the family for the stranger, or the homogeneous for the heterogeneous is no better than the outmoded idea of Japan as a family, with the Emperor acting as 'father of the people', or the world as a family with all people being brothers and sisters. Therefore, the multi-triangular image in Figure 2.1 is a much better representation of the subversion of binary in Banana's stories. The opposing terms of the binary are here resolved in the figure X^n at the apex of the triangle. The X^n represents an incessantly appearing 'something' that is no longer bedroom or kitchen, something other than sexual desire or food desire. It represents something that is neither heterogeneity nor homogeneity, and neither stranger nor family. What, then, is the X^n in Banana's fiction? We will discuss this in the following section.

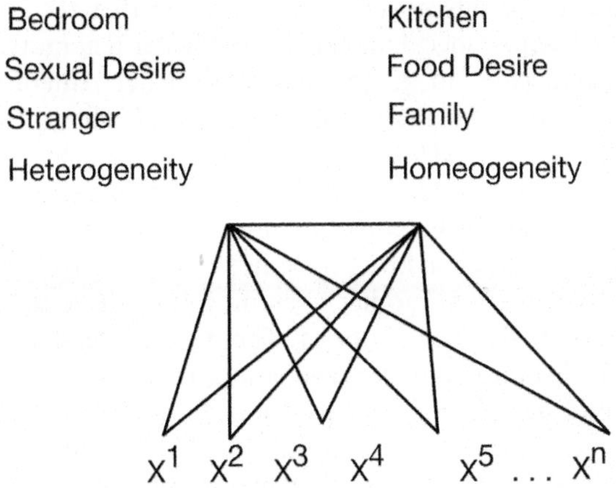

Bedroom	Kitchen
Sexual Desire	Food Desire
Stranger	Family
Heterogeneity	Homeogeneity

$$x^1 \quad x^2 \quad x^3 \quad x^4 \quad x^5 \dots x^n$$

Figure 2.1   Yoshimoto Banana's subversion of modernist binary oppositions

Oedipus versus Amaterasu

> Then Amë-nö-uzume said: 'We rejoice and dance because there is here a deity superior to you'. While she was saying this, Amë-nö-ko-yane-nö-mikötö and Puto-tama-nö-mikötö brought out the mirror and showed it to Ama-terasu-opo-mi-kamï. Then, Ama-terasu-opo-mi-kamï, thinking this more and more strange, gradually came out of the door and approached [the mirror.] Then the hidden Amë-nö-Ta-dikara-wo-nö-kami took her hand and pulled her out. Immediately Puto-tama-nö-mikötö extended a siri-kumë rope behind her, and said: 'You may go back no further than this!'
>
> (*Kojiki*: trans. Philippi 1968: 85)

In Yoshimoto Banana's fiction, just as places and desires exchange their functions, characters often switch their roles in the family. In *Kitchen* when Yuichi's mother dies, his father, Yuji, makes up his mind to become a woman. By changing his name to the female name Eriko, undergoing plastic surgery and dressing himself in women's clothing, he transforms himself into a woman. S/he then buys a transvestite bar where s/he works as the Mama, or manageress, and raises her/his son Yuichi, as his mother. In the character of Eriko, there is a transformation from father into mother. This exchange of roles within the family is not confined to that of father–mother. In *A Sad Premonition* (*Kanashii yokan*, 1988c) Yayoi, the narrator–heroine, realises in the course of events that Yukino whom she has thought to be her aunt is actually her elder sister. When their parents were killed in a traffic accident, they were adopted into the family of one of their parents' friends. Yayoi who witnessed her parents' death suffered from amnesia, and Yukino, although she was also legally adopted into the same family, insisted on living separately, pretending to be Yayoi's aunt.

Furthermore, in a more recent short story 'Sound of Silence' compiled in *The Body Knows Everything* (*Karada wa zenbu shitteiru*, 2000b) Banana repeats the situation. In this novella it is suggested that the heroine's elder sister who is fifteen years older than her is actually her real mother. When the elder sister/mother decides to go to Canada with her American boyfriend leaving her younger sister/daughter in Japan, the heroine has mixed emotions. She thinks: 'If she were my elder sister, I would feel just loneliness, but if she is my real mother…'. Then, suddenly, she is seized with a dark and passionate jealousy. But soon these mixed emotions resolve themselves into the calmer feelings associated with familial love (Yoshimoto Banana 2000b: 183).

The aunt–sister or sister–mother metamorphosis is one of the most attractive elements in these two stories. The readers' tender emotions are engaged when the distance between Yayoi and Yukino in *A Sad Premonition*, or the heroine and her elder sister/mother in 'Sound of Silence' suddenly contract from that of niece–aunt to younger–elder sister in the former, and from that of younger–elder sister to daughter–mother in the latter. But the change of role from aunt to elder sister in *A Sad Premonition* and from elder sister to mother in 'Sound of Silence' can be interpreted in a different way in the light of its relation to Eriko's father–mother transformation in *Kitchen*.

One of the fundamental ways in which self-identity is established is in its early stages through the role of the child in the family. One's self-identity is established in one's childhood mainly through playing the role of daughter or son in relation to parents, younger brother or younger sister in relation to older siblings, and niece or nephew in relation to aunts or uncles. Hence, we can argue that the metamorphosis or transformation of family roles in Banana's fiction threatens to disorient the current form of self-identity constructed in intra-family human relations. That is to say, by means of transforming relations from father-son to mother-son (Eriko–Yuichi) or from niece–aunt to younger–elder sisters (Yayoi–Yukino) or further from younger–elder sisters to daughter–mother ('Sound of Silence'), the characters in Banana's stories deconstruct their current self-identities. This is, however, still not the whole story. Let me explore this transformation of family roles a little further.

Yoshimoto Takaaki, Banana's father, considers the issue of metamorphosis when he remarks that in his daughter's stories male/female, father/mother, and relative/friend are often exchangeable (Yoshimoto Takaaki and Banana 1997: 124–125, 137–138). We can discover in this exchangeability not only the deformation of one's prior identity formed in the family but rather the disappearance of the particularity or uniqueness of the modernist concept of self-identity. For modernists one's identity must be unique and nothing can be substituted for it, but in Banana's fiction this uniqueness almost disappears. However, it must be stressed that Banana's stories are not trying to completely erase this uniqueness, but to attempt to here again deconstruct the distinction between uniqueness and commonality.

Looking at this issue from a different perspective, as Banana herself mentions, we can argue that she is trying to expand her love in an undiscriminatory manner, from one to another, from male to female, and even from human to animal (Yoshimoto Takaaki and Banana 1997: 137). We might surmise that Banana's intention is to establish human relations as widely as possible even at the risk of superficiality, rather than limit them in a closed, albeit profound, domain. These kinds of human relations well reflect an antithetical attitude, not only against the compelling forces of human compassion represented by people in traditional settings, but also against the modernist ideals of deep human relations. For example, Yuichi in *Kitchen* is described as being incapable of caring more for a girl than he does for a fountain pen (Yoshimoto Banana 1988a: 29).

In this sense, Banana's characters share the same inclination as Murakami Haruki's heroes. In contrast to Murakami's characters – especially in his early works – who attempt to detach themselves from others, Banana's characters try to deconstruct the relations between friend/relative or family/stranger. In so doing, Banana's narrative is changing the significance of 'love' itself, from narrow and deep to wide and shallow, just as many of Murakami's characters prefer shallow etiquette, or being a gentleman, to the experience of profound love.

The exchangeability of friend/relative or family/stranger further opens up new possibilities in relationships: namely incest. In the novel *A Sad Premonition*, following Yayoi's discovery that she is an adopted daughter of her present family, she begins a sort of love affair with Tetsuo, a son of her adoptive family, in which the theme of incest, not between biological but psychological siblings, is hidden. The theme of incest is also dealt with in *N.P.* (1990), in which Sarao Takase and Sui (father and daughter) and Otohiko and Sui (stepbrother and stepsister) love each other. This incestuous desire can also be found in the relation between Sakumi and Ryūichirō (Sakumi's late sister's lover, that is, her previous pseudo-brother-in-law) in *Amrita* (1994a). Furuhashi Nobuyoshi finds the incest motif also between Ningyo and Arashi (Arashi is Ningyo's father's adopted son) in *Fleeting Bubbles* (*Utakata*, 1988b), Yoshihiro and Marie (cousins) in 'Night and Night's Travellers' ('Yoru to yoru no tabibito'), a short story compiled in *Asleep* (*Shirakawa yofune*, 1989b) (Furuhashi 1990: 64). John Whittier Treat also sees a quasi-sibling, quasi-sexual relationship between Mikage and Yuichi in *Kitchen* (Treat 1995: 290).[5] What does this incest motif mean in Banana's stories?

As Gayle Rubin suggested in her study of feminism, the incestuous desire or kinship sexual desire can reconfigure the existing binary opposition between erotic sexual desire towards strangers and calm and tender emotions towards family (Rubin, G. 1975: 199). Judith Butler, however, in the later dialogue with Rubin confesses doubting the possibility of a reconfiguration of desire. Butler says:

> there was a belief that if you could reconfigure and change your kinship arrangements that you could also reconfigure your sexuality and your psyche, and that psychic transformation really followed directly from

the social transformation of kinship arrangements. And then when everybody had done that and found out that their psyches were still in the same old pits that they had always been in....Maybe there is something intractable, maybe there is something more persistent.

(Rubin with Butler 1998: 42)

Although I do not know what Butler had in mind when she mentioned 'something', I believe that nothing is intractable, and nothing is permanently persistent. Thus, I believe, reconfiguration of kinship sexual desire is not only necessary but also possible.

John Whittier Treat, in his analysis of *Goodbye Tsugumi* (*Tugumi*), discusses the pseudo-sibling/incestuous relationships in Banana's novels. He says that the 'pseudo-sibling relationship is always powerful in Banana's fiction: seldom sexual, never Oedipal, nothing but snug and non-threatening, the pseudo-sibling relationship engenders a kind of lateral parity that contrasts with the hierarchal schema of a patriarchal family organisation' (Treat 1993: 370–373; 1995: 291). Mitsui Takayuki also mentions the lack of erotic desire in the pseudo-sibling relationships in Banana's fiction, as well as the lack of Oedipalised family, and interprets this as Banana's attempt to heal the psychological wounds inflicted in human relations through a sort of friendly affinity experienced in the pseudo-sibling relationship. He regards *Kitchen* as a story about children who accept the collapse of the modern family or the appearance of the postmodern family in which Oedipal desire has disappeared. Banana's characters, though they are trapped in this situation, do not attempt to recover the Oedipal family, nor do they intentionally try to subvert it; they are simply indifferent to it, and watch the changing family with surprise (Mitsui and Washida 1989: 84–102). They consequently find the subversion of Oedipalised or patriarchal power relations in the family narrated in Banana's fiction.

In contrast to their interpretation that finds a lack of Oedipalised desire in the incest in Banana's fiction, I would like to focus on the reformation of the family/strangers distinction in the incest motif in these stories. By transforming sexual desire into food desire, Banana's fiction, as we have seen, first obscures the distinction between strangers and the family. And now, through the incestuous erotic desire, which unites two homogeneous family members, Banana's fiction attempts to deconstruct the current concepts of family and strangers, based on the incest prohibition. In this way the incest in Banana's stories, just like the exchange of food and sexual desires, reconfigures existing human relations founded on the family/strangers distinction, not from the outside but from inside the family. Through psychological incest, to use an expression from Jameson and Jencks, boundaries within and around the family are broken and the borderlines are literally transgressed, and 'something else' is created which is no longer family, strangers or self. Let me explore this point a little further.

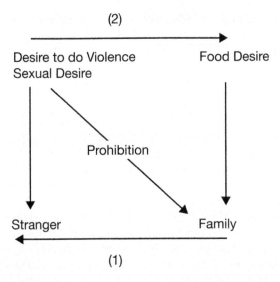

Figure 2.2   The deconstruction of incest.

There seem to be at least two different kinds of incestuous desire. One is to treat a family member as if she or he were a stranger and project one's erotic desire on to her or him, and the second is to transform sexual desire into something like food desire and manifest it in a relationship with a family member (Figure 2.2). The two types of desire, although they have the same result, are very different from each other. The former is, as has been mentioned, a desire to communicate deeply and unite with strangers as 'Others', as well as the desire to do violence: the desire bound by struggle against and unification with the 'Other'. It is in a sense an antinomic contrast between simultaneous individualisation and totalisation or differentiation from and identification with the Other. In this domain incest is depicted as an emotional, romantic and erotic love between brother and sister or mother and son that is strong enough to break the taboo even at the risk of their lives. The latter is, in contrast, the relation between the similar, homogeneous family members. In this realm they have sex as if they were dining together. Although the partners engage in sexual activity, what they are expressing is not a strong erotic desire, but a familiar friendship or the calm and tender sentiments that they share in their everyday lives together.

Relating to these two different kinds of incestuous desires, let me explore here two different human desires. Deleuze and Guattari find in the Freudian Oedipal triangle a symbol of modern society, or an archetype of capitalist society in which the rule of the game is to aggregate the surplus by means of rivalry and competition (Deleuze and Guattari 1984: 265). In the triangular Oedipal rivalry between father and son competing for the mother one can see a representation of modern capitalist society which is ruled by power struggles and aims at development and evolution.[6] In contrast to this incestuous

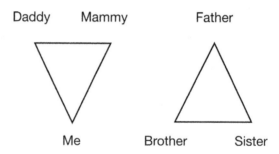

Figure 2.3   Two representations of incestuous desire.

desire of rivalry represented by the inverted Oedipal triangle, Hasumi Shigehiko finds a different pattern in contemporary Japanese novels. He finds an incestuous isosceles triangle between 'father–brother–sister', specifically narrated in Nakagami Kenji's *The Sea of Kareki* (*Kareki nada*, 1977) and in Ōe Kenzaburō's *The Game of Contemporaneity* (*Dōjidai gēmu*, 1979) (Figure 2.3). Hasumi remarks that in *The Sea of Kareki* the triangle is finally dissolved into the family bloodline (Hasumi 1994: 213–214).

Let me first trace this idea back to Japanese mythology. The brother–sister incestuous union in Book 1 of the *Kojiki*[7] is suggested repeatedly and successively between Izanagi–Izanami and Amaterasu–Susanoo (Figure 2.4). Susanoo, the forefather of the Izumo clan in the *Kojiki* story, indulges in incest and violence and is insulted, abused, and denounced as nothing more than a criminal and a social outcast, resulting in his expulsion from heaven. The emperor's royal blood derives from the goddess Amaterasu, Susanoo's sister, who is killed by Susanoo and reborn through a renewal ritual. Amaterasu's soul is regarded as the ancestral soul of the imperial family and it is believed that this passes into each new emperor's body. That is to say, in the *Kojiki* there are two aspects of incest: a sacred rebirth and a criminal act are enacted separately – the former by Amaterasu and the latter by Susanoo.

We can argue that in comparison with *Oedipus the King* where the incest is closely associated with murder and the sacred rebirth is not narrated, in the *Kojiki*, the two aspects of incestuous unions, separate characters, Susanoo and Amaterasu, act out violence and sacred rebirth. This point can be related to two different interpretations of incest: (1) the transformation of family members into strangers – diametrical desire of erotic sexual act and violence – and (2) the transfiguration of sexual desire into something like food desire.

In *Oedipus the King* the incest is certainly interpreted in the first manner. Whereas in the *Kojiki* Susanoo plays the former and Amaterasu, the latter role.[8] What then is the desire underlying incest (2) in the *Kojiki*? It seems that what is apparently desired in Amaterasu is to allow the ancestral soul, particularly the soul of one's parents, to be reborn into the body of one's offspring. That is, the underlying desire is one of rebirth. One of the beliefs

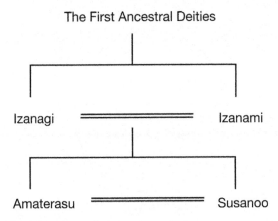

Figure 2.4 Brother–sister incest in Japanese mythology

underlying this desire is that grandparents' souls are reborn in their grand-children's bodies (Murakami F. 1988).

This desire to be reborn or to see someone else reborn apparent in the Amaterasu–Susanoo incest myth can be found not only in classical Japanese literature, but also in many modern and contemporary Japanese novels. As Hasumi points out, both in Ōe Kenzaburō's *The Game of Contemporaneity* and Nakagami Kenji's *The Sea of Kareki* the ancestors are clearly invoked to be reborn through the ritualistic brother–sister incest. In this case, the brother-sister incestuous isosceles triangle would be represented better as a circle. At the top of the circle is the ancestor's soul, at the two ends of the horizontal diameter are the brother and sister, and at the bottom are the offspring. The overall figure shows an eternal repetition of rebirth (Figure 2.5). The desire underlying this circle is not a power struggle between father and son competing for the mother as depicted by Deleuze and Guattari and René Girard that provides the foundation for the development and evolution of modernist ideology. Rather, it is an eternal circle that ensures the rebirth of the ancestors' souls in the bodies of their offspring, or the rebirth of grandparents' spirits in the bodies of their grandchildren.[9]

Relating to this kind of cyclic desire of rebirth, the study of the dichotomy of cyclic time and linear time can be referred to. As one of the central figures having studied this dichotomy, Mircea Eliade explains cyclical time as traditional and primitive, and linear time as modern. He also asserts that the linear, progressive conception of history became predominant in the century of Enlightenment and popularised in the nineteenth century by the triumph of the ideas of evolution. Eliade further suggests that human individuality's creative spontaneity is what constitutes the authenticity and irreversibility of history (Eliade 1954: 46, 112, 145–147).[10] The conflict between individualisation and totalisation or differentiation and identification, which, we suppose in the previous chapter about Murakami Haruki, appeared with the modernist ideologies of the

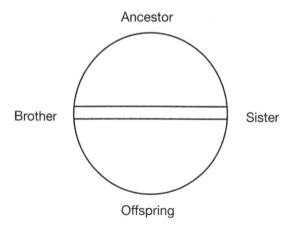

Figure 2.5   Eternal repetition of rebirth

Enlightenment and evolution, is therefore closely related to the dichotomy of cyclic time and linear time. That is to say, individuality and the concept of linear time for aim and purpose are coterminous; both of them become clearly visible in the modern time. We will return to this issue later when we discuss African, Asian and Native American consciousness in the next chapter.[11]

Going back to our discussion of the relations between Banana's incest motif, the concept of rebirth, cyclic time and the desire underlying them, the question I would like to address is why people pray for their ancestors' rebirth in cyclic time. What desire underlies this rebirth? It is possible to interpret this in many ways and it may be hard to come to a single conclusion. Despite René Girard's rejection of the idea (Girard 1977: 105), it is difficult to rule out completely the desire to preserve one's family bloodline, which lies behind rebirth. A yearning for eternal life is also another possibility that deserves consideration. Concerning the meaning of rebirth, Eliade emphasises its aspect of transition toward a higher condition of humanity.[12]

Among many possible interpretations, I would like to focus here on one of the primary aspirations hidden behind the Amaterasu circle in relation to one of Banana's key terms: the desire for nostalgia (*natsukashisa*).[13] In stark contrast to the longing for an ideal future represented by the Oedipal triangle, what the Amaterasu circle represents seems to be a yearning to see familiar persons again. This is illustrated in the scene cited in the epigraph of this section: after Amaterasu's concealment of herself in the heavenly rock-cave, which in *Kojiki* suggests her own death, the deities in *Takama no hara* heaven brought out a mirror and lured her from the cave. They wanted to see her again.[14] And, this is also what Banana's key term nostalgia (*natsukashisa*) is longing for.

For instance, in Banana's story 'Night and Night's Travellers' ('Yoru to yoru no tabibito') the heroine Shibami happens to see the son of her late brother Yoshihiro and his former girlfriend Sarah in a hotel lobby. The boy's familiar face evokes her enormous nostalgia for Yoshihiro (Yoshimoto Banana 1989b: 167 (J), 63–64 (E)).[15] Although it is rebirth that is narrated here, what is desired is not the rebirth itself, but the sense of nostalgia. In contrast to Nakagami Kenji's *The Sea of Kareki*, in which, as Hasumi remarks, the theme of rebirth is closely connected to the continuation of the family bloodline, in Banana's stories the emphasis is placed not on the family bloodline, but on the underlying desire for nostalgia.

In *Kitchen*, in a delicate equilibrium between a sense of independence and belonging, or between the happiness of being alone or of being together, what unites Mikage and Yuichi is neither their future hopes nor their present sexual unity, but here again nostalgia. It is the recollection of the time they spent together that enables them to establish a deep sense of understanding. In the penultimate scene of *Kitchen*, in the contemplative atmosphere and the ensuing silence in the room in the inn, Yuichi and Mikage are supported by their memories.

Deborah Garrison points out the fact that in *Kitchen* the reader learns of many key events in the story only in retrospect. She supposes that the reason is 'because it is only in retrospect that Mikage comes into full possession of their significance'. In her concluding remark Garrison says 'In fact, she [Banana] makes you wonder if bounce-and-shine is still a standard feature in the artistic youth of other nations' (Garrison 1993: 110). I would like to add one further point here. Mikage is obsessed not only with understanding the significance of past events, but also with retrospection or nostalgia itself. And furthermore, that is why she makes us wonder if bounce-and-shine is still a standard feature in our desire.

Nostalgia (*Natsukashisa*) is also a key term in *A Sad Premonition* (*Kanashii yokan*). The heroine Yayoi who is suffering from amnesia often almost recalls some past event, a memory sweet and lovely. The story follows Yayoi's journey from Tokyo to Karuizawa, and to Mount Osore, chasing after the past nostalgic memories preserved by Yukino – her aunt/elder sister. It is significant that Mount Osore is a place for recalling the dead (Ivy 1995: 141–191). Yukino is also depicted as a person who has a nostalgic desire in the sense that she loves to see a familiar person again and again in a TV video series. Masahiko loves Yukino because she reminds him of something nostalgic, memories of his late mother. As I will mention soon, in Banana's recent books such as *Adultery and South America* (*Furin to nanbei*, 2000a), *The Body Knows Everything* (*Karada wa zenbu shitteiru*, 2000b) and *Rainbow* (*Niji*, 2002b) nostalgia (*natsukashisa*) also appears as a key term.

As Treat and Mitsui mention, the power struggle or desire to evolve to achieve a goal as represented by the Oedipal triangle certainly disappears in Banana's novels. The desire for preserving the purity of the bloodline by being reborn also vanishes. But nostalgia, hidden in the Amaterasu circle, still remains. We should not underestimate this immense nostalgia, which underlies not only the pseudo-sibling/incestuous relationship but also many other human relations in Banana's fiction.

Why is Banana so obsessed by the nostalgic desire? What does the sense of nostalgia mean in Banana's stories and in the current cultural context? Nostalgia first comes from familiarity – from shared lives and memories. Born from reliving again and again the memories of shared events, nostalgia is an emotion directed towards homogeneous partners. When one has not seen the people familiar to one for a long time, one naturally feels nostalgia. Indeed, it is the emotion that reminds us of the dear old past memories shared by our homogeneous group.

Yet, significantly, a lot of Banana's characters feel nostalgia towards strangers from their first meeting. Yuichi in *Kitchen* is first attracted to Mikage because she reminds him of Woofie, a dog he used to have. That is, for Yuichi, Mikage is from the first meeting a nostalgic figure who reminds him of his late dog. In *N.P.* when the narrator–heroine Kazami first meets Saki and Otohiko at a party, she feels nostalgia. She tells herself:

> I was overwhelmed by the sensation that I had actually met them before in my dreams, but then, in the next moment, I came back to my senses, aware that anyone who saw these two would feel the same way. They were, in some sense, a couple who evoked nostalgia, a longing for home.
>
> (Yoshimoto Banana 1990: 2)

When Kazami first meets Sui she thinks, 'It was hard to believe that I had just met her. I felt as if we had been together for a long time. She felt so familiar to me, like a childhood friend' (71). All of them feel like they have known each other for a long time, and all of them evoke feelings of familiarity and nostalgia in each other (27, 69). A character feeling nostalgia towards a stranger is an element repeated in Banana's later works, too. In *Hachi's Last Girlfriend* (*Hachi-kō no saigo no koibito*, 1994c) when a heroine Mao first meets Hachi, she thinks she knows him well (Yoshimoto Banana 1994c: 16). The heroine of the short story 'Sycamore' ('Puratanasu') compiled in *Adultery and South America* (2000a) starts loving her sixty-year-old boyfriend because his clothes smell like those she remembers from her grandfather's wardrobe (Yoshimoto Banana 2000a: 96).

The above examples show that Banana's main characters are from the very beginning homogeneous. Banana does not narrate the troubled way in which heterogeneous people struggle to create homogeneous relations. The characters in Banana's stories are from the first encounter already homogeneous. One might be tempted to criticise her narrative style as too easy-going. But we can also argue that in using the idea of nostalgia towards a stranger, Banana's fiction here again attempts to reconfigure the modernist homogeneous/heterogeneous binary opposition. It also reminds us of the subversion of the modern idea that human relations should move from heterogeneous to homogeneous.

This feature is thus related to the contrast of the sexual/food desires, which, as we have noted, also functions to deconstruct the homogeneous/heterogeneous dualism. Just as Mikage and Yuichi in *Kitchen* eat together on occasions when modernists would have sex, a lot of Banana's characters feel nostalgia on first meeting with heterogeneous people, in which situation modernists would most probably feel erotic attraction or hostility. In addition to being a medium for deconstructing the binary notions of homogeneous/heterogeneous or family/strangers, it seems to me that the concept of nostalgia is also able to subvert modernist discourse and help us glimpse a postmodern and feminist view. I shall explore these ideas in the next section.

Nostalgia versus castration fantasy

> Only by the concurrent or mutually opposing action of the two primal instincts – Eros and the death-instinct –, never by one or the other alone, can we explain the rich multiplicity of the phenomena of life.
> (Sigmund Freud 1964, 'Analysis Terminable and Interminable' vol. 23: 243)

> These considerations make it possible to regard the fear of death, like the fear of conscience, as a development of the fear of castration.
> (Sigmund Freud 1991, 'The Ego and the Id' vol. 11: 400)

In order to explore Banana's nostalgia further, and also to search for the connecting link between Banana's work and feminism and homosexuality, some explanations of its theoretical background is helpful. Let us first look at the linguistic background of the Japanese adjective nostalgic (*natsukashii*) before moving on with our discussion on the connection between nostalgia and feminist endeavour. The word '*natsukashii*' evokes in many Japanese native speakers a deep emotional response. In English, 'nostalgia' means 'yearning for a past period' (*OED*). The etymology is the Greek *nostos* (return home) + *algos* (pain). In contrast, '*natsukashii*' derives from the verb '*natsuku*' which means to get used to being with or to become attached to something/someone. Thus, in its original meaning, a *natsukashii* person was someone with whom one felt comfortable.

Some of the Japanese 'sensation/emotion' adjectives indicate a sort of correspondence in various ways between the outside world and a person's inner psychology – the subject and object of the emotion. The present usage of '*natsukashii*' (so nostalgic that I am reminded of something from the past) is one of these; others include the classical '*aware*' (so impressive that I am moved), '*hazukashii*' (so admirable that it makes me feel inferior) and '*yukashii*' (so charming that I am attracted by it). On the whole these adjectives tend to produce in the native Japanese mind a strong emotional response toward the unity between the subject and object.

However, with regard to the present discussion, it is also important to understand that the object of nostalgia is now lost. One of the hidden desires underlying nostalgia is this sense of an imagined past unity that has now disappeared. The term establishes a distance between the subject and object: they are temporally and spatially apart, but mentally and imaginatively united. Were subject and object to be tightly conjoined, then nostalgia would lose its meaning. Therefore, '*natsukashisa*' (nostalgia) in a sense results in the decline of deep physical affections.

Susan Stewart describes nostalgia by saying that its motif is the erasure of the gap between nature and culture, and hence a return to the utopia of biology symbolised by the walled city of the maternal (Stewart, S. 1984: 23–24). I would like to focus on Stewart's understanding of nostalgia as the inability of the sign to 'capture' its signified and of narrative to be one with its object, as a driving force behind nostalgic longing. Nostalgia is not directed towards an object before one's eyes. It bypasses face-to-face communication and orients itself towards a signified that exists only in the past. Thus, nostalgia in a sense castrates desire because of the impossibility of its being realised.

The direct confrontation between subject and object characteristic of modernism inevitably results in either identification or differentiation. However, because of the impossibility of this direct confrontation in nostalgia, the modernist double bind of individualisation and totalisation can be eroded. Erotic desire, for instance, is conceived of directly in relation to its object and struggles with it, resulting in either unification or differentiation. Nostalgic desire, in contrast, deconstructs this binary opposition and provides a certain distance both between the desire and its object and the desire and the image of the object. That which arouses one's nostalgic emotion is a copy of an original, which has now disappeared.[16]

What exactly does nostalgia long for? In this regard, let me first explore the relationship between nostalgia and the Freudian concept of fantasy. Referring to Laplanche and Pontalis' studies of fantasy (Laplanche and Pontalis 1973: 317–318; 1986: 26–27) and also to Judith Butler's subsequent argument on fantasy (Butler 1993: Ch. 3, 267–268), the similarity between fantasy and nostalgia seems apparent in that both stress the impossibility of a return to primary satisfactions, that an original object is lost, and that both dissimulate that loss in the imaginary recovery and articulation of the lost object. The difference lies only in the perceivable and conscious longing to return to the impossible primary satisfaction evident in nostalgia.

Concerning Freudian fantasy or to be more specific castration fantasy, it is crucially important to refer to Gayle Rubin's classic study of gender identity. By interpreting the work of Lévi-Strauss and Freud, Rubin in her 1975 paper pays attention to the pre-Oedipal phase in which children of both sexes were psychically indistinguishable (Rubin, G. 1975: 185–186). In Freudian theory for both girls and boys the most crucial point determining the possibility of satisfaction in the Oedipal and castration stages is regarded as superiority/inferiority consciousness, and one of the processes we can find at work between the Oedipus complex and the latency period described by Freud, is the process whereby the child is captured in the net of power systems referred to as phallogos which is significantly attributed to the gender and sexuality distinctions.[17]

In the Oedipal and castration stages the child's desire as mythical and pre-symbolic intention is repressed and articulated according to the symbolic desire of the Other and directed into encoded channels. Among them, of particular importance for our discussion, are two desires: one is the desire to repeat past experiences in an incestuous autism (the death drive in its extreme case), and the other is the erotic desire and desire to actively and energetically progress to the future on the basis of superiority/inferiority consciousness (including the repetition for mastery).[18] The former longs for the pre-castrative state (castration fantasy) and the latter causes the threat of losing itself (castration anxiety).[19] It is natural to suppose, as Rubin suggested, that in the child's desire before the Oedipal stage these two types of desires co-exist fused without being distinguished. It seems, however, crucial to retrospectively distinguish these two desires. As cited in the epigraph at the top of this section, each of them reciprocally acts as a defence against the other.

We can now argue that the nostalgia frequently narrated in Banana's fiction represents a desire to usher the post-castrative subject into the pre-castrative setting in which the distinction between masculinity and femininity or phallic authority and envious obedience built on the matrix of the Other's symbolised desire have not yet been articulated. In this context the castration fantasy and nostalgia are construed as the desire to return to the original stage of fusion in which heterosexual/power-oriented desires and bisexual/incestuous autistic desires co-exist without being distinguished. It is the desire to go back to the pre-Oedipal, original pre-castrative state, in which distinctions between masculinity and femininity, authority and obedience, and even between superiority and inferiority did not exist. This is the desire to renounce sexuality and this is exactly the place some feminists are, following Rubin's suggestion, looking for.[20]

In Banana's story 'Newlywed' – from the short-story collection *Lizard* (*Tokage*, 1993) – the old, homeless guy who suddenly transforms himself into a beautiful woman makes the protagonist feel as though he is witnessing something familiar:

> This being sitting next to me felt somehow familiar, like the scent of a place, before I was born, where all the primal emotions, love and hate, blended in the air. I also could sense that I would be in danger if I got too close. Deep inside, I felt timid, even scared, not about my own drunkenness or fear that my mind was playing tricks on me, but the more basic sensation of encountering something much larger than myself, and feeling immeasurably small and insignificant by comparison. Like a wild animal would when confronted by a larger beast, I felt the urge to flee for my life.
>
> (Yoshimoto Banana 1993: 12)

This place before he was born can be conceived of as the phantasmic setting in which the threat of castration did not yet exist. It is the state before he, as an individual being, enters into the site of the desire of the Other – where all the primal emotions, love and hate, blend in the air. He feels deep inside the danger of getting too close, and becomes timid, even scared, probably because it is a situation in which individual identity could disappear.

When Yayoi, in *A Sad Premonition* (*Kanashii yokan*), recalls the nostalgic figure of her aunt/elder sister Yukino, she mentions a dark magical female force of nostalgia (*natsukashisa*).

> What brought me as far as here is neither that she is my elder sister, nor that she disappears without any notice, but it is a dark magical female force she bears. She hides behind her hair, sweet voice, and thin fingers that play the piano, an overwhelming nostalgia (*natsukashisa*). Those who have lost their childhood surely know it very well. Deeper than the night, longer than eternity, something far away.
> (Yoshimoto Banana 1988c: 107; my translation of the original Japanese)

Here again, those who have lost their childhood will recognise the nostalgia in the figure of Yukino, because it derives from the pre-Oedipal or pre-castrative stage in which the child could be part of the chaotic whole. It is also worth noting that in this story the force leading the subject to the pre-castrative setting is called a dark magical female force. In Banana's stories it is in this magical female force that the immense nostalgia is primarily stored.

The image of a river vividly represents the sense of nostalgia. The water flowing past us is definitely not the same water we saw the last time we visited the riverbank, but its unchanging figure recalls the previous time we saw it. At the same time it makes us aware of a transient and evanescent changing world where the momentary rivalry and evolution seem to be nothing but a stream. A present copy makes us recall the past original that is lost. But this original loss is only tangible retrospectively, because a chaotic mass of fusion can only be articulated from the viewpoint of symbolic order.

The image of the river is significant in Banana's 'A Strange Tale from Down by the River' ('Ōkawabata kidan'). The heroine Akemi quits her life of sexual adventure and makes her mind up to live an ordinary married life. Then, she happens to realise that one of the factors that led her to follow a life of sexual abandon was her unconscious memory that she had been thrown into the river by her mother. Tormented by her husband's love affair with another woman, Akemi's mother had once become hysterical and thrown the infant Akemi into the river in front of his eyes (Yoshimoto Banana 1993: 160–162 (E); 1994b: 245–246).

To be thrown into the river is symbolic in at least two senses. It signifies rejection by her mother, which is why she desired someone with whom she could unite. Another reading suggests that through transcending her mother's psychological state in which both love and hate, and selfish motives and kindness are in conflict, she goes back to the pre-castrative stage represented by the river through the symbolic act of being thrown into it. Hope for Akemi lies in neither moving on relentlessly nor in repeating the same patterns endlessly, but in following a fate that is in flux, represented by the river (Yoshimoto Banana 1993: 174). The force of the river that summons Akemi to its banks must be, in a sense, the force pulling her towards the pre-castrative stage (174). That is why she can find her own sheltered place in the room near to the river and feel comfortable with her boyfriend who has given up his business ambitions (133, 170).

Kurosawa Ariko points out that we still cannot find the missing link that connects the 'Yoshimoto Banana Phenomenon' (Banana's immense popularity among female readers in the late 1980s) and the issues being problematised by feminists (Kurosawa 1990: 151). But, one of the factors which relates Banana's fiction with feminism must be this deviation of desires of the Other by going back to the pre-castrative phase. Banana's stories go around and around flowing ceaselessly like the river. They are always playing a placid homogeneous family game with homogeneous family members. In this game however they are certainly deconstructing the symbolic order of the Other.

One of the important issues being problematised by feminists is the male/female distinction that is closely connected with the power structures and superior/inferior consciousness produced by the Oedipus and castration complexes. In this situation, Banana's characters' nostalgia attempts, if unconsciously, to go back to the pre-Oedipal and pre-castrative stage in which no distinction exists. This must be one of the main reasons why many women confessed their psychological wounds have been healed by reading Banana's novels.[21]

However, it should be mentioned that Banana's characters who long for nostalgia lack something. Akemi, when she decides to marry her boyfriend, thinks:

If there was something to worry about, it was that an important piece was missing from my life. Even though I would literally throw myself into things, I was eternally skimming the surface, never truly hearing or seeing the substance. All along, I'd look for surface beauty to hide the emptiness. But perhaps that's what hobbies are for, in the final analysis.

(Yoshimoto Banana 1993: 133)

Kazami in *N.P.* explains it in more intelligible terms:

My way of looking at the world is so nearsighted. If no one said anything, I'd probably just live like I do now year in and year out, and feel complacent about everything around me. Plus, I don't see that many people. Something is definitely missing – I don't know what, maybe compassion for people who are suffering, a sense of adventure, interest in other people

(Yoshimoto Banana 1990: 74)

Banana's characters lack compassion for and interest in other heterogeneous people as well as a sense of adventure. While compassion for and interest in other people lead one to a paranoid diametrical desire towards strangers, the lack of a sense of adventure castrates the desire for progress and evolution. Perhaps, as Yoshimoto Takaaki points out (Yoshimoto Takaaki and Banana 1997: 123–124), what they want is not a human relation on the basis of love and hate or unification and competition, but a situation in which they feel at home. It is a nostalgic setting, and in this sense we can sense an ambivalent significance of feminist nostalgia. It, as the term 'castration fantasy' well suggests, castrates erotic desire and the desire to progress.

It should also be mentioned, however, that Sakumi, the narrator-heroine of Banana's novel *Amrita* (1994a) gradually attempts to escape the recurrent cycle. In the abundant nostalgic feelings pervading the story she understands that the resonant cycle has brought about a different change in her. She has been pushed so far away that she can never go back. When she comes to Saipan, Sakumi becomes aware of this.

> Ever since coming to the island I realized that something inside me was, without question, out of place. Over the course of a few weeks that confirmation grew stronger by the day as I took in air almost too painful to breathe and recalled sights so nostalgic my chest started to ache. I knew returning would be impossible.
>
> By now I'd been pushed too far into my own revolutions, and I would not be allowed to go back and do things over again. Cells containing my expectations for what lay ahead in my unknown future rotted away in my heart like some evil form of cancer.
>
> I would never return.
>
> (Yoshimoto Banana 1994a: 209)

Though it is true that moving on from nostalgic longing is suggested in this passage, albeit in a reluctant manner, it is still not overtly expressed.

This situation basically does not change in Banana's later stories. In *Marika's Long Night* (*Marika no nagai yoru*) (1994d) Marika, who has multiple-personality disorder, attempts to escape from unpleasant memories by playing lots of nostalgic people's characters as her own. Her various characters finally resolve into one, and it is suggested at the very end of the story that she overcomes the illness. *Honeymoon* (1997) features a twenty-three-year-old woman called Manaka who married her husband Hiroshi when they were both eighteen. They had been neighbours since they were seven years old. Although their unsociable and secluded relationship is about to open to the world in their second honeymoon to Brisbane, here again the movement occurs only at the end of the story.

Many of the short stories compiled in *Adultery and South America* (*Furin to nanbei*, 2000a) and *The Body Knows Everything* (*Karada wa zenbu shitteiru*, 2000b) and also the later story *Rainbow* (*Niji*, 2002b) deal with adultery which basically represents the heterosexual, paranoid and diametrical desire towards strangers. But, the major motif underlying these stories is again the reproduction of nostalgic memories and nostalgic persons – nostalgia for one's mother, father, grandmother, grandfather and old friends. Here again, the interest in other unknown people and the longing for adventure is no more than allusive.

In 'Small Darkness' ('Chiisana yami') compiled in *Adultery and South America*, for instance, the heroine's mother has suffered from claustrophobia since, as a child, she was caged by her mother in a small paper house for two weeks. The heroine's father cannot come home early when his family awaits him. Being monopolised by deep love scares both of them. Claustrophobia in this story is used symbolically as a disease caused by an ambivalent desire for, and fear of, meeting strangers. Looking at her parents' characteristics, the heroine reflects on herself.

> What is the small darkness in my mind? I am not a person who cannot go home early when expected to do so. Neither am I frightened of being boxed in. But, I think someday the darkness will surface from deep in my mind. That is what people mean by 'grow up'. How shall I face it? How shall I deal with it? I am still young and fearless. I am even looking for it. I want to see it.
>
> (Yoshimoto Banana 2000a: 83; my translation)

That she is not suffering from claustrophobia now means that she is happy with closed circumstances and with familiar persons. Thus, looking for claustrophobia has two meanings. One is to be deeply loved by someone to the extent that she feels claustrophobia, and the other is to have a desire to meet strangers. Here again the longing for unknown things is declared, but it does not invite further progress. It is just mentioned at the end of the story.

The same thing can be said about the last story in *Adultery and South America*, 'Out of the Window' ('Mado no soto'). When her lover is looking out of the window, the heroine finds his back very similar to that of the teddy bear that her grandmother gave her. She starts feeling nostalgia towards him. Outside the window he is looking through is Iguacu Falls, in Brazil. Later when she looks down the falls from a helicopter, she feels a strong power of two different strengths, male and female, or Yin and Yang, which have been creating the earth (Yoshimoto Banana 2000a: 176–177). This is the awe of the heterosexual power of two different strengths confronting each other. But, once again this is the end of the story.

In Banana's fiction the various possibilities are open both to the characters and the narrators, and perhaps to the author and the reader, too. But at the moment concerning the contrast between the familiar persons and foreign others, the narrators' attitude, as well as that of the characters, is not to arouse interest in other heterogeneous people as they are, but to invite them into her familiar place.

Homosexuality versus heterosexuality

> In the ancient world so few people cared to categorize their contemporaries on the basis of the gender to which they were erotically attracted that no dichotomy to express this distinction was in common use. People were thought of as 'chaste' or 'unchaste', 'romantic' or 'unromantic', 'married' or 'single', even 'active' or 'passive', but no one thought it useful or important to distinguish on the basis of genders alone, and the categories 'homosexual' and 'heterosexual' simply did not intrude on the consciousness of most Greeks or – as will be seen – Romans.
>
> (John Boswell 1980: 59)

In the last section of this chapter I will first briefly explain the relationship between postmodernism, feminism and homosexuality, especially lesbianism, and then analyse Banana's fiction from the viewpoint of lesbianism or homosexuality. Many theorists point out the interrelations between postmodernism, feminism and homosexuality (lesbianism). For some feminists to remove discrimination against women involves treating them as men and thus forcing them to join the Oedipal triangle – the modernist pattern of capitalism and patriarchy. They therefore have adopted postmodern theories in order to enable them 'to articulate alternative ways of thinking about (and thus acting upon) gender without either simply reversing the old hierarchies or confirming them' (Scott 1990: 134).[22] Some other feminists explore the possibility of dismantling the gender hierarchy in the thought of such so-called postmodern philosophers as Adorno, Derrida, Lacan and Levinas (Cornell 1992a, 1992b).

In modern society, people are forced to confront the binary opposition between the forcible demands of progress and evolution symbolised by the Oedipal triangle in the form of rivalry or power struggle, and the desire for incestuous autism, overtly prohibited but implicitly present, represented by the Amaterasu circle. We can find in the feminist movement the potential to subvert this binarism in modern patriarchal capitalist society. Following these theories, feminists now seem to have, ideologically, almost completed the paradigm-shift of deconstructing the modernist dualism based on male perspectives which includes reason/emotion, culture/nature, homosexual/heterosexual, man/woman, and so forth, and are now practically or politically attempting to realise the emancipation of women from dominant male discrimination.

Homosexuality is also related to feminism in terms of deconstructing power structures. Many theorists have provided a theoretical basis for studies of both homosexuality and feminism as well as for the interrelation between them (Sedgwick 1991; Wittig 1992; Halperin 1995). As has been mentioned, Gayle Rubin's study is vitally important here too. As early as the mid-1970s Rubin sought the possibility of emancipation for women in a reformation of kinship (Rubin, G. 1975: 169–204). Lacan's formula that our desire is the desire of the Other also played a crucial role. Before Lacan's work became widely known, it had been tacitly accepted that gender was a culturally encoded distinction, whereas sexuality was, in a sense, a natural or innate desire. But the Lacanian formula subverted this distinction – sexuality itself was seen to be constructed as heterosexual by the symbolic order in which power relations were subordinated. As Michel Foucault argues and Gayle Rubin agrees, sexuality or desire is not a pre-existing naturally given biological entity, but rather it is a historically constructed social practice (Foucault 1978–1986 I: 105; Rubin, G. 1984: 276). Although, as Judith Butler mentions (2001: 426–427), the distinction between the concepts of sexual difference, gender and sexuality has the difficulty of determining where the biological, the psychic, the discursive and the social begin and end: the definitions of all these concepts are always to be constructed and reconstructed. Thus, the deconstruction of (hetero)sexuality is here again not only possible but also necessary. But what sort of new desire can be produced by homosexuality?

Adrienne Rich in her 1980 article points out the possibility of lesbian continuum in which all women experience orgasmic sensation in suckling at their mother's breast, in suckling their own child, touching and handling each other (Rich 1980: 650–651). As Biddy Martin writes, Rich argues for the primacy and naturalness of a woman's erotic bond with another woman (Martin 1988: 87). Lesbianism in this sense is located in a pre-castrative, free-from-power-struggle feminist site.

Concerning this identification between feminist and lesbian theories in a pre-castrative setting, however, Cheshire Calhoun argues that the such feminine identity is itself a historically constructed product. Calhoun maintains that lesbian became and remains conceivable, representable, in virtue of the creation of a new category of individuals who were outside of the sex/gender categories 'woman' and 'man'. She insists on separating lesbian theory from feminist theory, because lesbians' insistence on the political value of their performing masculinity and femininity disables feminists from challenging masculine–feminine power relations (Calhoun 2000: 39, 53, 69). Calhoun is arguing here that the male domination of the patriarchal system which feminism is attacking, and the heterosexual domination which lesbian and gay theory is attempting to reconfigure are in different categories; and that sexual outlaws to heterosexual dominance (lesbian and gay) and gender outlaws to patriarchal norms (feminist) must be distinguished.[23]

Since the focus of our discussion is not feminist/lesbian/gay theories *per se*, but the analysis of Yoshimoto Banana's stories from the viewpoints of feminism, lesbianism, gay theory and homosexuality, we will not go further with their argument. It must suffice here to confirm both the theoretical similarity between feminist theory on the patriarchal system and lesbian and gay theory on heterosexual domination, plus the theoretical difference between feminism, which looks for the pre-castrative site, and the lesbian who has different sexual and erotic orientation. Then, how is lesbian sexuality in Banana's stories different from heterosexuality? Is it also different from the pre-castrative position sought by some feminists and some of Banana's characters introduced in the previous section?

As Banana reveals in the afterword to her novel *N.P.*, her main literary themes are, among others, lesbianism and love within the family (Yoshimoto Banana 1990: 193). She often includes homosexuality in her stories. Eriko's transformation of his/her family role from father to mother in *Kitchen* can, from this perspective, be interpreted as the transformation from man to woman, which leads the reader to imagine homosexuality and lesbianism. Banana's interest in homosexual characters continuously appears in her fiction from her early works until recent stories 'Hard-boiled' (*Hard-boiled, Hard-luck*, 1999) in which the lesbian love between the heroine and Chizuru is depicted, and *Kingdom* in which Kaede and Kataoka are homosexual (Yoshimoto Banana 2002c).

One of the points in Banana's stories that draw our attention to homosexuality is the transvestite and transgender language she uses. In *Moonlight Shadow*, Banana's earliest published novella written in her university days, the main character Hiiragi begins to wear his girlfriend's sailor-suit school uniform after she dies in a traffic accident. In the last scene of the story Hiiragi appears without the girl's uniform, his return to normal clothes is interpreted as his having recovered from the pain of having lost his girlfriend. But his figure in the girl's school uniform, walking fast along the lane, is certainly attractive not only as an object of sympathy, but as a figure that creates something new, or something else. He could be, as Cheshire Calhoun describes, a new category of individuals who are outside of the sex/gender categories 'woman' and 'man' (Calhoun 2000: 69). The homosexual and transsexual figures Banana describes, like Eriko and Chika in *Kitchen* or Hideo in *SLY* (1996), are also depicted as men who wear female dress and/or speak in female language. They are in a sense playing the game of gender ambiguity. In a society like Japan in which gender distinctions are clearly expressed in terms of clothes (i.e. girls and boys school uniforms) and language (i.e. male and female final particles) transvestism and gender-coded language are very effective means of subverting gender dualism.

Judith Butler finds a critical potential in 'drag' performativity for deconstructing prevailing notions of gender and sexuality. Drag, for Butler, is 'not a secondary imitation that presupposes a prior and original gender', because "imitation" is at the heart of the *heterosexual* project and its gender binarisms', and 'hegemonic heterosexuality is itself a constant and repeated effort to imitate its own idealizations' (Butler 1993: 125; emphasis in the original). She consequently claims that all gender is like drag. What then is the fundamental difference between the homosexual and heterosexual projects? How can sexuality be more specifically deconstructed? Which methods can be most gainfully employed?

Although Butler rejects the notion that lesbian sexuality exists outside the economy of phallogocentrism (Butler 1993: 85), elsewhere in the same book she claims that 'there is a lesbian desire radically different from a heterosexual one, with *no* relation to it, that is neither the repudiation nor the appropriation of heterosexuality, and that has radically other origins than those which sustain heterosexuality' (Butler 1993: 128; emphasis in the original). It seems that Butler is suggesting that we should attempt to find a lesbian desire that is radically different from a heterosexual desire. As I mentioned before, Cheshire Calhoun also insists that the lesbians have created a new category of individuals outside the sex/gender categories 'woman' and 'man' (Calhoun 2000: 39, 69). But in what sense can lesbian desire be radically different?

In terms of the discussion outlined previously, we can regard homosexuality as a kind of homogeneous relationship. This point, as suggested by Rubin, associates gay men and lesbians with incest. Homophobia is no less related to incestuous claustrophobia (feelings of disgust or terror regarding incest) than to such other prejudices against oppressed groups as ethnic minorities or women. The intolerance of homosexuality or homophobia and the emotion hidden behind the prohibition of incest, that is the incest taboo discussed previously, have something in common. Both prohibit sexual relations among the homogeneous; the former among the same-sex, and the latter among the same family. Furthermore, the distinction between familiarity and strangeness is also evident in the fact that the homicide of kin is tacitly accepted as a worse crime than the murder of strangers.

The underlying distinction is, as has also previously been discussed, between eros directed at the stranger, which causes an intense emotional and physical excitement, and friendship and kindness felt towards the homogeneous group, which implies a common life with shared feelings. In this way, it can be said that we are culturally encoded to feel erotic desire towards a heterogeneous opponent and familial love or friendship towards a homogeneous person through the symbolic order of the Other. Therefore, we experience a homophobia/incest taboo when feeling erotic desire towards a homogeneous person, and extreme guilt when expressing violence towards kin.

Concerning the relations between homosexuality and homogeneity, and heterosexuality and heterogeneity, I shall mention here reservations made by two scholars. One is Cheshire Calhoun who suggests that it is a mistake to equate heterosexuality with the orientation of sexual desire, and the taboo on lesbianism and homosexuality with a taboo on same-sex desire and sexual activity. She argues that heterosexuality is a way of organising social life around the male–female couple and that couple's family. The heart of institutionalised heterosexuality is, for her, in the institution of the family itself (Calhoun 2000: 46). But, it seems to be reasonable to suppose that by means of shifting heterosexual domination to heterosexual/homosexual coexistence, the concept of family itself is inevitably changing.

Ueno Chizuko expressed another reservation from a different perspective. She once approved of the relations between homosexuality and homosociality and cautioned us by saying that homosexuality/homosociality tends to be contaminated by misogyny and hatred of heterogeneity (Ueno 1986: 14).

But later, following Sedgwick (1985: 1–5; 1991: 87–88), Ueno differentiates these two concepts, and insists that misogyny and xenophobia or hatred of heterogeneity are only related to homosociality, whereas homosexuality is free from them (Ueno 1998a: 244). But, one of the points on which this book insists is the future possibility of discarding violence – the possibility found in the overlapping common ground of homosexuality and homogeneity. Certainly it is an extremely dangerous place, in the sense that, as Ueno points out, fascistic and ethnocentric identification and hatred of the Other are located there. But the most beautiful thing is often positioned next to the most dangerous thing. If we can clearly distinguish between the beauty and the danger in the common ground of homosexuality and homogeneity, we may be able to find the place in which the desire for violence is overcome.

Just like incest, now, there are at least two possible modes of homosexual desire. One treats the same-sex object as if she or he were of the opposite sex and projects erotic desire on to her or him (1). The second transforms the erotic desire that is heterosexually oriented, transforming the desire of the Other into familial love or friendship, while maintaining sexual activity directed at a same-sex partner (2) (Figure 2.6). In both cases, it seems clear that homosexuality has the potential to subvert the differentiation between familiar and strange objects by eroding the homogeneous/heterogeneous opposition: in the former by changing the object of sexual desire, and in the latter by transforming the desire itself. In homosexual desire (1), however, although the partner is of the same-sex, the connection between the erotic desire and sexual conduct is basically a heterosexualised one. In contrast, we can find in homosexual desire (2), like in incestuous desire (2), a deviation in the association between desire and conduct linked by the Other. Herein lies a possibility for 'something new', which consequently leads to the castration of our erotic desire.

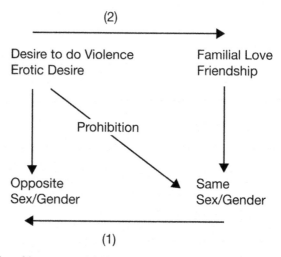

Figure 2.6   Modes of homosexual desire.

One of the desires of the mythical, real, pre-symbolic intention that is castrated by the desire of the Other might be this homosexual desire (2). Just as Butler's insistence on 'drag' performativity reveals the process whereby the distinction between the 'inside' and 'outside' truth of femininity produces a contradictory formation of gender, homosexual desire (2) also deconstructs the heterosexualised genders by cutting the connection between *eros* and heterogeneity, and *philia* and homogeneity. Now, which desire can be found in Banana's fiction – heterosexualised desire (1) or pre-castrated desire (2)?

The theme of lesbian erotic love in Banana's fiction occurs as early as 'An Experience' ('Aru taiken') compiled in *Asleep* (*Shirakawa yofune*, 1989b). The heroine Fumi and her rival Haru love the same man. They hated each other while they were competing for the man's love. But after Haru's death in Paris, her dead spirit comes to visit Fumi every night in her dreams accompanied by an angelic and nostalgic melody. Fumi, having realised that it is Haru's ghost who is calling her, visits a medium who can talk to spirits of the deceased. With his help Fumi waits for Haru's apparition in a room in a dream-like coma. Haru appears there and says that it was perhaps Fumi whom she loved at that time, and that she wanted to kiss her. They realise that they loved each other more than they loved the man.

In *Hachi's Last Girlfriend* (*Hachi-kō no saigo no koibito*, 1994c) Hachi's former girlfriend also deep-kisses his future girlfriend Mao (Yoshimoto Banana 1994c: 7). It is symbolic that Mao calls Hachi's former girlfriend 'mother' and when she met 'mother' for the first time she thought that she had met her before. That is, the 'mother' is a nostalgic person for Mao and they are from the very beginning homogeneous kin. In *N.P.* another female character, Sui, gives an erotic kiss to the heroine Kazami (Yoshimoto Banana 1990: 156). In this story Sui and Otohiko, stepsister and stepbrother, love each other and in the last scene of the novel the love between Kazami and Otohiko is suggested.

Haru and Fumi, Mao and 'mother', and Sui and Kazami, all of them are in a sense rivals in love. But in their rivalry, instead of the desire to do violence, they discover a common connection, for both love the same man. Instead of competing and fighting, they gradually realise that they have something in common which they find reassuring, or in other words we could say that they have a nostalgic desire for each other.

In *Hard-boiled* (1999), a later story which deals with lesbian love, the lesbian relationship between the heroine and Chizuru is basically the same as in previous stories. Though the story narrates that Chizuru is erotically attracted to the heroine, and that the heroine is her passive sexual partner, they are fundamentally not like heterosexual lovers but more like intimate close friends. Also significant in the story are a husband and wife living upstairs from Chizuru's apartment, who leave the windows open while having sex in their bathroom. As they make love they talk about their children's education (Yoshimoto Banana 1999: 71–73). They are homogeneous family members and they have sex as if they were dining together. Although they engage in sexual activity, what they are expressing is not a strong erotic desire, but the familiar friendship that they share in their day-to-day lives together. This kind of homosexuality can be categorised as homosexual desire (2) in the above Figure 2.6.

There is, however, another aspect to the female–male–female love triangle depicted in Banana's stories. As has been mentioned, relating to the concept of 'homosociality', and based on a critique of Gayle Rubin, Eve Sedgwick discovers in the trope of a man's struggle against another man for the hand of a woman, the structure of male traffic in women. Women are used by men as exchangeable objects, as units of currency, for the primary purpose of cementing relationships with other men (Sedgwick 1985: 123). She writes that:

> In the presence of a woman who can be seen as pitiable or contemptible, men are able to exchange power and to confirm each other's value even in the context of the remaining inequalities in their power. The sexually pitiable or contemptible female figure is a solvent that not only facilitates the relative democratization that grows up with capitalism and cash exchange, but goes a long way – for the men whom she leaves bonded together – toward palliating its gaps and failures.
>
> (Sedgwick 1985: 160)

We can find in Banana's love triangle stories of exactly the opposite structure: the female traffic in men.

From this perspective, *N.P.* can be interpreted as a story of the relationship between Kazami and Sui cemented by Shoji and Otohiko. The story starts with a love affair between Kazami and Shoji ending with the latter's suicide, followed by the incestuous love between Sui and Otohiko. When chatting with Kazami, Sui reveals that she had had a love affair with Shoji before he met Kazami (Yoshimoto Banana 1990: 57). Sui says 'I knew that you were dating Shoji. Otohiko spotted you with him at that party and told me who you were. Ever since then, I've wanted to meet you. I was depressed about coming back to Japan, but I felt a little better when I remembered that you were here' (62). Sui seems to be attracted by Kazami more than by Otohiko through Shoji. Later Sui gives Kazami a piece of Shoji's bone that she stole at his funeral (103–104). This symbolic action clearly indicates, in a reverse of the dynamic pointed out by Sedgwick, the structure of the female traffic in men – the use of men by women as exchangeable objects for the primary purpose of cementing relationships between two women – Sui and Kazami. The use of men as a currency between women is confirmed again in the last scene of the novel where, by leaving Otohiko, Sui lets Kazami have him.

Hachi's Last Girlfriend can also be interpreted in this formula of 'female traffic in men', in the sense that Hachi's former girlfriend and his future girlfriend, the heroine Mao are connected by their boyfriend Hachi. It is symbolic here again but in a different sense that Hachi's former girlfriend is called 'mother' and killed in a traffic accident, and that when Mao looks at Hachi's back, she thinks it is like a father's back (she does not know who is her own father) (Yoshimoto Banana 1994c: 41). In this story, though the narrative style is very concise and less elaborate, the Oedipalised and patriarchal power is feminised; it flows not from father to son through mother, but from 'mother' to daughter (Mao) through 'father' (Hachi).

It is true that we can sense in this story, as well as *N.P.*, a feminist power struggle against patriarchal domination. This reading consequently leads us to the conclusion that Banana's fiction attempts to replace male dominance (or male homosociality) with female dominance (or female homosociality) by means of power struggle. However, though the death of 'mother' and erotic desire towards 'father' is certainly narrated in *Hachi's Last Girlfriend*, the general emotion underlying the work is not deep and strong, but as in many of Banana's stories, shallow and light. Emphasis is placed not on the hidden desire to kill her mother and marry her father, but on the familiar, nostalgic and comfortable feelings of etiquette and kindness.

We should therefore read these stories as an attempt to reconfigure the erotically charged heterosexual desire to do violence against the stranger with the friendly, gentle and incestuous lesbian sexual desire experienced in relation to the family. Then, we can conclude that lesbian love narrated in Banana's stories is fundamentally not very different from the pre-Oedipal and pre-castrative child's desire before it is heterosexually constructed by the symbolic order in which power relations were subordinated. Banana's stories make us wonder if strong erotic desire is still necessary for us. Like Banana's characters, can we not engage in sexual activity without discharging and appeasing our erotic desire and the desire to do violence?

In modern society, which is structured by the concepts of individuals, families, nation-states, ethnicity, etc. we inevitably encounter heterogeneous/homogeneous, inside/outside, interior/exterior, superior/inferior, and majority/minority binaries everywhere. When we discard these binaries, we may be able to release ourselves from the ambivalent desire contained in these double binds. But in that case it is almost certain that we will also lose our erotic desire and the energy to progress that is affiliated to the desire to do violence. Without the 'Other' we cannot support the desire to do violence, but at the same time without the 'Other' we also lose erotic sexual desire. In other words, we lose our sexual identity. What happens if we lose our identity?

A number of critics have cautioned about the problems resulting from this loss of identity. René Girard considers that the crisis facing typically modern societies can be defined as the elimination of differences. He argues that in this state of relative indifferentiation the present process of disintegration, when compared with primitive societies, is gradual, and kept more or less in rein with seemingly no catastrophic outbursts of violence, although no resolution of any kind is taking place. Nonetheless, he also sees in this situation ever-increasing tension and multi-sided familial and nonfamilial rivalries in a more and more competitive world (Girard 1977: 189–190, 206).

As we will see in Chapter 4, Karatani Kōjin also warns us that a lack of heterogeneity results in solipsism. He divides human relations into two categories: relations between those who have a common code (a common language game) and those who do not. While communication among the former results in introspection, in the latter it results in relations between teaching and learning or selling and buying. In order to criticise the solipsism produced in the former paradigm, Karatani insists that we have to invite the 'Other' who belongs to a different language game into the singular culture (Karatani 1992b: 10–12).

With regard to sexual difference, Judith Butler also remarks on the importance of refiguring the 'outside' as a future horizon, one in which the violence of exclusion is perpetually in the process of being overcome. But she is careful enough to mention that of equal importance is the preservation of the outside, arguing that 'to include, to speak as, to bring in every marginal and excluded position within a given discourse is to claim that singular discourse meets its limits nowhere, that it can and will domesticate all signs of difference. If there is a violence necessary to the language of politics, then the risk of that violation might well be followed by another in which we begin, without ending, without mastering, to own – and yet never fully to own – the exclusions by which we proceed' (Butler 1993: 53). This is particularly important in the argument against the insistence of globalisation. Concerning identity politics, Butler also insists:

> None of the above [the despair evident in some forms of identity politics] is meant to suggest that identity is to be denied, overcome, erased. None of us can fully answer to the demand to 'get over yourself!' The demand to overcome radically the constitutive constraints by which cultural viability is achieved would be its own form of violence.
>
> (Butler 1993: 117–118)

It seems certain that identity cannot be erased totally. Yet it also seems clear to me that identity can be transformed and furthermore, the lack of heterogeneity does not necessarily result in the domination of homogeneity. For homogeneity is constructed in relation to heterogeneity and vice versa. As Stuart Hall mentions, the 'positive' meaning of any term is constructed through the relation to the Other, the relation to what it is not, to precisely what it lacks (Hall 1996: 4–5). If one of the two disappears or is deconstructed, the Other cannot remain uncontested: it must also be transfigured. What we should try to achieve is neither homogeneity nor heterogeneity, but the incessant reconfiguration represented by the capital X^n defined in the first section of this chapter.

Ōtsuka Eiji interprets Banana's *Kitchen* and *A Sad Premonition* (*Kanashii yokan*) as stories of children who attempt to create a puberty rite themselves in a society in which this rite of passage has disappeared (Ōtsuka 1990: 114–124). In puberty rites, young people are supposed to learn the types of behaviour considered appropriate among adults in their society. These must be constructed on the basis of distinctions between individuals, family, relatives, tribe, ethnicity, etc. grounded on the homogeneous/heterogeneous dualism. To become mature means in a sense to develop the ability to distinguish different attitudes to people in different categories – a familial love to family and relatives, an erotic desire and the desire to do violence to strangers, etc. Ōtsuka's interpretation suggests that adults cannot now initiate a puberty rite because they have lost the confidence in their own maturity or rather they are not satisfied with it, and people are now giving up this type of human relations, but still cannot find a new way of behaving.

We can confirm here the binarism 'erotic desire/desire to do violence/desire to progress = heterogeneity/strangers/lovers' versus 'friendship/familial love/incestuous autism = homogeneity/family/friends'. In the process of deconstructing this binarism, it is necessary to withdraw the prohibition from the combination of the crossed line that connects erotic desire and the desire to do violence with homogeneity. Otherwise, people are deprived of the chance to discharge and appease their erotic desire and the desire to do violence. The resulting Figure 2.7 is a graphic representation of the kind of human relations in Banana's stories.

We have so far seen how Banana's stories attempt to deconstruct the binaries between sexual and food desire, how they try to transgress the borderlines between cultural, gender and sexual otherness and familiarity, and consequently how they strive to subvert the distinction between heterogeneity and homogeneity in human society. We have also discerned the *eros*, the desire to do violence, exogamous rivalry, and vital, energetic and triangular movements characteristic of heterogeneity, plus *philia*, incestuous autism, and the calm, quiet and narcissistic circular repetition characteristic of homogeneity. Furthermore, as a methodological possibility, we have noted the potential to overthrow the binary oppositions in psychological incest and homosexuality, and moreover in conceiving nostalgia towards heterogeneous opponents. What Banana's fiction suggests is that relentlessly deconstructing these binary oppositions can cause something new to emerge. By interchanging family with strangers and vice-versa, friends with lovers and vice-versa, or same-sex opponents with opposite-sex opponents and vice-versa, the characters in Banana's fiction keep on attempting to create new human relations. In this new situation, the erotic desire and desire to do violence gradually disperse into undifferentiated, anti-cultural surroundings.

It might be helpful at this point to recall the comparison between Murakami Haruki's and Yoshimoto Banana's stories. Both Murakami and Banana attempt to deconstruct the polarised oppositions between fascistic totalitarianism and violent discrimination, which are based on the distinction,

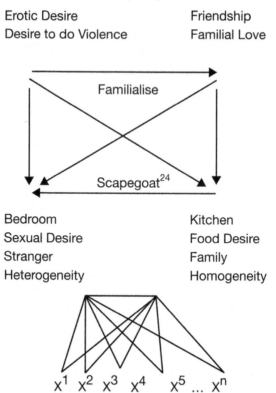

Figure 2.7   Human relations in Banana's stories

made between homogeneous family and heterogeneous strangers. Banana, as we have seen in this chapter, attempts to discover heterogeneity within the family and homogeneity among strangers. She does this by conceiving nostalgia towards strangers, and at the same time by acknowledging erotic desire among family members. In her recent work, *Kingdom* (2002c, 2004), too, she is still going in the same direction by narrating the heroine Shizukuishi's love affair with Nobayashi – who is about ten years her senior – as if they were an aged married couple. Shizukuishi also has a familiar, friendly love for Kaede, a good-looking, gay, fortune-teller. In this story Banana seems to keep on reconfiguring erotic desire by deconstructing the connection between the heroine's sexual desire for a young, good-looking man, and her calm and tender emotion for a considerably older person, as well as the erotic desire to the same sex opponent.

In contrast, as we have seen in the previous chapter, Murakami Haruki first tries to keep his distance from both homogeneity and heterogeneity as in the town of *The End of the World*. After *Dance Dance Dance* in 1988, however, he changes his stance from detachment to commitment and now faces directly the modernist binary desire for deep love and the desire to do violence.

3 Yoshimoto Takaaki and the subaltern

Intellectuals and the people (*taishū*)

Yoshimoto Takaaki (1924–) has been one of Japan's leading figures in the fields of philosophy and cultural and literary criticism from the 1960s until today. The critic Washida Koyata has argued that Yoshimoto is, in fact, the greatest of Japan's modern thinkers and that his work should at least be made available in English (Washida 1992: 3, 483). Michel Foucault, too, after holding a round-table discussion with Yoshimoto in 1978, also expressed his hope that Yoshimoto's work would be translated into French or English (Yoshimoto T. and Foucault 1984: 48).

Yoshimoto's writing touches upon a number of issues that are also being debated by Western theorists. For instance, he problematises the relationship between Japanese intellectuals who adopt Western theories and approaches in order to analyse Japan and the Japanese people themselves, who live submerged in the traditional round of daily life without striving to analyse it. This contrast between the intellectuals and the people (*taishū*) has been pointed out by postcolonial writers in other cultures, too. Also, Yoshimoto's notion of 'Collective Fantasy' (*kyōdō gensō*) which he first expounded in 1968, although conceived independently, shows similarities to Saussure's linguistic theory of arbitrariness and differentiation, and Merleau-Ponty's intersubjectivity, as well as Benedict Anderson's later study *Imagined Communities* (1983). What Yoshimoto suggests is one possible way in which the dualistic tendencies of modernism might be reformulated. It can be further argued that Yoshimoto's work, in particular his analysis of power structures, is closely related to debates within structuralism, post-structuralism and postmodernism, and the aforementioned discussion held with Michel Foucault is particularly interesting in this regard.[1] Also, the way in which Yoshimoto contrasts African and Asian forms of consciousness with European consciousness provides a challenging insight into the way in which current global ideology has been constructed and suggests ways in which it might be reformulated.

However, as far as I know, only a few of Yoshimoto's writings and other critics' studies on him are available in English. These include his poem anthology *Ten Poems For Transposition* (*Ten'i no tameno 10 pen*, 1995), Lawrence Olson's journal article that focuses on Yoshimoto's early works (Olson, L. 1978) and Leith Morton's introduction of Yoshimoto's thought in his book *Modern Japanese Culture* (Morton 2003). Although Yoshimoto's language is particularly difficult to understand even for Japanese native speakers, and it is easily anticipated that the translation would be an extremely difficult task, I share the view with Washida and Foucault that his work should be available in different languages. The aim of this chapter is thus to look for connections between his work and recent postmodern and postcolonial theories, and to introduce Yoshimoto's ideas to English-speaking readers, so as to offer a critical basis for future study.

The critic Takeda Seiji divides Yoshimoto's major works into two categories falling roughly in chronological order. The first is his study of Japanese political converts (including the pre-war Communists, the fascist imperialists of the China–Japan and Pacific Wars, and the post Second World War democrats), as well as his study of the responsibility for the war, and his criticism of post-war Japanese literature. The second phase of Yoshimoto's works, according to Takeda's categorisation, includes Yoshimoto's criticism of the basis of universality of thought, wherein he presents his own foundation for universality contrasted with the pragmatism of post-war (Japanese) democracy and Marxian scientific objectivism (Takeda 1996: 59–60).

In his criticism of Japanese proletarian writers before and after the Second World War 'A Criticism of "Democratic Literature"' ('"Minshushugi bungaku" hihan') (1956) Yoshimoto, a Marxist writer himself, presents two stages of setback in their movement, marking 1937–1940 as the turning point. In the first stage Japanese proletarian writers were repressed by the imperial government, isolated in jails, and forced to retract and convert. In the second stage, utilising the proletarian theory they had picked up from their European studies, they intentionally followed and supported the Japanese imperial authority (Yoshimoto IV: 119).[2] Yoshimoto strongly criticises the opportunism of the Japanese intellectual proletarian writers who advocated Communism in the pre-war era, imperialism during the war, and finally democracy in the post-war period.

In his work, he reviews the individual case of each convert and in the process drastically reformulates the question 'How could they do that?', by asking instead, 'Why was it inevitable that they should act in this way?' This reformulation raises two important issues. First, Yoshimoto discerns in the problem of the converts a kind of aloofness that separated these intellectuals from the mass of the people, a situation that he later considers to be universal. Second, he doubts the legitimacy of Western theories when analysing, examining and criticising non-Western cultures.

Following on from the above criticism of the convert, in an essay entitled 'On the Convert' ('Tenkō ron', 1958), Yoshimoto presents two major ways in which the Japanese intellectual proletarian writers converted. One pattern involved the return from Western logic to a Japanese way of seeing things. Yoshimoto places Sano Manabu (1892–1953) and Nabeyama Sadachika (1901–1979) both of whom converted from Communism to imperialism in this category. The more these writers employed Western logical or rational ways of thinking, Yoshimoto insists, the more they came to regard the situation in Japan as illogical or irrational. Therefore, they attempted to change Japan according to Western logic. However, when confronted with the difficulty of doing this, at first they ignored reality, and when compelled to face it by the imperial police force, they changed their position. They came to see the situation in Japan which, on the basis of Western logic had seemed irrational, to be rational and coherent when viewed from the perspective of the Japanese Emperor system. Hence, they came to see the validity of the Japanese way of doing things through a new appreciation of Japanese daily life.

The second type of convert includes Kobayashi Takiji (1903–1933), Miyamoto Kenji (1908–) and Kurahara Korehito (1902–1991) who did not in fact convert but rather criticised those who did. Yoshimoto, however, categorises them as a kind of convert. He maintains that when they realised the lack of correspondence between Western theories and Japanese realities, unlike the first type of convert, they did not return to the Japanese tradition, but instead continued to follow Western logical procedures without attempting to apply them to Japan. Neither kind of convert, then, attempted to apply Western theories to Japan; the difference between them is that while the former repudiated Western theory and returned to a more traditional Japanese view, the latter continued to uphold Western logic, but not in application to Japan. While the former writers lost the battle with Japanese feudalism, the latter avoided fighting in the battle altogether (Yoshimoto XIII: 17–22). From Yoshimoto's perspective, in both cases those Japanese intellectuals who employed Western logic and theories failed because they did not base their understanding on the people who were living a traditional Japanese life.

Consequently, Yoshimoto regards this contrast between the intellectuals and the people as the confrontation between the logocentric West and the pre- and/or post-modern East, and suggests that logic or theories derived from Western cultures are not suitable for analysing the situation in Japan (Yoshimoto XIII: 17). Yoshimoto isolates two issues here. First he is concerned with the disparity between Western logic and non-Western situations: the former is represented by intellectuals who attempt to follow Western logic and the latter by indigenous people who live their lives in terms of non-Western experience. Second, he expresses doubts about the validity of the standard by which the former evaluates the latter.

From this point of view, Yoshimoto criticises the Japanese political scientist Maruyama Masao's analytical methodology[3] in his essay 'On Maruyama Masao' ('Maruyama Masao ron').[4] In this essay Yoshimoto first of all attacks the rupture between Maruyama's intellectual mode of thought and ordinary Japanese people's lives. He remarks on the fact that

Maruyama, at the beginning of his book *Studies in the Intellectual History of Tokugawa Japan*, cites a passage from Hegel's *Reason in History*. From this Yoshimoto assumes that Maruyama is well acquainted with the Hegelian notion that the historical process is the progress of the reason of the world spirit. In contrast to Maruyama who focuses on the Hegelian concept of reason (rationality) itself, Yoshimoto is more interested in analysing why Hegel was so interested in the notion of reason.

By quoting a passage from the same book by Hegel, Yoshimoto draws attention to the factors that motivated Hegel to investigate the essential destiny, the absolute aim and the true result of the world's history. He then notes that the primary motivation underpinning Hegel's investigation is the history of the slaughter-bench at which the happiness of people, the wisdom of states and the virtue of individuals have been victimised. Hegel's fundamental question is for what principle, for what final aim have these enormous sacrifices been made (Hegel 1900: 21).

Yoshimoto criticises Maruyama in that, although his writing is rationally based and employs the Hegelian dialectic well, he has failed to clarify the relations between the intellectuals and the people, which was one of the fundamental questions directing Hegel's investigation of the role of reason in history. In Maruyama's theory, the history of thought is regarded as something that dialectically proceeds automatically and independently from the reality of the Japanese people. This is, for Yoshimoto, one very conspicuous example of the discrepancy between Western logic and the Japanese situation. Consequently Yoshimoto is arguing that Maruyama cut the connection between the Hegelian theory of dialectic and the European situation that produced it, and mistakenly applied the former to a totally different situation (Japan).

The essential question raised by Yoshimoto – whether theories born in the West based upon Western cultures can be applied to Japanese everyday experience – arises whenever two different cultures meet, and has been widely discussed by other postcolonial writers. Ashcroft, Griffiths and Tiffin write that the idea of 'post-colonial literary theory' emerges from 'the inability of European theory to deal adequately with the complexities and varied cultural provenance of post-colonial writing. European theories themselves emerge from particular cultural traditions which are hidden by false notions of "the universal"' (Ashcroft *et al.* 1989: 11). The term 'postcolonial' is not confined to English writing. As defined by Ashcroft, Griffiths and Tiffin, postcolonial criticism 'points the way towards a possible study of the effects of colonialism in and between writing in English and writing in indigenous languages in such contexts as Africa and India, as well as writing in other language diasporas (French, Spanish, Portuguese)' (Ashcroft *et al.* 1989: 24).[5]

What Yoshimoto has problematised is not exactly the effect of colonialism appearing in between writing in English and writing in Japanese (indigenous language), but rather, the problems that emerge when thinking in Western languages and experiencing in Eastern ways; otherwise expressed as the discrepancy between European theories and Asian realities. Finally, it is clear that Yoshimoto's analysis has much in common with other critics in many non-Western cultures who are urging that the relationship between intellectuals and the people be clarified and are throwing doubt on the universal applicability of Western theories and logic.

With regard to India, the historian Ranajit Guha remarks that the historiography (the history of historical writing) of Indian nationalism has for a long time been dominated by elitism. This elitism, both colonialist and bourgeois-nationalist, is the ideological product of British rule in India, and has survived the transfer of power and been assimilated into neo-colonialist and neo-nationalist forms of discourse in Britain and India respectively. For Guha, what historical writing of this kind cannot do is to provide an explanation of Indian nationalism for Indian people, for it fails to acknowledge, far less interpret, the contribution made by the people on their own, that is, independently of the elite, to the making and development of their nationalism.

Furthermore, Guha asserts that what has clearly been left out of this unhistorical historiography is the politics of the people. Parallel to the domain of elite politics there existed throughout the colonial period another domain of Indian politics. In this domain the principal actors were not the dominant groups of the indigenous society or the colonial authorities but the subaltern classes and groups constituting the mass of the labouring population and the intermediate strata in town and country – that is, the people (Guha 1982: 1–4; see also Spivak 1988: 283–284). There is, to some extent, a correlation between the elite and the subaltern classes described by Guha in India and the situation described by Yoshimoto in his argument about Japanese intellectuals and the people.

With regard to Africa, where the concept of Négritude claims a distinct Black culture and identity, Nigerian writer Wole Soyinka, Nobel prize winner for literature in 1986, comments that what is wrong with this notion is that it involves

> the contrivance of a creative ideology and its falsified basis of identification with the social vision. This vision in itself was that of restitution and re-engineering of a racial psyche, the establishment of a distinct human entity and the glorification of its long-suppressed attributes...Négritude, having laid its cornerstone on a European intellectual tradition, however bravely it tried to reverse its concepts (leaving its tenets untouched), was a foundling deserving to be drawn into, nay, even considered a case for benign adoption by European ideological interests.
> (Soyinka 1990: 126–134; see also Ashcroft *et al.* 1989: 21–22 and Holdstock 2000: 135, 141)

Soyinka is arguing that the notions of an ethnic psyche and a distinct human entity with long-suppressed attributes are a contrivance based on the very intellectual tradition they are attempting to subvert. Once more, Soyinka's argument clearly parallels the points which Yoshimoto and Guha have raised.

In Japan the cross-cultural problem can also be found in nativist (*kokugaku*) scholars' criticisms of Chinese Studies as early as the Edo period (1603–1867). One of the key representatives of this school, Motoori Norinaga (1730–1801), writes:

> The Chinese heart (*karagokoro*) means not only to love Chinese customs and respect the nation, but also to discuss good and evil or truth and falsehood, and judge the reasons behind them on the basis found in Chinese books...It seems reasonable to suppose that the human heart is fundamentally not different between Japanese and Chinese, and there-fore that there must be only one criterion of good and evil or truth and falsehood. But to say so is also the Chinese way of thinking. Thus, it is very difficult to free ourselves from the Chinese heart....Since there are many cases in which what they judge true is not really true, and what they assess false is not actually false, it cannot be said that there is only one criterion of good and evil or truth and falsehood
>
> (Motoori 1968: 48–49;[6] see also Hirakawa 1976: 47)

It is significant here that Norinaga is arguing that the Chinese theories them-selves have emerged from particular cultural traditions, which assume false notions of the 'universal'. This tactic of relativising the absoluteness or universality of reason is currently very popular and it is from this perspective that postcolonial writers are challenging the 'universality' of European theory.

Apart from the cross-cultural problem that exists between China and Japan, the cultural confrontation between the West and the East also has a long history in both Japan and China. It has been discussed in terms of 'East Asian ethics and Western technology' (*tōyō dōtoku seiyō geijutsu ron*) by Sakuma Shōzan (1811–1864) in Japan. In China, Chang Chih-tung created the slogan 'Chinese learning for basic principle and Western learning for practical utility' (*Chung-hsueh wei t'i, hsi-hsueh wei yung*) in his *Ch'üan-hsueh p'ien* (*Exhortation to study*) in 1898 (Min 1989: 51–88).

These ideas were further developed in Meiji Japan by such intellectuals as Mori Ōgai, Natsume Sōseki, Nagai Kafū, Takamura Kōtarō and others who left Japan to study in Europe. Hirakawa Sukehiro, in his research on Japan–Europe cross-cultural problems, has a high regard for the contribu-tion made by Mori Ōgai, arguing that he held two different perspectives – Western and Japanese (Hirakawa 1976: 132, 278). But what does this really mean? Does it indicate that Ōgai had the ability to analyse Japanese situa-tions according to Japanese theories, and European situations following European theories? Or does it suggest the flexibility to utilise appropriate theories in different situations? Given that Ōgai's attitudes were very much founded on the notion of Enlightenment, although as we will see later in

Chapter 4 in his later writings Ōgai appears to be attempting to subvert Western logic, it seems to me that despite Hirakawa's high esteem, Ōgai's aim is no different from those who attempt to analyse Japan through Western logic and theories.

It is important not to insist on too strong a dualism between Western logic and non-Western situations. The contrast between 'elite/intellectuals/ideology' versus 'the people/subaltern classes/ethnic psyche' should not be replaced with the confrontation between the West and the non-West. For, first of all, this would lead us towards nationalism and ethnocentrism, and further, it is important to remember that just as there are elites in non-Western countries, 'the people' also exist in Western countries. Also, we should problematise the notion that the elites and intellectuals in any culture to a certain extent correspond with each other and contrast with ordinary people. For, as we have noted, many intellectuals themselves feel the necessity to communicate with ordinary people. Hence, what we have to do is not simply analyse Western logic and non-Western situations independently, but clarify what differences exist between the intellectuals and the people on the one hand, and what similarities they share on the other.

Until now many critics have treated the distinction between intellectuals or elites and the people in terms of individual differences. For instance, a common criticism is that such and such a person is intellectual and has there-fore failed to understand the people's emotion or psyche. But the contrast should be considered not so much as a conflict between different individuals, but rather as a confrontation between different ideologies. It is not very helpful to stigmatise a specific person or culture as being intellectual or analytical and then argue that this assumes a certain aloofness or inability to empathise with the people. Rather, we should remember that there are various contradictory ideologies inherent in any individual or culture. Concerning this point, Yoshimoto mentions that more or less we all have both the intellectual's and the common people's aspects (Yoshimoto XII: 15).

Furthermore, we have also to take care not to presuppose the *a priori* existence of Western and non-Western cultures. Taking translation as an example, Sakai Naoki writes:

> it is not because two different language unities are given that we have to translate (or interpret) one text into another; it is because translation *articulates* languages so that we may postulate the two unities of the translating and the translated languages as if they were autonomous and closed entities through *a certain representation of translation.*
>
> (Sakai 1997: 4 (J), 2 (E); emphasis in the original)

Following Sakai, we can argue that it is not because two different culture unities are given that we have to communicate with each other; it is because communication articulates cultures so that we may postulate the two unities of the addressing and addressed cultures as if they were autonomous and closed entities. In order to avoid the enclosure of each culture, it must be useful to set the vertical axis, which measures elite and non-elite subaltern people, as well as the horizontal axis, which assesses the geographical differences. Bearing the above in mind, let us now address Yoshimoto's analysis of the relationship between elites/intellectuals and the people.

The primary contrast between the intellectuals and the people in Yoshimoto's theory can best be described as the confrontation between the leader and the follower, or, in Nietzsche's terms between the strong and the weak, the master and the slave, the noble and the herd. If we regard this contrast as conflicting ideologies within one individual, however, it appears as two different human desires – the desire to become strong, noble, a master and a leader, and that to be weak, a follower, a slave and a group member. In this paradigm the advanced/intellectual individual is contrasted with the follower/subaltern. In his essay 'What is the Situation?' ('Jōkyō to wa nani ka', 1966) Yoshimoto characterises the difference between intellectuals and the people in the following manner. The people are grounded on the basic realities of their everyday lives; because they have no concept of a social structure, they are not aware of the social issues affecting them. On the contrary, the world-view of intellectuals is dominated by abstract theory quite independent of everyday social realities; consequently the mass of the people tends to be objectified as a problem in need of enlightenment (Yoshimoto XIII: 340).

In this definition Yoshimoto regards as intellectuals those who have the desire to obtain power in order to advance, and as the people those who have the desire to remain where they are. And furthermore, by attacking the intellectuals' alienation, Yoshimoto opposes the monopoly of the intellectual/strong/logos over the people/weak/pre- and post-logos in the form of the Enlightenment project. It is from this standpoint then, that Yoshimoto criticises Maruyama Masao who he considers places the intellectual/advanced/logos over the subaltern/follower, in the form of the Enlightenment project. As Washida Koyata remarks, one of the points Yoshimoto is criticising in Maruyama's thought is the Enlightenment scheme which assumes that the elite or advanced or intellectual (or top of the pyramid to use Yoshimoto's phrase) must enlighten, educate, lead and guide the people, regardless of their individual preferences (Washida 1992: 154–206).

Gayatri Chakravorty Spivak attempts to show that resisting the use of 'elite' methodologies on 'subaltern' material is symptomatic of an epistemological/ontological confusion by criticising the Big Three Systems of class, race/ethnos, and sex/gender. This confusion is based on the idea that just as the subaltern *is not* elite (ontology), the historian cannot *know* through elite method (epistemology). This is, for Spivak, part of a much larger confusion which questions whether men can theorise feminism, white people can theorise racism, or if the bourgeois can theorise revolution.

Spivak attempts to resolve this confusion from two perspectives. First, on a practical level, the collectivities implied by the above second group of nouns must start claiming subaltern identity and participating in the production of knowledge about themselves, even though, by so doing, they thereby become complicit in the structures of privilege that contaminate the first group. Otherwise, we must remain in the field of continuing colonisation. Second, more theoretically, the notion that only the subaltern can know the subaltern, or only women can know women and so on, is unsupportable for it predicates the possibility of knowledge on identity. Knowledge is made possible and is sustained by irreducible difference, not identity. That is, no programme of knowledge production can presuppose identity as origin. Consequently, Spivak urges us to go beyond the ontological/epistemological confusion that pits subaltern being against elite knowing, beyond the nativist's resistance to theory when it is recognisably different from her or his own unacknowledged theoretical position (Spivak 1987: 251–268).

The most significant difference between Spivak and Yoshimoto is that while the former encourages the subaltern to gain more power through knowledge of others and of themselves, and to ultimately upstage the elite, the latter urges the elite to come down to the level of the subaltern. Elsewhere in the interview by Frances Bartkowski, Spivak says:

> What we are asking for is that the hegemonic discourse, the holders of hegemonic discourse should de-hegemonize their position and themselves learn how to occupy the subject position of the Other rather than simply say, 'O.K., sorry, we are just very good white people, therefore we do not speak for the blacks'.
>
> (Spivak 1990: 121)

But it seems apparent that what Spivak is asking of the holders of hegemonic discourse is to learn how to occupy the subject position of the Other as the object of their knowledge, while maintaining their own position of the subject of knowledge intact.

In contrast, what Yoshimoto is asking of intellectual elites is to integrate or identify with subaltern people as part of themselves. Behind this contrast it is possible to discern Yoshimoto's personality and the empathy he feels towards the weak. Yoshimoto's apparent empathy with the subordinated is one of the most attractive features of his work. In analysing the work of Miyazawa Kenji, a writer of children's stories, for instance, Yoshimoto remarks that Miyazawa's writing expresses a limitless love and respect for the common people. Yoshimoto defines the common people in Miyazawa's work as those who unconsciously and unselfishly do good deeds, and sacrifice themselves and show mercy to others (Yoshimoto T. 1996a: 227–228).

Yoshimoto's compassionate look not 'at' but 'from' or 'with' the common people is evident throughout his work. Nevertheless, it must be admitted that in the present era of globalisation, irrespective of personal or social differences, power relations tend to override empathy. This is the reason why Spivak insists that we should obtain power through knowledge. Yoshimoto also apprehends this point. The relation between the power structures in which we are inevitably trapped and the empathic emotions we also unavoidably experience is brought up in his essay 'An Essay on the Gospel According to Matthew' ('Machiu sho shiron').[7] In the last part of the essay, concerning the seemingly hypocritical aspect of Christianity, Yoshimoto insists:

> Christians in the present day are free to say to the poor, alienated people, 'We sympathise with you. We intend to save you and we are practising our intention. We are your friends'. They have the right to say this of their own free will. But regardless of their intention, they are unable to deal with the fact that in reality they are supporters of the present order, and helping the enemy of the poor, alienated people. In the absoluteness of relation the meaning of helping people parts from one's emotion, and moves into the whole mechanical system...

> You can believe in revolutionary ideas, even though you are getting along well in the world. Or you can hate revolutionary ideas, although you are being forced to keep irrational laws in poverty. The free will has discretion to take either one of the two courses. But what decides your situation is nothing but the absoluteness of relation.
>
> (Yoshimoto IV: 105–106; my translation)

What does Yoshimoto mean by the term 'absoluteness of relation'? His use of this term is sufficiently multivalent to have evoked various interpretations from many critics. Isoda Kōichi cautions us by saying that Yoshimoto's concept of 'relation' is not necessarily reducible to power relations. He seems to interpret the idea as that which leads us to the various dilemmas in human society (Isoda 1990: 314). But it seems clear that in Yoshimoto's essay the crucial element that imposes the dilemmas upon us is the relation between power structures and human emotion or empathy. He insists in this essay that human relations through power structures are more decisive than those based on individual human emotion. It is impossible to reconcile the conflict between one's individual free intention to help people, and the power structures in which one must unavoidably oppress weaker people. No matter how sincerely the strong wish to help the weak, they can do nothing within a situation in which they are precisely the ones that reduce those less strong to a position of weakness. Beyond the level of right and wrong, true and false, good and evil, and beautiful and ugly, we are controlled by power structures.

It is now widely acknowledged that desires and emotions are subject to power relations. Obviously, most human relations in the modern period have become embedded in power structures. The more powerful knowledge, language, ideology, gender, sexuality, or culture of the majority often appropriates, colonises and exploits the weaker minority until seemingly nothing of the latter remains. In order to survive under the prevailing law of the jungle we have to be strong. This is the ideology underlying the idea of globalisation. Do we have then to follow Spivak in encouraging the subaltern to gain more power and fight with the elite? Is it not possible to help the weak as they are? If it is possible, how then can we save the weak and why should we? Yoshimoto's writings, in which he explores power relations in detail and then stresses the importance of the weak, can provide some answers to the above questions.

In 'Japanese Nationalism' ('Nihon no nashonarizumu', 1964) Yoshimoto sees contemporary intellectuals as playing a role that hides the authorities' intentions and appeases the people's grudges. He considers that the duty of intellectuals is to seek the missing link that connects themselves, not to the authorities, but to the people. Yoshimoto expresses this by saying that intellectuals must always integrate the people into themselves. What does this mean? If we regard both the authorities and intellectuals as displaying a desire to gain power, to advance and to become strong represented by the logos, then the people can be understood to show a desire to follow, to stay and to become weak, represented by the pre- and post-logos. Then it becomes clear that what Yoshimoto means by 'to integrate the people into the intellectuals' is a rejection of both positions; it is an attempt to create 'something new' from the discrepancy created by the confrontation between theory and reality. As his daughter Banana is attempting to create 'something new' by substituting the family for the stranger, or the homogeneous for the heterogeneous, father Yoshimoto Takaaki is also trying to subvert the distinction between the strong and the weak, or the elite and the subaltern. But the question remains unanswered: why should we preserve the weak in the first place? Are there reasons other than philanthropic, charitable and benevolent ones?

Language, self and ethnicity

In order to create any kind of culture, each society has its own form of fantasy (*gensō*) through which it interprets reality. Between the fantasy and reality, or ideology and perception, there is an inevitable discrepancy. By the term 'discrepancy' I mean the incongruity that occurs in the ideological process of bringing perceived real experiences into articulation. No matter how elaborate the fantasy is, it cannot fully represent every aspect of a situation, or to put it another way, once the real experience has been articulated, there still remains some aspect that is left unformulated. Moreover, the form of fantasy created in one culture is not necessarily suitable to express the realities of another. Yet, regardless of the applicability or inapplicability of the terms of one culture for interpreting another, when a weaker culture comes face to face with another stronger culture, the former inescapably accepts the latter's fantasy.

In this sense, we can argue that what Yoshimoto discerns in the problem of Japanese converts is this process of a weaker culture accepting the representations of a stronger culture. The situation is further complicated by the fact that the indigenous culture maintains its own relation between fantasy and reality

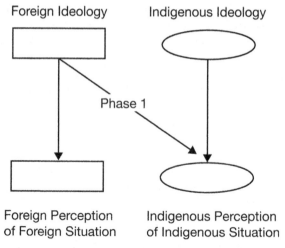

Figure 3.1   Foreign and indigenous cultures: Phase 1.

that is different from that of the foreign culture. This situation can be represented graphically as in Figure 3.1. When the foreign ideology is stronger than
the indigenous, in the first phase, the weaker adapts to the stronger. More
important, however, are the second and the third phases depicted in Figure 3.2.
We can posit along with Althusser that ideology interpolates individuals as
subject (Althusser 1984: 44), and that, following Lacan, our desire is the desire
of the Other (Lacan 1977a). Thus, in the second phase indigenous individual
perception shifts so as to fit the foreign ideology, and then, in the third phase,
the indigenous ideology reformulates itself so that it is in accordance with the
indigenous perception which has been adapted in terms of the foreign ideology.
Hence, both indigenous perception and ideology come to be assimilated into
the foreign form. What Yoshimoto, together with Guha, Soyinka and many
other postcolonial writers, attempts to preserve is the indigenous perception of
the indigenous situation which cannot be articulated in terms of the foreign
ideology and which is destined to disappear in the second phase.

Introducing Franz Fanon's *Black Skin, White Masks*, Homi Bhabha
insists that it is not the colonialist Self or the colonised Other, but the
disturbing distance in between that constitutes the figure of colonial otherness (Bhabha 1994: 45). For Bhabha, the problem of colonial identity
appears only in the hybridity of the colonialist and colonised. As Bart
Moore-Gilbert interprets it, Bhabha sees in *Black Skin, White Masks* 'the
crucial insight that the identity of neither party to the colonial relationship
is "original". Rather, each side needs and depends on the other in order to
constitute itself (if only by distinguishing itself from what it is not), whether
as colonizer or colonized' (Moore-Gilbert 2000: 458).

However, in the case of Japan the situation is more complicated, because
Japan has, in the process of modernisation, never been colonised by a Western
power until the end of the Second World War in 1945. The occupation of

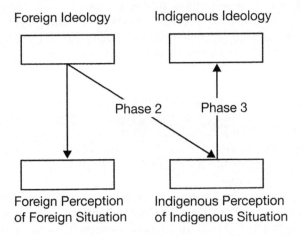

Foreign Ideology   Indigenous Ideology

Phase 2   Phase 3

Foreign Perception   Indigenous Perception
of Foreign Situation   of Indigenous Situation

Figure 3.2   Foreign and indigenous cultures: Phases 2 and 3.

Japan by the USA in the mid-twentieth century was, compared to the
Western powers' colonisation of other countries in the sixteenth to nineteenth centuries, shorter in term – lasting no more than seven years until
1952. But it appears that the Japanese people's perception of modernisation
since 1868 has been greatly affected by Western ideology, whereas the West
has not been greatly affected by Japanese ideology. Therefore, compared
with the relationship between directly opposing coloniser and colonised, the
relationship between Japan and the West was less reciprocal and more one-
sided. This means that the process from Phase 1 to Phase 3 in Figure 3.1 and
Figure 3.2 should have appeared in a more genuine and purer manner.

As Jace Weaver notes, indigenous cultures are living and have always been
dynamic rather than static; the only cultures that do not change are dead
cultures (Weaver 2000: 227–228). Although Weaver goes on to say that
European colonialism has always posited indigenous societies as dying and
dead, and it is certainly important to notice this, we also need to posit that
any culture must continue to exist despite coming into contact with other
cultures. Sometimes the opponent cultures are colonisers and some other
times they are not, but at all times and without exception they must be either
stronger or weaker than one's own culture. Therefore, rather than remain
static, a culture may need to change in order to survive in contact with other
cultures. But such change is one thing; preventing a weak culture from being
colonised by a stronger one is another.

It is necessary to be somewhat cautious here, so as not to give in to
nationalism, ethnocentrism or racism. In order to avoid falling into blind
chauvinism, it is necessary to clarify why it is necessary to preserve an
indigenous individual perception that cannot be articulated in terms of a
foreign ideology. The necessity lies neither in the desire of the indigenous
people to remain in their own limited sphere, nor in some supposed special
value of indigenous perception, for indigenous perception is no more

precious than foreign perception. Rather, it is necessary to preserve multiple perspectives in order to prevent everybody in the world from being subsumed in a monolithic global culture. Attempting to preserve indigenous perception simply because it is precious, means we cannot escape the enclosure of modernist ideology. Yet, on the other hand, if we allow the above two processes described in Figure 3.1 and Figure 3.2 to proceed unchecked, without attempting to protect indigenous experiences, it is obvious that one day everything will fall prey to the strongest ideological logic producing a global culture without boundaries. Since the only cultures that do not change are dead cultures, in order to keep on living, the negotiation between progress, which needs the strong, and divergence which needs co-existence with the weak is essential.

The principles of the French Revolution, of liberty (that requires emancipation of the weak from the strong people's despotic oppression), equality (that demands a lack of discrimination between the weak and the strong) and fraternity (rather than rivalry in the power structure), are in marked contrast to the rule of the jungle or the survival of the fittest. Perhaps the ability to admire strong people and care for the weak are input a priori into our life. The reason why terms like liberty, equality and fraternity seem beautiful to anyone's mind is most probably that they are seen as the hidden key to open the door for the continuation of life. In the process of evolution, we have never completely extinguished the weak; always the strong and the weak have co-existed. Otherwise there would not be various species in this world. We have to maintain this system.

As has been mentioned, Judith Butler has also remarked that preserving the outside is as important as refiguring it; otherwise, singular discourse meets its limits nowhere, and it domesticates all signs of difference (Butler 1993: 53). As we have noted in the previous two chapters, Murakami Haruki and Yoshimoto Banana suggest subverting the distinction between homogeneity and heterogeneity, either by means of adopting an indifferent stance towards both of them (Murakami Haruki), or conceiving *eros* towards homogeneous partners and *philia* or nostalgia (*natsukashisa*) towards heterogeneous opponents (Yoshimoto Banana). In contrast, Yoshimoto Takaaki warns us not to allow ourselves to be subsumed under a stronger heterogeneity, in order to avoid being trapped in a universal global homogeneity. Bearing the above in mind, it is necessary to ask what sort of indigenous perception of a native situation was or still is in danger when confronted with a universal or global ideology. Although many aspects of an indigenous culture come into play in this encounter, language clearly plays a central role.

It is evident that a foreign language produced by uniquely foreign ways of articulating experience cannot adequately express indigenous ideologies, desires, emotions or psyches articulated in an indigenous manner. To learn a foreign language requires deconstructing one's indigenous experiences formulated by one's native language, and re-expressing them in terms of the foreign culture. In this regard, it is significant that Yoshimoto, in his criticism of Maruyama Masao, refers to the following passage from the novelist Tayama Katai's (1872–1930) short story *One Soldier* (*Ippeisotsu*, 1908) as an example that represents the opposite side of Maruyama Masao's way of thinking. At the end of this story, a soldier, Katō Heisaku, is dying in a room, looked after by two other soldiers.

'I am very sorry.'

'It really is a pity. Where is (this guy) from?'

The soldier searches his pockets. (I notice/He notices) that (the soldier) takes out (my/his) regimental tally-book [*guntai techō o hiki dasu no ga wakaru*]. In his eyes the soldier's weather-tanned rough face and the figure that approaches the candle on the table in order to read the book are reflected. The voice which reads that Mikawa Province, Atsumi District, Fukue Village, Katō Heisaku...can be heard. Once again the hometown village appears before the eyes. Mother's face, wife's face, the big house surrounded by *keyaki* trees, the gentle shore out back, the blue-green sea, the familiar fishermen's faces.[8]

Yoshimoto criticises Maruyama by accusing him of lacking a sense of identification with the characters in the above passage. The difference between Maruyama's and Tayama's writings is neither between the intellectuals on the level of theory and the people on the level of everyday experience, nor between the author's scientific approach to the people as an object and the artistic narrator's empathy with the character. It is rather the difference between experiences expressed in language tinged with foreign sentiments and in typically native language.

In Japanese the personal pronoun is often not supplied, and in general the verb and adjective that show psychological movements only indicate the speaker's mental activities. Thus, the sentence '*guntai techō o hiki dasu no ga wakaru* (*guntai techō* = regimental tally-book, *o* = object marker, *hiki dasu* = to take out, *no ga* = nominaliser + object marker, *wakaru* = to notice)' is ambiguous. It can mean either 'I notice that he takes out my regimental tally-book' or 'He (Katō) notices that he (the soldier) takes out his (Katō's) regimental tally-book' – the former is the character's monologue, and the latter is the narrator's voice. Hence, in Japanese, the character's and the narrator's different voices are merged in one sentence without clear distinction (Murakami F. 1996: 65–80). It is difficult, if not impossible, to articulate this kind of ambiguity, which covers two different voices, in languages that have a different system. It is clear that a language such as English, which requires the almost mandatory use of personal pronouns and has a rigorous tense system, cannot easily express the identity between 'I' and 'she/he' or between 'now' and 'then'.

To the extent that Maruyama's translated books have been well received, his language is in a sense Westernised Japanese. There are some scholars

whose work is acclaimed worldwide, whereas the work of others is acknowledged only in their own society. Maruyama Masao is a representative of the
former, while Yoshimoto, along with Yanagita Kunio, whose work will be
discussed later, fall into the latter category. This phenomenon must partly
derive from the kind of language they use.

Wole Soyinka discusses a similar situation in Africa. He criticises the false
ideological contrast between analytical European and intuitive African, or
between Negro emotionality and Greek rationality, and presents Birago
Diop's poem 'Breath', as an example which conveys an important, even
fundamental aspect of the world-view of traditional Africa (Soyinka 1990:
129–133). 'Listen more to things/ Than to words that are said./ The water's
voice sings/ And the flame cries/ And the wind that brings/ The woods to
sighs/ Is the breathing of the dead./ Those who are dead have never gone
away…'. Two lines are repeated at the beginning of odd stanzas – 'Listen
more to things/ Than to words that are said'. By citing these lines of Birago
Diop, Soyinka seems to be implying something similar to Yoshimoto. Once
the indigenous experiences formed without language are articulated in
words, or once the indigenous emotions constituted by the indigenous words
are re-articulated by words tinged with foreign sentiment, the subtle texture
of the former is immediately lost. Yet, it must be added once again that if we
simply confine ourselves to our native language, we cannot go beyond our
ethnocentric enclosure. Hence, we have to avoid two extreme inclinations:
giving up our indigenous emotions in favour of the language of the stronger
culture, or isolating ourselves in our native language.

Apart from important differences in what can and cannot be articulated
through language, another crucial aspect of cross-cultural encounters is the
difference of the form of the self: the contrast between individual uniqueness and the sense of commonality with other people. The origin of
Yoshimoto's idea of the self can be seen developing as early as the series of
critical works he wrote on Miyazawa Kenji, written in 1945 just after the war
(Yoshimoto XV: 275–433). In this study Yoshimoto compares Kenji with
Natsume Sōseki, both of whom spent their lives in splendid isolation
(Yoshimoto XV: 404, 407). For Yoshimoto, however, the sense of loneliness
felt by Kenji and Sōseki are very different. Sōseki's isolation seems to derive
from the inconsistency he felt between the self (self to be seen, self-as-
object) and self-consciousness (self to see, self-as-subject) inside him, and his
inner repulsion against the people outside him, whereas Kenji's seclusion
was realised while maintaining a harmonious unity with the people around
him. But, contrary to expectation, Yoshimoto finds in Sōseki a warm
humanistic love, and discovers in Kenji a certain cold-heartedness. He
concludes his argument by saying that he cannot endure Kenji's loneliness
(Yoshimoto XV: 353, 403–404). Washida Koyata remarks on this indifferent
attitude of Kenji's, and suggests that what Yoshimoto is arguing in this essay
is not that Kenji's isolation cannot be endured, but that Kenji's indifference
must not be tolerated (Washida 1992: 25).

At this stage, it is important to re-examine the meaning of warm humanistic love. The fact that Sōseki can love people both deeply and warmly shows that he has a clear awareness of a unique part of his self which is different from people around him. Also, it shows that he is torn between the polarised axes of individual differentiation and totalitarian identification, and therefore he is strongly attracted to some people and deeply repelled by others. As we have seen in the previous two chapters, this is a typical characteristic of a modernist emotional attitude held towards heterogeneous others. Just as knowledge presupposes irreducible difference, not identity, so too does love. Most probably Sōseki learned this while studying in England where he felt doubly tormented by being placed between two cultures – the West and the East, and was torn between the two modernist polarised desires of individual differentiation and totalitarian identification.

In contrast, what stands behind Kenji's indifference is an extreme egalitarianism, that is, the awareness that to love all people without discrimination really means to love nobody, and consequently to lose love. Given that Yoshimoto remarks on a sense of Buddhist resignation as one of Kenji's characteristics, and also the fact that he highly esteems Kenji, it seems likely that Yoshimoto sees in Kenji's indifferent cold attitude towards people the potential to overcome the modernist double bind of individualisation and totalisation. This modernist attitude precisely corresponds with the modernist idea of humanism, in the sense that both value uniqueness and commonality in human beings. Kenji certainly cannot be called a humanist. As Yoshimoto points out, Kenji in his fairy tales depicts the life and death of animals from their own viewpoint, and does not value human nature above that of the animal (Yoshimoto T. 1996a: 35, 38). Yet we also know that he achieved an enormous sense of egalitarianism through his sacrifice of humanism.

As Yoshimoto has suggested, it is significant to note the difference between Christianity and Buddhism here. Christianity respects highly the angelic side of people on the one hand, and disdains the evil and animal aspects of human nature on the other, whereas Buddhism attempts to discard both. Unfortunately, it is beyond the scope of this study and also beyond my ability to elaborate on these differences other than to point out the various problems created by Christian humanism based on European culture and those arising from Buddhist resignation in the East. The contrast can be seen between the diametrical dualisms of Christianity, such as good versus evil, self versus others, universality versus uniqueness, and differentiation versus identification, and the apathetic indifference of Buddhist resignation. Perhaps what we have to seek for is, yet again, neither one nor the other, but something different, something new.

A development of Yoshimoto's argument about the self can be found in his criticism of Maruyama Masao in 'The End of Fictitious System' ('Gisei no shūen'), an article published in 1960 two years before his paper 'On Maruyama Masao' discussed above. Before Yoshimoto's 1960 essay,

Maruyama had published his own article entitled '15 August and 19 May' ('8.15 to 5.19') in the journal *Chūō kōron* (August 1960). In this article he traces the changes in the characterisation of the Japanese people from subjects of the emperor during the war, to two different understandings in the post-war era. Of these new understandings, one stresses the individualisation that underscores individual rights and private benefits, and the other is characteristic of the active revolutionary movements which value the society's interests over the individual's benefits. Maruyama argues that before the 'Anti-Security-Treaty Movement (*Anpo tōsō*)' of 1959–1960 the stress on personal benefits had resulted in political apathy, and thereby indirectly helped the authorities to suppress revolutionary tendencies, but that the Anti-Security-Treaty Movement had provided both streams with a good opportunity to communicate with each other (Maruyama M. 1960).

These two directions which Maruyama has pointed out in Japanese society are precisely the two diametrical poles of modernism discernible in Sōseki's, as well as Murakami Haruki's and Yoshimoto Banana's work: individual differentiation and totalitarian identification. Compared with Sōseki, who was psychologically tormented and torn between these two polarised desires, we find in Maruyama a calm, reasonable, detached and objective viewpoint. At first sight Maruyama's assertion looks like Miyazawa Kenji's posture of indifference, but they differ in one crucial way. While for Kenji, individuality and totality are both fundamentally excesses, for Maruyama both are crucial for a mature and democratic society. In order to overcome feudalistic family bonds, we first have to foster individuality. However, in order to act politically, Maruyama argues that one needs to form a party, not on the basis of authoritarian or patrimonial domination, but on rationality. Namely, Kenji considers individuality to be as illusory as totality, but Maruyama attempts to foster individuality for the purpose of emancipating people from feudalistic totalism, and in order to avoid losing solidarity, he insists on the importance of being united rationally.

In Maruyama's mind, to be individual requires the responsibility to respect others' individuality, and democracy means to be able to negotiate in a fair manner with others for the purpose of creating a better society. In contrast, apathy, for him, is irresponsible, since, without concern for others, one cannot realise one's own individuality. Maruyama's argument is therefore based upon the distinction between the individual and the total, and presupposes an idealistic concept of a universal good society. The good society consists of good individuals, and, if we judge by the standards set by rationality, it must be good for all individuals. If people do not appreciate what is good for them, they need to be educated, so that they can appreciate what is good and what is bad on the basis of rationality.

This is a crucial foundation of Western rationalism which Maruyama attempts to preserve, but which Yoshimoto, together with Kenji, wishes to reject. We can discern two different factors that cause Yoshimoto to criticise Maruyama's sense of individuality and solidarity. The first is that while

Maruyama presupposes that there is a distinction to be made between self and others, and that this distinction is invaluable, Yoshimoto regards both as illusory, excessive and superfluous. Therefore, for Yoshimoto, 'apathy' is a more favourable condition than individuality in the sense that it can avoid the double bind of individualisation and totalisation. For Yoshimoto, to empha- sise individuality involves being enmeshed within the sphere of the binary opposition between individuality and totality. Judging from Yoshimoto's high esteem for Kenji's apathetic indifference, it seems likely that, from this perspective, Yoshimoto calls the democracy that Maruyama imagines, fake, and insists that genuine democracy must be established on the principle that gives priority to the political 'apathy' (Yoshimoto XIII: 67–68).

Second, Yoshimoto criticises democracy in Maruyama's sense for oper- ating under a power system. Democracy based upon rationality and majority rule establishes meritocratic hierarchies wherein a person is valued in terms of the strength of their rationality: a logocentric power game. Consequently it is the very binary opposition between individualism and totalitarianism made on the basis of power structures that Yoshimoto is attacking. No matter how reasonably or rationally one attempts to negotiate with others, one cannot go beyond dualism and power relations. Yoshimoto aims to repudiate all these in favour of an egalitarian and indifferent 'apathy'.

This contrast between individualism and totalitarianism in relation to power structures is closely connected with two aspects of the self (uniqueness and commonality) and also related to ethnocentrism and globalism. As Spivak has pointed out, one of the characteristics of scientific knowledge is its distinction between subject and object. Knowledge presupposes an irreducible difference, not identity, between subject and object (Spivak 1987: 251–268). In the modern period there has been a tendency to try to detach the object from the subject as clearly as possible, taking consciousness as the subject. Even when we try to understand ourselves, we set up our own consciousness as an object for scrutiny. Contrary to this trend, however, the modern Japanese philosopher, Nishida Kitarō (1870–1945), insists that the Japanese subject is constituted not in individuality, but in society, and occupies a realm in between the Western sense of subject and object (Nishida 1988: 348).

Watsuji Tetsurō, in his study of Japanese ethics, develops Nishida's idea, pointing out that the etymology of the Japanese term *'ningen'* originally means both 'people' and 'in-between people'. He insists that human exis- tence is a unity of both the personal and societal aspects of one individual. Watsuji also argues that the concept of the individual as constituted by both personal and communal aspects can be found in such Western philosophers as Aristotle, Kant, Cohen, Hegel, Feuerbach, Marx and others (Watsuji 1934: 31; see also Sakai 1997: 104 (J) 87 (E)). This understanding can also be seen in Georg Simmel's idea of singleness and uniqueness (Simmel 1971: 224), and Merleau-Ponty's notion of intersubjectivity (Merleau-Ponty 1962). Hence, we can argue that in both Western and non-Western cultures, the idea of distinguishing subjectivity as uniqueness and intersubjectivity as

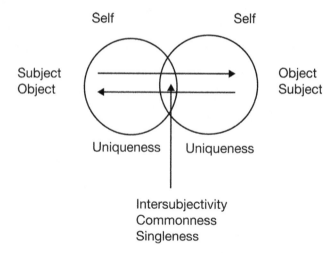

Figure 3.3   Relationship between individuality and communality

commonality, has a long tradition, though the degree to which this is emphasised differs between cultures.

The relationship described above between individuality and communality can be represented diagrammatically in Figure 3.3. As Sakai Naoki cautions us, we should not forget that individuality cannot be clearly resolved into communal and unique aspects. No matter how we attempt to categorise ourselves, there is inevitably produced a 'surplus' that is irreducible to the dual structure of the whole and the individual, this is in our terms something new which consequently has potential to subvert the distinction (Sakai 1997: 119 (J) 98 (E)). Bearing this surplus in mind, however, we can still argue that the individual has communal and unique aspects as well as the potential to exceed the distinction.

Both Nishida's and Watsuji's understandings tend to highlight the inter-subjectivity as a communal construction of selfhood. Hence, they emphasise the sense of ethnic singleness felt by a native people, and stress the unique-ness felt by one ethnic group when it confronts another. It is easy to see here the risk of ethnocentrism when intersubjectivity is understood to be confined to a single ethnicity. Other than the central contrast between inter-subjectivity and uniqueness in oneself, those Japanese who studied in Western countries such as Mori Ōgai, Natsume Sōseki, Nagai Kafū and Takamura Kōtarō,[9] must also have encountered the problem of universality and locality that is represented in Figure 3.4. Of importance is that, if our sense of commonality or universality with others is lost in an international situation (Figure 3.4), then we tend to substitute for it in the intersubjective or common aspects of ethnicity (Figure 3.3).

Yoshimoto is well aware of this danger of becoming ethnocentric. In his study of Takamura Kōtarō, he insists that it was his failure to compromise the oppositions between the unique and common aspects of the self and

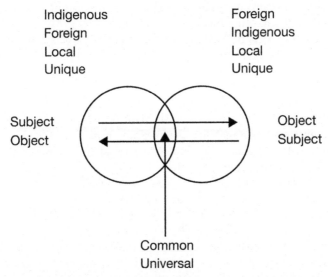

Indigenous   Foreign
Foreign   Indigenous
Local   Local
Unique   Unique

Subject   Object
Object   Subject

Common
Universal

Figure 3.4   Representation of universality and locality.

between universality (the intellectuals) and locality (the people) that led him to support extreme imperialism (Yoshimoto VIII: 104–106, 117–118; see also Washida 1992: 74). Thus intersubjectivity appears as commonality, just as homogeneity is manifested at various levels such as family, country, nation-state, ethnic group, gender, etc. It is apparent, then, that we are aware of two extreme tendencies: being trapped in ethnocentrism through an over-emphasis on commonality and intersubjectivity shared with others in the same ethnic group, and becoming trapped in a worldwide monolithic global subjectivity.

A theory of collective fantasy (kyōdō gensō ron)

Yoshimoto Takaaki published *A Theory of Collective Fantasy* (*Kyōdō gensō ron*) in 1968. The book is the second part of his theoretical trilogy, which was preceded by his theory of language presented in *What is Beauty for Language?* (*Gengo ni totte bi to wa nani ka*, 1965), and followed by his theory of mind developed in *An Introduction to the Theory of Mental Phenomena* (*Shinteki genshō ron josetsu*, 1971). Though all three theories are important for understanding Yoshimoto's thought, I shall concentrate here on his theory of fantasy which had an important impact on almost all the fields of cultural studies in the 1970s and 1980s in Japan.

In *A Theory of Collective Fantasy*, Yoshimoto asserts that the Marxian concept of 'superstructure' (political and legal relations or such social ideologies as religion, art, ethics and philosophy) is the domain of fantasy (*gensō*). He divides the concept of fantasy into three categories: collective fantasy (*kyōdō gensō*, including religion, law, the state and the nation); conjugal fantasy (*tsui gensō*, involving sexual relations); and self-fantasy (*jiko gensō*, or the self–self and self–other relation, art and literature) (Yoshimoto T. 1982b). The significant aspects of Yoshimoto's theory of fantasy can be summarised as follows. First, he classified all wide-ranging cultural phenomena into three broad categories (collective, conjugal and self), and clarified the relations between them. Second, following Marx and Engels, he insisted that the domain of fantasy was, to a certain extent, independent of economic relations and could develop autonomously. Third, his use of the term fantasy (*gensō*) suggested the possibility of freedom from a dark unknown force, which previously had been considered to be an inherent condition of society. And finally, by introducing the notion of collectivity (*kyōdō*), he provided a theoretical basis for dealing with the mass of people.[10]

Yoshimoto's concept of collective fantasy presupposes the Saussurian idea of 'arbitrariness', seen in the notion of fantasy, which implies that the domain of culture is contingent. His notion of collective fantasy also corresponds to the Merleau-Pontian concept of intersubjectivity, in that his stress on collectivity suggests that if we collectively attempt to change cultural phenomena, we can do so. However, although Yoshimoto's theory does seem to derive, in part, from these two Western philosophers, it was, in fact, conceived independently. For, although a few specialists in Japan had studied Saussure, it was not until Maruyama Keizaburō's pioneering introduction to the work of Saussure in 1981 (Maruyama K. 1981), that Saussure was fully understood in Japan. Also, Merleau-Ponty's work was not introduced to Japan until the mid 1960s. Therefore, it seems clear that Yoshimoto created his theory independently without reference to any previous studies in Western countries. It is understandable, then, that Yoshimoto's theory should be so highly regarded in Japan, as being an original achievement comparable to significant theories in Western philosophy.

In Yoshimoto's theory, self-fantasy originally and fundamentally opposes collective fantasy. In his 'Japanese Nationalism' (1964) and also in his lecture at the Dōshisha University entitled 'What is the Situation?' ('Jōkyō to wa nani ka') (1966) Yoshimoto differentiates between writing and speaking activities, and concludes that the individual consciousness of each person is formed analogically through writing and rewriting activities based upon introspective and retrospective consideration. This inevitably goes against the mass consciousness, which is formed on the basis of speaking and taking part in the normal activities of everyday life (Yoshimoto XIV: 134–136). In Yoshimoto's theory, however, though self-fantasy originally and fundamentally opposes collective fantasy, the former is destined to be finally included and assimilated into the latter. With regard to the confrontation between self and collective fantasies, Yoshimoto says:

> Man was originally not a social being. Although we were independent and wanted to be 'individual' by freely eating and thinking, we unavoidably created a 'societal' communality. And once created, the 'societal'

communality started acting more or less as a restraint to each 'individual' who had created it.

('Individual, Family and Society', '*Kojin kazoku shakai*' Yoshimoto IV: 465;
my translation)

The notion of self-fantasy obviously contains the figure of the intellectual, but behind the concept of collective fantasy at least two different aspects can be discerned – the people and the dominating authority. When Yoshimoto insists that the self-fantasy is necessarily defeated and assimilated into the collective fantasy, most probably he is describing the process whereby the self is caught up in power structures. This seems to be based on his personal experiences. During the China–Japan and Pacific Wars, Yoshimoto encountered the enormous power of the collective fantasy of the Japanese people, which, under imperial authority, swept over each individual person's self-fantasy and formed a sort of national consensus. He says:

> During the War, until the end, there was the presupposition that sociality preceded individuality. In other words, you may say that the individual interest should be disregarded for the benefit of the nation-state or society. It was by no means possible to subvert this idea. Though in those days I persistently experienced the inconsistency or conflict between the individual and the society or nation, I could never resolve it. When I attempted to elucidate it in an extreme way, I had always to conclude that the benefit of the nation or society took priority, and compared with it, the individual will was a small matter. There were, as far as I could see, no circumstances that could destroy it.

> How did the post-war mentality begin? It started with the supposition that we had to negate the idea that society or state – that is, communality – preceded individuality.

(Yoshimoto 1990: 10; my translation)

This was a crucial moment for Yoshimoto. Faced with the collapse of the dominant value system, Yoshimoto had to reconsider the legitimacy of good and evil or truth and falsehood. Hence, the motive behind Yoshimoto's theory of collective fantasy is now apparent: he first had to understand why the self-fantasy of all Japanese people, including himself, was easily manipulated by the collective fantasy during the war, and second, he had to account for why, if collective fantasy was, to a certain extent, grounded in the people, self-fantasy could be released from the dominating authority of the collective fantasy without losing the connecting link with the people.

For Yoshimoto, in contrast to the self-fantasy, the conjugal (or sexual) fantasy always stands against the collective fantasy, and they never compromise each other. Conjugal fantasy in Yoshimoto's theory is not confined to the male–female or husband–wife sexual relations, but includes parents', children's and siblings' relations, in other words, the family as a whole. A significant point in Yoshimoto's theory of collective fantasy lies in his distinction between family and community. As Karatani Kōjin points out, Yoshimoto's conjugal fantasy is a calm and comfortable human relationship in which the individual can be lost without experiencing alienation (Karatani 1979a: 97–98).

In Yoshimoto's theory the self cannot maintain itself in opposition to a society that consists of strangers. No matter how hard an individual fights against society, the struggle is doomed to failure for an individual cannot bear such loneliness. In contrast, however, the family based upon conjugal relations (though in this relation too the individual must also compromise) can stand against the community by forming a sort of fortress of homogeneous members. Although the family comes about from heterogeneous sexual relations, it results in homogeneous human relations. It is in the context of the homogeneous family that the self can resist society's attempt to reduce individuality to a state of homogeneous bondage. The most important aspect of Yoshimoto's theory of collective fantasy is, then, his theory of the family.

Figure 3.5 illustrates this. In Yoshimoto's theory, both the self-collective fantasy and the self-conjugal fantasy move in the same direction: from the heterogeneous to the homogeneous. The difference is that the former is based on cultural or social differentiation, whereas the latter is based on distinctions of gender and sexuality and ensuing blood relations. Yoshimoto sees in the family, or, in other words, the homogeneous relations resulting from sexual desire experienced by heterogeneous genders, a calm and comfortable relationship in which the individual can lose the sense of self without being alienated or appropriated. However, he considers the

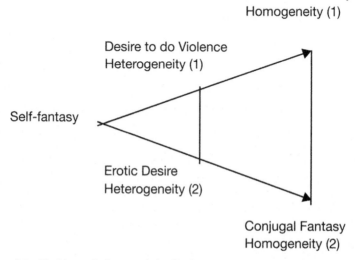

Figure 3.5   Yoshimoto's theory of the family

homogeneous relations created by culturally heterogeneous people to be a compelling force towards estrangement. Yoshimoto claims that the family has a unique quality that cannot be subsumed into society.

We can therefore argue that Yoshimoto, in his concept of conjugal or sexual fantasy, imagines an erotic desire that excludes the desire to do violence or express itself through power structures. That is, for Yoshimoto, homogeneity (1) and (2) in Figure 3.5 are different in nature. While homogeneity (1) results from the power struggle and succeeding alienation, colonisation and exploitation, homogeneity (2) is a sort of utopian human erotic relation which does not have any desire to do violence, and he considers that it can be attained in the family.

We have to be careful here in dealing with this point. First, it seems to be more pertinent to say that people have both unique and communal aspects, not only sequentially but also spatially. Although it might be usual for human relations in general to start from the heterogeneous and move towards the direction of the homogeneous, we can presuppose neither complete heterogeneity, nor perfect homogeneity, nor a one-way traffic from heterogeneity to homogeneity.

Yoshimoto considers the relationship between the self and collective fantasies, and probably that between the self and conjugal fantasies too, to be temporal and continuous sequences from heterogeneous to homogeneous relations (the former forcible and the latter without exploitation). But it seems better to regard them spatially; namely, the individual simultaneously experiences subjectivity as being heterogeneous towards strangers, and inter-subjectivity as being homogeneous with regard to the collective and/or conjugal fantasy. The idea that human relations necessarily move from the heterogeneous to the homogeneous seems to be a typical characteristic of modernism, in the sense that familiarity and strangeness are crucial distinctions made in modernist human relations. This is the point actually, as we have seen, his daughter Banana later attempted to subvert.

Second, although Yoshimoto finds in the family an ideal human relationship in which there is no power struggle, and therefore, no exploitation, it seems somewhat optimistic. If, as Karatani Kōjin argues, the family for Yoshimoto is a place for calm and comfortable relations where the individual can become lost without being alienated, then from the feminist point of view, Yoshimoto's understanding can be criticised for being androcentric. The family is, rather, a place where *men* can escape from the bonds of exploitation, but where *women* are exploited and appropriated (Mitchell 1984: 34–39). Likewise, Yoshimoto's vision of the relations between self and society as nothing but power relations, also seems to be exaggerated. We can at least imagine and therefore should not give up on the ideal of human relations without exploitation in society (Kohama 1999: 240).

Hence, both the family and society can be a site of exploitation and appropriation, as well as a place for creating the possibility of ideal human relations. If we follow the above argument, then, it seems unlikely that there is any fundamental difference between homogeneity (1) and (2). Or, in other words, we should claim that, following Georges Bataille (Bataille 1986: 16), in the modern period, the desire to do violence (homogeneity 1) and the 'pure' erotic desire (homogeneity 2) are almost inextricably merged.

Having pointed out the above, however, there is still one issue that cannot be overlooked. That is, if homogeneity (1) and (2) were the same, we would not have the incest taboo. As long as incest is prohibited, as we discussed in the previous chapter, we have to grant that the distinction between familiarity and strangeness exists more or less in any human culture. Thus, it would be misleading to regard Yoshimoto's concept of the family as typically and exclusively chauvinistic.

For instance, Juliet Mitchell writes that throughout history women have been appropriated as sexual objects. She also discerns nothing but a lexicon of reification in contemporary sexual vocabulary. She is making these observations in a domain in which erotic desire is closely linked with the desire to do violence, as in Bataille's theory (Mitchell 1984: 34–35). However, the strength of the bond between the desire to do violence and erotic desire might differ in culture and in time. Then, this indicates that we have to reconsider Bataille and restrict his formula, so that the domain of eroticism is the domain of violence only in modern society. Not surprisingly, Yoshimoto disagrees with Bataille, arguing that:

> Bataille neglected the fact that the 'Other' who appears in one's eroticism is a unique 'Other', that is, the peculiarity is an inevitable condition for this 'Other', whereas the 'Other' who witnesses one's death does not have any specific aspect. Therefore, in his theory, one's juvenile eroticism in pseudo-death and rebirth is without any deep insight directly connected to death.
>
> (Yoshimoto T. 1981: 53; my translation)

In this passage, although Yoshimoto's expression is, just as in others, elusive, we can surmise that Yoshimoto claims here that there are two different types of the 'Other'. One resides in homogeneity (1) which is an anonymous Other who witnesses one's death, and the second is characteristic of homogeneity (2), a unique Other constituted as the object of an individual's eroticism. Yoshimoto insists that Bataille has overlooked the difference between them.

It is true that the family is exactly that which we have to overcome when we overthrow feudalism and foster the development of an individual self. But, as we have seen in Yoshimoto Banana's stories' attempt to subvert the family/stranger distinction, the deconstruction of family might be necessary now as part of the postmodern process of subverting the forms of desire. Of interest for the present discussion is that, as Ueno Chizuko has also mentioned (Ueno 1986: 2), there might be potential in Yoshimoto's theory of distinction between collective and conjugal fantasies for deconstructing the modernist binary opposition between self and Other. As we have noted in the previous chapter, what Bataille's formula has overlooked is the possibility of *eros* without violence in the form of incest among homogeneous people.

A reformulation of desire is now urgent, so as to refigure the 'Other' and overcome the violence of exclusion. In order to deconstruct desire, it is necessary to find a new pleasure or enjoyment and to reform the ways connecting desire and its object. If *eros* and violence, unification and discrimination, or longing and disdain select the 'Other' as their object, re-forming desire offers the possibility of transgressing the boundary between self and Other. In order to achieve this, the concept of kinship that is conjugal fantasy, set in between the self and collective fantasies, in Yoshimoto's terminology, must play an important role.

However, we have to be cautious here. If an ideal erotic relation without the desire to do violence felt between heterogeneous opponents is unattain-able, Yoshimoto's theory of family becomes nothing but chauvinism and discrimination. From this perspective, it is possible to argue that what Yoshimoto Banana is attempting to do is to move one step forward along the way paved by her father. That is, in order to avoid the risk her father Takaaki runs in inviting *eros* into the homogeneous family sphere, leaving violence in the heterogeneous stranger's domain, the daughter, Banana, conceives *philia* or nostalgia (*natsukashisa*) towards the heterogeneous strangers.

In order to understand the uniqueness of Yoshimoto's theory of fantasy it is helpful to refer to the discussion held between Yoshimoto and Michel Foucault mentioned previously. This round-table discussion was held on 25 April 1978, interpreted by Hasumi Shigehiko, and published in the journal *Umi* (July issue, 1978) (Yoshimoto T. 1982b: 309). In the discussion, Yoshimoto first raises the question of how to deal with Marxism. Foucault, in his book *The Order of Things*, maintains that Marxism exists within the confines of nineteenth-century thought like a fish in water, in that it is unable to breathe anywhere else (Foucault 1994: 261). Yoshimoto, however, argues that we must not give up Marxism. His assertion is based on two claims. One is that we cannot ignore the importance of the individual will that was advocated by Hegel and further stressed by Marx, second is that our analysis must be grounded on causality. This implies that we must main-tain the will to realise the ideal Marxian society, because if the will can act as the cause, it will surely someday be achieved, just as the cause results in the effect (Yoshimoto T. and Foucault 1984: 8–13).

Foucault continues the argument with Yoshimoto by providing reasons why we have to go beyond Marxism. He points to three aspects of Marxism that are closely linked to power structures. First, it functions discursively, producing truth in the discourse of scientific knowledge; second, it is teleo-logical, since the truth is discursive not only in the past but also in the future. Third, it exists as a political movement in the sense that it is widely regarded as a state philosophy or class ideology. The traditional European critique of Marxism has centred on its truth or falsehood, whether it fore-sees the future correctly or not, or how Marxism differs from Marx's own ideas. This kind of critique is, Foucault declares, fruitless, for it cannot go beyond the power of truth and its effect.

Foucault presents three strategies for breaking through the above impasse. First, by looking at Marxism in the context of nineteenth-century thought, its teleological force is reduced, that is, by rejecting the supposition that Marx expressed the truth and placing his theory in the historical context, the discursive power of Marxism as a scientific or teleological discourse is lessened. Second, Foucault maintains that since Marxism has been preoccupied with its role as a political ideology, it has consequently overlooked many important problems such as the process of institutionalisation in which under a regime of 'rationality' certain people are understood to be problematic and are confined to a variety of institutions, such as prisons, hospitals and clinics. Therefore, by analysing these problems that have been overlooked by Marxism, we can reduce Marxism's political power. And last, by connecting the above issues like institutionalisation to the social movements of protest and resistance, Foucault urges us to regain what has until now been monopolised by Marxism and Marxist political parties (Yoshimoto T. and Foucault 1984: 13–22). It is clear that Foucault's arguments about Marxism in this discussion relate to many of his philosophical preoccupations.

Both Foucault and Yoshimoto share the paradox that in order to create an ideal society in which there are no power structures, it is necessary to use power. When faced with this dilemma, Foucault tries to subvert power itself by means of a strategic codification of resistances, whereas Yoshimoto embarks on an analysis of the fantasy that creates power structures. The relationship between power and resistance for Foucault is therefore, in a sense, equivalent to the relationship between Yoshimoto's collective and self-fantasies.

However, they differ in at least one point. While for Foucault, power is manifest in the direct opposition between the strong and the weak to the extent that the former physically and intellectually oppresses the latter, the relation between Yoshimoto's collective and self-fantasies focuses instead on commonality and uniqueness, and the way that the former assimilates the latter. Thus, we may be able to argue that both Foucault and Yoshimoto are fighting on the side of uniqueness and weakness in the struggle against the stronger power of commonality. Nevertheless, it is clear that their approaches (to analyse human fantasy for Yoshimoto and to subvert power by the codification of strategic points of resistance for Foucault) are sufficiently different that we cannot ignore their specific cultural perspectives.

Karatani Kōjin, in his evaluation of the discussion between Foucault and Yoshimoto, focuses on rationality and says: 'For Yoshimoto the law or nation-state is part of "collective fantasy"...whereas for Foucault the law is rationality or language.... The logic which supports the authority in Japan is not "rationality" but "fantasy"' (Karatani 1979b: 173). What, then, is the relation between rationality and fantasy, both of which act as power structures? As Karatani notices, there is here a cross-cultural problem. Following on from Karatani's criticism, we may be able to argue that it is a basic

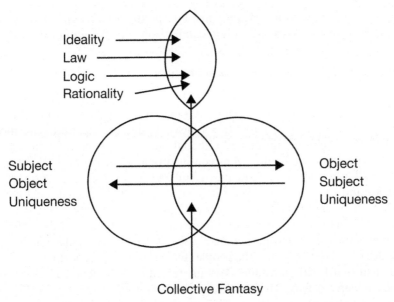

Figure 3.6   Rationality and collective fantasy.

contradiction between Western and Asian ideologies which underlies the cross-purposes between Foucault and Yoshimoto.

It seems that Foucault argues on the basis of a pre-given law, logic, theory and rationality, whereas Yoshimoto considers all these to be collective fantasy. But rather than attributing their difference to a fundamental distinction between fantasy and reason, we should suppose instead, that we have given two different names – rationality and collective fantasy – to one object (Figure 3.6). Rationality is applicable to everyone, since it is judged by the collective fantasy. Thus, we can argue that what Western ideology has achieved is to cast out sympathetic or empathic identification in the domain of intersubjectivity from the human unconscious and name this ideality, logic, law and rationality. By so doing, it has emancipated us from simple ethnic identification in the domain of the blind unconscious intersubject, through stressing the universality of logic and rationality. Yet, this process has come to be criticised as a form of phallogocentrism, for, it results in a forced progress based on a strong-is-good mentality that further results in a universal monolithic culture.

It is apparent that what we have to surpass is both the idea of a universal logic, or rationality in the sphere of ideality, and the empathic identification in the domain of the intersubject. For Yoshimoto, the problem is how to escape the intuitive power of collective fantasy which tends to cover the self-fantasy, whereas for Foucault, the issue is how to subvert rationality which is thought to be a universal standard, so that the more rational you are the stronger you become. Put simply, Foucault critiques phallogocentrism (rationality) whereas Yoshimoto criticises fascistic totalitarianism (collective fantasy). This point is important when interpreting the distinct characteristics of African and Asian cultures in comparison with Western ones.

African, Asian and European consciousness

With reference to Hegel and Marx, Yoshimoto distinguishes three patterns in the evolution of human thought – African, Asian and European. Though closely following Hegel's and Marx's ideas, Yoshimoto's patterns are more analytical, not chronological, and although they are apparently named after ethnic types, they are by no means confined to any one people.[11] We should expect all three forms – African, Asian and European – to share some aspects, and each system to have its own unique face, original focal point, and distinct combinations. We should also suppose that everyone has African, Asian and European characteristics, although with different emphases, just as everyone possesses aspects belonging to the intellectual (the desire to be strong) and the people (the need to be dependent).

I shall first briefly introduce Yoshimoto's idea of African consciousness, which is derived from Hegel's theory (Yoshimoto T. 1998b).[12] Yoshimoto first sees in Hegel's notion of African consciousness outlined in his book *The Philosophy of History*, a perspective characteristic of absolute modernism, that is a viewpoint that looks at world history as a uni-linear process of development and progress towards an ideal condition. From this evolutionary perspective, Yoshimoto argues, Hegel sees African people's savagery and barbarity as a primitive state in which the people are not yet 'enlightened'. Yoshimoto insists that:

> if you take the standpoint of the history of nature, it [Hegel's analysis] is certainly the right way of looking at the situation. But, from the viewpoint of the history of human inner spiritual existence, it [what Hegel positively analysed] is exactly the process whereby we have been oppressed by the outside civilisation, torn into pieces, wounded and invaded by the outsiders. We can further argue that it is therefore a history in which we have created a stiff rationality in order to remove from the inside that which was eroded by the outside.
>
> (Yoshimoto T. 1996b: 12–13; my translation)

In this criticism, Yoshimoto's intention to take the African (and also the Asian) consciousness into consideration is obvious. He is attempting to recover in the African (and also in the Asian) type of consciousness the possibilities and potentials repudiated in the process of European modernisation in the form of the Enlightenment project imposed from the outside. What, then, has been gained and what lost in the process of Western modernisation?

First, Hegel mentions that African consciousness first and foremost lacks the concepts of God (Absolute Being, Higher Power) and Law (Universality), both of which are construed as idealised essences which exist independent of human society, and both of which are considered to control individual will in terms of absolute commands. It must therefore be asked what did European consciousness renounce in order to realise the concepts of God and Law? As we have seen, Hegel's fundamental understanding is that world history progresses from a state of wild savagery to a cultivated state in which the happiness of peoples, the wisdom of states and the virtue of individuals must be realised by the light of God and Law (Hegel 1900: 21). These abstract essences are considered to be universal ideals by Hegel, which means that he views them as equally applicable to all people and societies in the world. As ideals, Hegel considers that all people should follow them, and, if they follow regular steps, they will all reach the same goal some day. However, on the other hand, we may also be able to argue that, since these values are understood to be universal, they are imposed on individuals, irrespective of personal differences, from the outside. And, since they are regarded as ideal, all the people in the world are compelled to move in the same direction.

The second point considered by Hegel is consciousness of individuality. Hegel believes that the reason why African consciousness cannot attain the realisation of any ideals or universality, is because individual consciousness is not distinguished from the natural surroundings, therefore African people do not conceive of themselves as individuals, distinct from a universal or essential being (Hegel 1900: 93–97). For self-consciousness to arise, there must be the concept of the Other. Similarly, it is also true that the sense of a unique self cannot be realised without the notion of universality. Following on from this, the sense of individual incompleteness depends on the notion of an absolute being or higher existence. Hence, it is not surprising that characteristically African (and Asian) consciousness, which lacks the sense of universality, is inclined to the concept of oneness, empathy and unity with others and the environment. As noted earlier when we discussed Nishida Kitarō and Watsuji Tetsurō in the second section of this chapter, this sense of belonging is not abstracted through the application of concepts of logic, God, or Law, but established through the domain of the intersubject; that is the sense of something inherently shared.

We can therefore argue that this form of consciousness is not inclined to produce ideas of the Other, universality, absolute being, higher existence or ideals outside the self. Instead, African and Asian consciousness is characterised by the strong power of totality in the form of collective fantasy, and lacks enthusiasm for development, evolution and progress. Yet, it is also free from at least some of the structures that have contaminated people who have developed a distinct sense of self-consciousness.

In a recent study of African consciousness, T. Len Holdstock introduces the Zulu expression, '*umuntu ngumuntu ngabantu*' which means, Holdstock explains, that a person is a person through other persons. Holdstock says that this expression 'captures the essence of the African concept of the self well'. For the African consciousness, the individual cannot be human alone. One's personhood is dependent upon one's relationships with others (Holdstock 2000: 105).

Relating to this self-consciousness of African and also Asian cultures, it might be helpful here to refer to the Native American consciousness. A historian Donald L. Fixico notes that Native Americans and Anglo-Americans differ considerably in their value systems. Traditional Native Americans, Fixico reports, believe that they are part of a whole; they are not solitary; they prefer a culture stressing community more than individuality; they see the whole or the group and want to be part of it. Fixico concludes that to want to be a part of the whole and to see oneself as a small part of the 'one' refocuses the emphasis on group-ego rather than self-ego (Fixico 1996: 37–38). As Weaver, Fixico and Michael Kearney noted, Native Americans are inclined to see themselves in terms of 'self in society' rather than 'self and society'. It is an 'enlarged sense of self' that declares, 'I am We' (Weaver 1997: 39, 2000: 227; Fixico 1998: 205; Kearney 1984: 151).

Then, this is very similar to African and Asian consciousness. As Holdstock notes, there are many other cultures in the world that constitute the concept of self in social context, rather than as an individual psychological core.[13] As both Fixico and Kawai Hayao mention, it might be right to say that self-identity consciousness or individuality is specifically strong in English-speaking people (Fixico 1998: 210; Yoshimoto Banana and Kawai Hayao 2002: 72). As we have seen, this idea of individuality is closely related to the concept of progress in time's arrow (Eliade 1958: 46; Gould 1987: 12–13), and also to the ideas of individual freedom from traditional and archaic collective life or from the oppression of another, despotically strong, individual.

The third point that Hegel regards as a characteristically African feature is the worship of the dead (Hegel 1900: 94–95). Ancestor worship can be found almost everywhere in the world. From a modernist point of view, it can be regarded as a chronological stage: a feature that has gradually disappeared as societies progress from premodern to modern, or from animism or polytheism to monotheism. The development of Christianity is, in this sense, characteristic of Western culture. Departing from ancestor worship, animism and polytheism, Christianity established an ideal universal monotheism, or, rather, the notions of the ideal and universal already pre-existent in Greek philosophy made possible the creation of Christianity.

A consciousness grounded in individuality, universality and ideality must overcome the idea of ancestor worship and unification with nature and others, in favour of a future ideal represented by the Christian God of Western culture. Ancestor worship, in contrast, indicates first, the identification between oneself and one's ancestor, second, the tendency to lose oneself in nostalgia, and third, the inclination to be enclosed in incestuous family relations, and to lose the energy to progress towards the future and foreign places, in other words, autism. In addition, ancestor worship also encourages a tendency to believe in a fascistic totality. Yet, it is also true that ancestor worship is free from some of the idealistic struggles characteristic of Christianity. Hence, the imperative is here again to transcend both idealistic religion and ancestor worship.

Apart from the absence of individuality and the tendency towards autism, there is one other aspect of African consciousness to which we have to pay attention. This is the inclination that a consciousness that lacks a sense of individuality, ideality and universality, has to understand the outside world by means of projecting its hidden power as images into the world of phenomena. This is the feature described by Hegel as *Fetich* (fetish): a kind of objective independence as contrasted with the arbitrary fancy of the individual (Hegel 1900: 94). This is the problem with fantasy that Yoshimoto describes. People who share this type of consciousness are united not by the ideal God or the universal Law, but by the common aspects shared among them. Hegel assumes the substantial objective existence of ideal essences such as God or Law, which exist outside the individual, and regards human beings' sensuous volition as a hindrance to recognising them. But, for Yoshimoto, God or universal Law is produced by an individual's sensuous volition (collective fantasy). We can find here a similar difference to that between Yoshimoto and Foucault. As we have seen, while Yoshimoto bases his analysis on the collective fantasy, Foucault is concerned with pre-given Law. Once again, it is necessary to repeat that what we have to repudiate is neither one of them, but both.

Yoshimoto's idea of Asian consciousness is derived from Marx's concept of Asiatic Mode of Production (AMP). In his often cited Preface to *A Contribution to the Critique of Political Economy*, Marx writes: 'In broad outline, the Asiatic, ancient, feudal and modern bourgeois modes of production may be designated as epochs marking progress in the economic development of society' (Marx 1970: 21). Among various definitions of AMP made by many scholars, if we highlight the points which are related to our discussion, we can raise: 1) the absence of private property in land, and land is owned by the community, 2) need for large-scale public projects such as irrigation organised by a central authority, and 3) the ruling class (the state officialdom) extracts the surplus product in the form not of money, but of tribute (O'Leary 1989: 16–18; Li 1996: 10–12; Kanth 1997: 200–210).

In 1853, on the topic of British rule in India, Marx describes how the European (modern) power oppressed the Indian (Asiatic) mode of production. However, he also points out the Oriental despotism and its undignified, stagnant, and vegetative life, and the inevitability of historical progress of India. He concludes his essay by saying 'The question is, can mankind fulfil its destiny without a fundamental revolution in the social state of Asia? If not, whatever may have been the crimes of England she was the unconscious tool of history in bringing about that revolution' (Marx 1975- XII: 133). This sort of statement invited the criticism that the concept of AMP is Eurocentric (O'Leary 1989: 24–25; Young 1990: 2).

Yoshimoto, however, compares Marx's view on progress with Lenin's idea on war expressed in his *Socialism and War* (written in 1915). In this book Lenin regards any war that brings about the overthrow of absolutism, feudalism and alien oppression as a progressive war (Lenin 1964: 299–300). Yoshimoto comments that while Lenin understands history as a uni-linear progress of Idea and anything which contributes this progress is good or right, Marx, when he writes about 'British rule in India' understands that historical progress or development is not necessarily parallel to the ideal of revolution or that of socialism (Yoshimoto *et al.* 2002: 122–125; original 1980–1981).

It seems that Marx is here rather nostalgically lamenting that the oppression of idyllic, stagnant and vegetative life in the Asiatic Mode of Production is probably an inevitable consequence of historical evolution. In contrast, Lenin is optimistically prizing progress. In Marx's writing, there still remains room to answer 'Yes' to his own question 'Can mankind fulfil its destiny without a fundamental revolution in the social state of Asia?' As Yoshimoto and many others have cited, in the draft of the letter to Vera Zasulich in 1881, Marx mentions the possibility of a future superior social system in a revival of the archaic type of communal property (Marx 1975– XXIV: 350). In any case, as can be seen in this criticism, Yoshimoto's idea of Asian Consciousness is closely related to the conflict between progress/development and stagnation, or in the linear time and cyclic time both that Murakami Haruki and Yoshimoto Banana call into question.

In her recent book, Spivak, by referring to Perry Anderson's study of Asiatic Mode of Production, cautions that at issue is not just the question of whether history is uni- or multi-linear, but a radical shift in perspective (Spivak 1999: 92). After the examination of the Islamic and Chinese social histories, Anderson considers that Asian development cannot be reduced to a uniform residual category after the canons of European evolution have been established. He concludes his essay by saying:

> Any serious theoretical exploration of the historical field outside feudal Europe will have to supersede traditional and generic contrasts with it, and proceed to a concrete and accurate typology of social formations and State systems in their own right, which respects their very great differences of structure and development. It is merely in the night of our ignorance that all alien shapes take on the same hue.
>
> (Anderson, P. 1974: 548–549)

Anderson's conclusion partly overlaps with Yoshimoto's methodology in that they consider that the canon of European evolution is not suitable for evaluating other cultures' situations. They, however, subtly differ in that while Anderson seems to be emphasising a culture's serious theoretical exploration of its own situation and the aspect of its differences of structure and development, this point is ambiguous in Yoshimoto's thought. Yoshimoto emphasises the contrast between elite and subaltern people rather than that between different cultures. As we have noted, Anderson's methodology suggests that one analyses one's own culture and society according to one's own cultural and social theories. There is the danger here of ending up with the ethnocentric enclosure of each culture and no communication between cultures. Perhaps what we should call for is not only a drastic shift in perspective but also feedback and dynamic interaction between different perspectives. That is not only to radically shift the perspective to analyse another cultures, but also to look at one's own culture from a shifted perspective.

Yoshimoto's concept of Asian consciousness is well expressed in his study of Yanagita Kunio. Washida Koyata argues that the concept of 'Asia' that Yoshimoto discovered in his reading of Yanagita Kunio, is a form of logic necessary for interpreting the domain of collective fantasy, which is different from the logic of empirical or experimental science (Washida 1992: 445–446).[14] Yoshimoto and the religion specialist Yamaori Tetsuo bring up the difficulty of a cross-cultural dialogue based upon understandings of logic or law, and collective fantasy.

> Yamaori: The co-existence in Japan of late capitalism and the emperor system is a problem for the future – how to explain it logically [to Western people]...It is related to the problem that makes the works of Yanagita Kunio and Orikuchi Shinobu[15] difficult to translate.
>
> Yoshimoto: Nevertheless, if I am asked to point out the big names among Japanese intellectuals since the Meiji era, I have no other choice than to mention Yanagita Kunio and Orikuchi Shinobu...
>
> Yamaori: I was in London two years ago. A specialist in religion there asked me which Japanese person since the Meiji era had most greatly influenced European society. Those who came to mind included Okakura Tenshin,[16] Nitobe Inazō,[17] Yanagita Kunio, Orikuchi Shinobu and Suzuki Daisetsu.[18] While I was wondering who would be the best example, the person said: 'It's Suzuki Daisetsu. In terms of the strength and depth of influence, and profundity of entering into European people's emotions, Suzuki Daisetsu is the most important'. I felt I had been caught napping.
>
> Yoshimoto: I somehow understand that kind of evaluation in Western countries. But from inside Japan, it is difficult to agree with it, isn't it?
>
> (Yoshimoto 1983–1993 IV: 480–481; my translation)

The difficulty of explaining Japanese traditions in Western terms is related to the problems that arise when attempting to translate the works of Yanagita Kunio and Orikuchi Shinobu into Western languages. With regard to the difficulty Western people have in understanding Yanagita, Ōiwa Keibō writes:

Many concluded that Yanagita's writing had gained such acclaim in Japan because of its literary and poetic qualities, rather than for any social-scientific value. An essay by Tsurumi Kazuko, in which she argues that Yanagita's works can make a unique academic contribution in the international community of social science, was greeted with scepticism by many graduate students in anthropology.

(Koschmann *et al.* 1985: vii)

Yoshimoto himself is all too familiar with this problem, and his interest in Asian systems of thought and his criticism of Yanagita Kunio should both be viewed in this context.

Having pointed out the importance of Yanagita's thought in analysing Asian consciousness, I should also immediately mention recent criticism of Yanagita by some Japanese scholars. For instance, Iwamoto Yoshiteru argues that Yanagita limited the object of his study to common people and intentionally occluded the investigation of the emperor system (Iwamoto Yoshiteru 1992). Murai Osamu, from a different perspective, argues that Yanagita searched for the origin of the Japanese people in islands to the south in order to foreclose his own failure to examine the Japanese agricultural policy of colonising Korea (Murai 1995).[19]

Their arguments were sensational and invited lively discussions. It is extremely important to criticise Yanagita's intentional avoidance of studying the emperor system and, if not his contempt, then his ignorance of Korean people. But Iwamoto's and Murai's criticisms, as both of them clearly mention, focus not on Yanagita's research methodology itself, but on the aim or purpose of his study. It is crucially important to make the subtle distinction between ethnocentrism and one culture's unique way of understanding, though the two are often tightly interwoven. Even if Yanagita should be criticised as being ethnocentric, the method of his study should also be properly acknowledged, if it so deserves.

Yoshimoto's analysis of Yanagita was published in his collected works *Yoshimoto Takaaki zenshū sen*, volume IV. In this study, Yoshimoto contrasts empirical (*jisshōteki*) with inherent[20] knowledge, and insists that Yanagita regards the latter as more important than the former (Yoshimoto T. 1986–1988 IV: 67). Although Yoshimoto's wording in this book is, just as in others, not easy to follow, we can argue that he is again contrasting logical and original identifications. Logical identification is gained by finding common aspects in two originally different things, whereas unconscious or original identification cannot be perceived, because the subject and object of knowledge are not different.

We should recall here again that, as Spivak argues, knowledge presupposes irreducible difference, not identity, between the subject and the object (Spivak 1987: 251–268); thus, the subject of knowing cannot gain knowledge about itself. This is similar to the relationship between sympathy and empathy. The logical identification or sympathy (feeling for someone) presupposes, as its essential component, the self–other distinction, whereas the unconscious identification or empathy (feeling with someone) presupposes the self-other fusion (Eisenberg and Strayer 1987: 5–6). Hence, it is not until the self distinguishes itself from the object that the original unconscious identification or empathy is perceived. That is to say, the unconscious identification or empathy can only be retrospectively recognised, when it has gone (Murakami F. 1996: 25–29).

Logic can be educated, fostered and trained, as can the ability to persuade others through rational power. While at the same time, one can also discipline, nourish, expand and refine one's empathic ability and convince others by its power. Yanagita emphasises the latter. Yoshimoto points this out when he says that the reader experiences *déjà vu* when reading Yanagita (Yoshimoto T. 1986–1988 IV: 9–11). Perhaps there is a scene that can be seen only by persons who have shared experiences. If a sight reminds me of another scene in the past I saw with you, and if the sight awakens the same scene in your memory, then this is a scene that can only be seen by you and me. On a cultural level, there must be some things that can only be perceived in a similar way by Japanese, just as there are things that only Europeans, for instance, can see in the same way. However, here again there is the danger of being confined in a nationalistic enclosure.

For instance, in 'A Meiji and Taishō History: Part of Aspects of Life' ('Meiji Taishō shi: Sesō hen'), Yanagita talks of colour and says that recently white has come to be used even in kitchen aprons (Yanagita 1960: 139–140; original 1931). With regard to the white apron, most Japanese people would remember seeing housewives and mothers doing their work while wearing white aprons. Yanagita continues: 'Originally, however, white was an awful colour. People in Japan used to wear white clothes only for festivals or funerals'. In Japanese people's minds, white is also associated with religion, especially *miko* Shinto shrine maidens who wear white and red clothes. They would recall the solemn feeling they had when they saw the *miko* on the spacious ground in front of a Shinto shrine. Shrines contain other white things – white gravel and many small pieces of white paper (people's fortunes) knotted around the green branches of trees. They now would realise that the solemn feeling they felt when seeing shrine maidens wearing white clothes has something in common with the emotion they felt when they saw their mothers wearing white aprons.

Having reached this point, they would easily understand Yanagita when he says that in the past Japanese people distinguished between festival occasions and their everyday lives, and felt keyed-up only during festivals, whereas now they no longer discriminate between the two. Yanagita argues that this is clear from the fact that in the past only shrine maidens wore white clothes on special occasions, whereas nowadays mothers wear white aprons to do their daily tasks. On the basis of this, we can further imagine if, when Japanese housewives and mothers wore white aprons while they performed domestic tasks in wartime, they, albeit unconsciously, considered these times as special occasions, and they themselves as *miko*. Perhaps Yanagita's logic is deficient here, but people who have seen mothers wearing white aprons and Shinto maidens wearing red and white clothes and felt a similar feeling on both occasions can easily understand what he means.

Bernard Bernier cautions us about the problems that arise in Yanagita's methodology that involves this kind of total identification with the object of study. He says:

> We are dealing here with crucial methodological problems that are present in any enquiry into a specific sector of social reality. Can (or must) the research[er] identify or empathize with the object of study? What interference will his beliefs cause in his enquiry? Must he try to understand the way people see their world from the inside or rather try to explain it as a 'social fact'? The questions just raised have to do with faith, comprehension and explanation. Briefly, I think there is, as far as enquiries into social reality are concerned, an essential difference between faith and comprehension. And I would argue that Yanagita's method, despite the fact that it has been presented as an attempt to comprehend people's beliefs from the inside rather than to logically explain them, is based on the selection of facts to prove what is already a deep belief. In short, I would argue that Yanagita's method is closer to theology than to social science.
>
> (Bernier 1985: 81)

Bernier concludes his essay as follows:

> Yanagita's appeal, as it appeared clearly at the workshop, is emotional. His way of writing, his personal feelings, appeal to the Japanese reader. But an emotional appeal can never be proof of the validity of any conclusion on a society. Human beings, including intellectuals, have been known to forget their critical judgment when an emotional appeal is made to them. One fairly recent and rather disquieting example is the overwhelming support of the German intellectuals for Nazism. Theories of racial uniqueness and superiority have a way of attracting people, including intellectuals, even though they are clearly unacceptable. These theories strike an emotional cord within people, but this does not mean that they are either true or useful.
>
> (Bernier 1985: 92)

We have to do our very best to attack theories which support ethnic superiority. However, the status of a universal, monolithic logic must also surely be subject to critique. Is it not important to attempt to understand another culture's different way of reasoning, even if it can only be expressed in terms of 'emotion'? Is it not the case that 'universal logic' is used as a weapon to conquer and colonise so-called 'emotional' or 'illogical' people and force them to progress in only one direction? I do, however, fully endorse Bernier's criticism of ethnic identity. The argument in this book, too, has criticised psychological unification, and insisted on the importance of maintaining a distance from extreme individual differentiation and totalitarian identification, or in other words, attempted to deconstruct the distinction between homogeneity and heterogeneity. Yanagita's method involves understanding the way people see their world from the inside, and his faith and belief are made on the basis of collective fantasy. But, we have also to denounce, as we have seen many times, not only Yanagita's emotional identification and empathy with the object of study, but also forms of logical comprehension and explanation that attempt to objectify and thereby repress the object of study.

Yoshimoto pays particular attention to Yanagita's concern with cases in which parents murder their children because of poverty, looking at these cases from the perspective of empathy.[21] Yoshimoto writes:

> In certain birth conditions and circumstances some people have no other way than to commit homicide or suicide. This kind of necessity is expressed in the protocol discovered by Yanagita. Yanagita presents cases in which fate leads a man through a series of events that end in homicide. Yanagita, as a student of law and society, believes that all the *laws* must inevitably establish punishment for a crime that every person, if he or she is placed in the same circumstances, will unavoidably commit. To Yanagita it seems the law of nature decrees that such conduct is human beyond human *laws*.
>
> (Yoshimoto T. 1986–1988 IV: 87; emphasis in the original; my translation)

Kant considers almost the same situation in his *Critique of Pure Reason*. He takes the example of a malicious lie through which a person has brought about a certain confusion in society. He asserts that one may seek its motivation in a bad upbringing, bad company, and in the wickedness of a disposition naturally insensitive to shame, plus carelessness and thoughtlessness. Kant, however, continues that even if one believes the action to be determined by these causes, one nonetheless blames the agent, and not on account of his unfortunate natural temperament, not on account of the circumstances influencing him, not even on account of the life he has led previously. Why? Kant answers by saying that:

> for one presupposes that it can be entirely set aside how that life was constituted, and that the series of conditions that transpired might not have been, but rather that this deed could be regarded as entirely unconditioned in regard to the previous state, as though with that act the agent had started a series of consequences entirely from himself. This blame is grounded on the law of reason, which regards reason as a cause that, regardless of all the empirical conditions just named, could have and ought to have determined the conduct of the person to be other

than it is. And indeed one regards the causality of reason not as a mere concurrence with other causes, but as complete in itself, even if sensuous incentives were not for it but were indeed entirely against it; the action is ascribed to the agent's intelligible character: now, in the moment when he lies, it is entirely his fault; hence reason, regardless of all empirical conditions of the deed, is fully free, and this deed is to be attributed entirely to its failure to act.

(Kant 1997a: 544)

For Kant the law of reason is more important than one's empirical conditions. In contrast, for Yoshimoto and Yanagita, conditions and circumstances take precedence over the law of reason. Consequently we can say that the Western concept of law does not pay attention to the *uniqueness* of the individual person (not the *importance* of the individual person). There are no two persons in the world who are exactly the same. But, if you take individual uniqueness into consideration, you cannot establish the law. That is, if a criminal were sentenced having taken into account his or her peculiar genetic background, birth condition, family background, ethnic characteristics, individual idiosyncrasies, education, social status, etc., then the legal system would collapse. The law must overlook each individual person's subtle uniqueness and, by presupposing that all persons have the same nature and ability, put everybody in an equal condition, under the aegis of equality before the law.

Regardless of the personal distinctions of the criminal, in principle, the same penalty must be imposed for the same crime. However, though each individual's particular nature is disregarded in this way, no one considers that, since everyone is treated as having the same nature, everyone does the same thing in the same situation. That is, the figure gained by discarding each individual's uniqueness before the law is not the commonality shared among people, but an ideal figure or a free individual who is supposed to have reason that exists outside our own selves. The concepts of freedom, equality, individuality and law are closely related and appeared simultaneously. As we have seen, freedom or liberty emerges as an emancipation of weak people from a small group of despotic strong people. The belief underlying this Euro-American consciousness is thus that every individual must be an equal and free individual and that society must be controlled not by the despot but by the Law.

In contrast, for Yoshimoto, as we have noted, the law does not presuppose an ideality outside the individual, but is based on collective fantasy. This collective fantasy also has the power to forcefully unite people, not by reference to ideals but on the basis of a shared commonality. For Yoshimoto (and Yanagita too), since the law is based on a shared commonality, unlike the idealistic law, it does not force people to progress in only one direction. However, it tends to confine itself to a shared commonality. Yoshimoto explains the Euro-American sense of law in the following manner. In order to resolve a conflict between A and B, one can set C beside them and deal with the conflict from the point of view of C. In this case, C can be, in a sense, an analogy for the law or nation-state or logic. This is the Euro-American way of thinking.

In contrast, Yoshimoto insists that for Yanagita Kunio, the nation is the place in which people come together to exchange surplus products. In this case, there is no third party, C, and the nation is another name for the commonality of people or collective fantasy (See Figure 3.6) (Yoshimoto T. 1996b: 37–41). As Yoshimoto clearly argues, unlike in Western ways of thinking, Asian consciousness recognises neither third party arbitration nor an abstract ideal outside the individual. However, on the other hand, Asian consciousness does have the fear of fascistic totality on the basis of commonality, and also it is almost impossible to move and develop in this system.

In conclusion, while Euro-American consciousness produces rivalry and competition for development and evolution, as well as a sense of idealistic totality based on rational laws and principles independent of society, African, Asian and Native American consciousness constructs the totality on the basis of collective fantasy inside each individual and inclines towards autism. How, then, can we discard rivalry and competition, escape from idealistic totality and forceful collective fantasy, and, at the same time preserve the vital movement for progress? These questions seem to be ones that Karatani Kōjin is currently struggling with and will be discussed in the following chapter.

4 Karatani Kōjin and the intercourse with the Other

Subversion of causal and motivational relations

It should now be clear that the essential problem we have to confront is the dichotomy between identification and discrimination, which emerges from the experience of uniqueness and commonality on various levels. An individual's own uniqueness/particularity is experienced in each self through such things as gender, sexuality, family, local community, country, nation-state, ethnicity, class and so on. But this experience of uniqueness necessarily leads to discrimination, as another's attributes are recognised as different from one's own. Yet, if the individual tries to avoid discrimination by retreating into a homogeneous community of similar selves, then the concept of the 'Other' will be lost, resulting in a state of solipsism or incestuous autism. How can this dilemma be resolved? How can a position beyond the antinomic distinction between ally and enemy, identity and discrimination, commonality and uniqueness, or generality and particularity be established, while simultaneously maintaining a sense of movement and progress? Or, in a broader sense, how can the dichotomous pattern of this antinomy be transcended?

So far, the literary works of Murakami Haruki, Yoshimoto Banana and Yoshimoto Takaaki have been analysed, focusing on the potential they contain for renouncing or repudiating discrimination. One possibility so far discovered is the subversion of typically modern ideologies of 'strong-(evolution)-is-good' and 'love-is-beautiful'. Another possibility is the deconstruction of family/stranger or homogeneity/heterogeneity in the form of solipsism through incest or by means of conjugal fantasy, in other words the realisation of *eros* without violence. These two methods result in a re-formation of desire.

Furthermore, we have discerned the prospect of emancipation in something which goes beyond both logic and rationality based on the subject–object distinction characteristic of European thought, and the African, Asian, Native American and some other cultures' consciousness of oneness, empathy and unity with other people and the surroundings in the domain of shared intersubjectivity. In contrast to the above approaches,

Karatani Kōjin looks at the same issues from a radically different perspective, that is, from the concepts of 'uniqueness', 'Other', 'difference' and 'singularity', albeit at the risk of being possessed by the desire to do violence. Let me first introduce Karatani's overall work.

Karatani began his career as a literary critic with a study of Natsume Sōseki in an essay entitled 'Consciousness and Nature' ('Ishiki to shizen'), which was awarded the *Gunzō* Prize in 1969 (Karatani 1979a: 9-63; 1992a: 9-69). Referring to T. S. Eliot who found in Hamlet's bafflement an inexpressible emotion (Eliot 1976: 145–146), Karatani in this essay sees in many of Sōseki's novels the same problem as Hamlet's: a problem inexpressible in terms of Western logic. For instance, in *Mon*, though the protagonist Sōsuke's anxiety is evoked by the triangular love affair he was involved in before his marriage, the reason for his distress cannot be sufficiently explained by the love problem. That is, although his uneasiness depicted in the novel is certainly occasioned by his past love affair, upon reading this novel most readers would doubt whether the love affair was an adequate reason for his distress. Furthermore, in *Kokoro* it is suggested that the reason for Sensei's suicide is his guilty conscience over betraying his friend K, and also his sense of resignation that the Meiji era has ended. But the novel gives the reader the impression that these factors do not fully explain the real reason behind his suicide.

Upon completing these novels of Sōseki, we are left wondering if there is something yet to be narrated, or if there is not some excess behind the characters' activities that cannot be sufficiently grasped by our intellect. In a sense, the characters' actions cannot be objectified in terms of the logical relation between, for instance, cause and effect, reason and consequence, or motivation and action. Consequently, as Shakespeare did with Hamlet, Karatani insists that we must simply admit that Sōseki tackled an insoluble puzzle and attempted to express the inexpressibly horrible – a problem that proved too much for him, or too much for our intellect. What concerns Karatani here is not the reason why Sōseki attempted to solve the insoluble puzzle at all, but to see in Sōseki, as T. S. Eliot had seen in Shakespeare, a problem that cannot be expressed in language. That is to say, Karatani argues that Hamlet and some of Sōseki's characters are caught up in a sense of something beyond rationality.

It is significant that Karatani considers Sōseki to be his predecessor. As we noted previously, Sōseki was a pioneer who was caught in the gap between Western logic based upon rationality, and a vague consciousness of another different order. Before studying in London, Sōseki had developed this vague consciousness of an order different from the Western intellectual tradition from his Chinese educational background. But, for Karatani, who does not have an intellectual background steeped in Chinese learning comparable to Sōseki, this gap appears simply as something inexpressible in Western terms. He calls it 'nature' in this essay, in contrast to 'consciousness', which is supposed to be formed by intellectual activity.

Karatani later mentions in a dialogue with Yoshimoto Takaaki in 1970 that his main concern is the theory of 'nature'. He says that 'nature' for him is something beyond the limit of 'consciousness', and that he attempts to deal with 'consciousness' from the perspective of 'nature' (Karatani 1987a: 6). If we translate 'consciousness' into 'logic' and 'nature' into 'something different from logic', then, what Karatani is trying to do is to analyse logic from the perspective of something different from logic. It is important to note here that, at the beginning of his literary career, Karatani was interested in problems that were inexpressible or unspeakable in intellectual terms. This has been one of his central concerns, which he later regards as the contrast between 'formalisation (consciousness)' and the 'Other (nature)', or 'interiority' and 'exteriority'.

Karatani discovered after Sōseki another predecessor in the person of Mori Ōgai. Karatani's essay on Ōgai appeared in 1974, entitled 'History and Nature' ('Rekishi to shizen'). It is interesting to note that in his essay on Sōseki, 'consciousness' was contrasted with 'nature', whereas in his essay on Ōgai, 'history' is associated with 'nature'. In Karatani's theory, 'consciousness' is an aspect of intellect, whereas 'history' is understood as a sequence of happenings reorganised by the consciousness of causality, and both of them are treated as opposing 'nature' – something beyond the Western tradition of intellectual, logical and rational theory. Just as Karatani saw in Sōseki's novels an attempt to express a problem inexpressible in intellectual terms, he later discerned an attempt to subvert causal and motivational relations in Ōgai's historical stories.

Ōgai, in his short essay 'History as It Is and History Ignored' ('Rekishi sono mama to rekishibanare') confesses that he dislikes artistic devices in historical novels and gives two reasons why – first, because he reveres the reality that is evidenced in historical records, and second, he believes that if the Naturalists[1] could write about life 'just as it is', then he could just as easily write the past 'just as it was' (Mori 1977 I: 151–152; original 1915). The reasons he gives, however, seem to be somewhat misleading or insufficient for understanding exactly what he really means.

With regard to Ōgai's rejection of artistic devices used in story-telling, Karatani argues that historical materials record nothing more than the surface of an incident, and that they are fragmental, unorganised, and even inconsistent. When Ōgai says that he hates arbitrarily changing 'nature' in his stories, he means not only that he does not want to distort historical fact, but also that he does not want to rearrange the originally inconsistent historical materials. In other words, Ōgai insists that he not only wants to be faithful to historical documents but that he wants to preserve the inconsistency and incoherence of the historical materials (Karatani 1989a: 164–166).

Following Karatani's analysis, we can argue that in spite of Ōgai's own insistence elsewhere in the above essay that he selects and organises his materials on a rational basis, the rationality Ōgai employs here is not reducible to Western rationality. Rather, what he feels is a sense of discomfort towards 'making up' a coherent and consistent story in the Western sense, when the materials are really fragmentary and contradictory. For Ōgai, rearranging the historical materials so as to produce a consistent and coherent story without any illogical flaw, is nothing but arbitrary, that is, it is rather 'irrational' in his own sense.

In what manner then does Ōgai narrate his story? In *Abe Family* (*Abe ichizoku*; original 1913), for instance, Ōgai depicts an act of self-immolation (*junshi*[2] or suicide) and explains the reasons why Chōjūrō made up his mind to commit *junshi*. Ōgai writes:

> If we were to probe more deeply into his motives, however, it would seem that besides his compulsion to commit *junshi* at his own request, he felt with almost identical intensity that others expected him to commit *junshi*; therefore, he was left with no other recourse but to do so, all the while seeking their approval. The reverse of the same motive was his fear that if he did not commit *junshi*, he would certainly be despised. Chōjūrō was a man of such weakness, yet he had not the slightest fear of death. This is why his aspiration to gain permission from his lord dominated his entire will, brooking no obstacle....Thinking of how kindly the surviving relatives of one who has committed *junshi* are treated by the family of their former lord, he felt he could die serenely, having left his family in a secure position. With these thoughts, Chōjūrō's face brightened.
>
> (Mori 1977 I: 42)

Ōgai explains that for Chōjūrō *junshi* is his own intention, but at the same time he feels compelled to commit *junshi* because others expect him to do so and if he failed, he would certainly be despised. These two motivations are usually incompatible. Citing the above passage from Ōgai's story, Karatani argues that although there are at least three motivations – autonomous, compulsive, and utilitarian – that cause people to commit *junshi*, Chōjūrō's motivation is depicted here in a manner that cannot be reduced to one of the three categories (Karatani 1989a: 174–175).

As Karatani argues, we can be pressured by either autonomous intention or outside compulsion, but, logically, we cannot be pressured by both of them simultaneously. There are some ways to logically solve this inconsistency. For instance, it is possible that Chōjūrō's motivation is sometimes autonomous, but at other times compulsive, or his intention is, if looked at from one perspective, autonomous, but if assessed from another viewpoint, compulsive. However, are there no cases in which we are motivated by autonomous and compulsive factors at the same time, irrespective of our standpoint?

The same issue can be discerned in another part of the above passage where Ōgai writes that Chōjūrō was a man of weakness, and yet he had not the slightest fear of death. Here again we cannot say that the protagonist is weak or strong. As in the previous case, we can argue that a person is cowardly in such and such a sense, but courageous in some other way. In

Chōjūrō's case, it seems clear that, in terms of his fear of being despised, he is weak, but in regard to his acceptance of death, he is by no means cowardly. Or, we can consider that in order to interpret the sentence 'Chōjūrō was a man of such weakness, yet he had not the slightest fear of death', the meaning of 'weak' must be defined more precisely. To be 'weak' means in this case to fear being despised, but not to fear death. There are surely many other ways of logically solving this paradox. But, just like the previous example of motivation, are there not cases in which we can be weak and yet simultaneously strong?

Something can be blue *or* yellow, but cannot be blue *and* yellow. Nevertheless, if we look at the issue in a completely different way, instead of saying blue and yellow, we can invent a new word: green. Likewise, in the above example from Ōgai's *Abe Family* we can question the semantic scope of words such as 'autonomous' and 'compulsive', or 'strong' and 'weak'. Analysis often involves breaking an issue down into its component parts. The way in which we reduce complex issues to their components is, if not arbitrary, often very culturally specific and involves setting up one view or perspective as the obvious, necessary or universal one.

Furthermore, we should not overlook the fact that time is in constant flux. The process of logical reasoning constantly slips away just at the moment when we believe it completed, because cause/effect and reason/consequence are in an unceasingly mobile dynamic. It seems right to argue along with Karatani (1989a: 160) here, that in the above passage what Ōgai describes is not the character's static motivation or stagnant cause which produces a certain effect later, but the moving process itself in which the motivation, cause and effect are ceaselessly affected by and amend each other.

It is obvious that without cause, there can be no effect. Yet, conversely, it is also true that without effect, there can be no cause, because the cause is only apparent once the effect is manifest. In other words, causal relations must be conceived retroactively in that we conceive of events temporally and thus look backwards in time in order to discern causality (Karatani 2000: 44). With regard to causal relations, it is apparent that the idea of causality presupposes at least two things. The first is that the multiple causes, which result in a singular effect, can be enumerated. If this were not so, if causal factors were uncountable, then the logic of causality would collapse. A Japanese proverb, which says that the blowing wind is profitable for the wooden bucket maker, illustrates this. The blowing wind raises a lot of dust, which blinds people who then become *shamisen* players (traditionally a job for blind people). This results in many cats being caught to make *shamisen* skins, which in turn results in a growing number of rats who eat wooden buckets. The ironic stance towards causality evident in the proverb should not be dismissed. Although a causal chain can be followed back indefinitely, we usually adopt a cut-off point arbitrarily. That is to say, the factors that we select when explaining causality depend largely on ideology. No matter how carefully, impartially and objectively we attempt to select a real or absolute cause, our selection cannot but be arbitrary.

The second presupposition underlying our sense of causality is that the same pattern of events can occur many times. For, if we were to suppose that nothing could be repeated, causality would become meaningless. Thus, in order to sustain the notion of causality, we have to admit that if we can enumerate the factors leading towards a certain event, they will always produce the same event. Yet, it can be argued that these two suppositions cannot be proven. To say that there is neither cause nor effect, or neither motivation nor resulting action is just as exaggerated as saying that there exists a clear distinction between the cause or motivation and its effect or result. The fact is that cause or motivation and effect or result are so closely connected and interdependent that it is impossible for us to neatly grasp and explain them in terms of our limited logic. Even if a causal relation exists, we cannot prove it because there are innumerable other factors underlying one small event, and furthermore exactly the same happening can never reoccur.[3]

People often contrast emotion with reason. But this contrast is problematic because there are many possible modes of reasoning. It is not that some cultures are without logical analysis but rather that different cultures have devised different ways of analysis. As we have seen in the previous chapters, both Sōseki and Ōgai were troubled by their encounter with Western logical analysis, a different mode of thought from what they were used to. Karatani finds in their bafflement a potential to go beyond the confines of Western intellect: a way of thought that deviates from the traditional flow of logical explanation appearing in between Western analysis and something different. Recently, this kind of criticism of Western (phal)logocentrism has been widely acknowledged, as has been noted in the previous chapters, especially since Foucault's development of the concept of a *heterotopia* in which people shatter or tangle common names, destroy not only the syntax with which we construct sentences but also that less apparent syntax which causes words and things (next to and also opposite one another) to hold together (Foucault 1994: xviii). Yet in the 1970s there were still many who argued that Western logic and rationality were universal.

While in the 1970s Karatani analysed logic (consciousness and history) from the perspective of something different from logic (nature), in the early 1980s he initiated, together with Asada Akira, an academic and critical discussion of Japan's post-structural and postmodern movements. The results are compiled in his book *Criticism and the Postmodern* (*Hihyō to posutomodan*) published in 1985 (in Japanese) and also in his contribution to *Postmodernism and Japan* in 1989 (in English). Given his interest in thought that deviates from the traditional Western intellect, Karatani's immediate response to postmodernism is easily understandable. Furthermore, as a visiting Professor at Yale University from 1975 to 1977, and at Columbia University from 1990, he was able to meet with Paul de Man, Jaques Derrida, Fredric Jameson and other contemporary critics who provided him with an opportunity to consider further the concepts of deconstruction and postmodernism.

His main argument concerning postmodernism in Japan in the early 1980s is, however, rather negative. He insists that postmodernism in Japan is no more than an intellectual storm blown over from the West which has no fundamental roots in the Japanese tradition. The Japanese critical discourse was 'blown off by it and lost consciousness and further even was not aware of it' (Karatani 1985a: 13). Before we (Japanese) discuss deconstruction, Karatani insists, we have to ask what construction in Japan is (Karatani 1985a: 17).

In his chapter 'One Spirit, Two Nineteenth Centuries' compiled in *Postmodernism and Japan* (1989a), Karatani again emphasises the difference between the West and Japan. He claims that the deconstruction of reason (*ri*) – one of the typical features of postmodernism – was in Japan already accomplished in the nineteenth century in a different context in the tradition of Itō Jinsai's (1627–1705) criticism of the rationalism (or logocentrism) of neo-Confucianism. It was succeeded by Motoori Norinaga's (1730–1801) rejection of Buddhist, Confucian and Taoist texts, in favour of a critique of rationalism based on an interpretation of ancient Japanese texts like the *Tale of Genji* and *Kojiki* (Karatani 1989b: 269; 1993b: 49). Karatani continues:

> A similar situation [to nineteenth century Japan] prevails in the Japan of the 1980s. Japan has become a highly developed information-consumption society, in which meaning is information and desire is the desire of the Other, because the 'subject' of the nineteenth-century West has never existed in Japan, nor has there been any resistance to the modern. In 1980s Japan (a Japan 'liberated' from its obsession with modernism), parody, pastiche, and collage have become dominant trends. But in the Japanese context, this amounts to a rehabilitation of the nineteenth century. It is a revival of that mood within which late Edo society saw itself as a 'paradise of fools'.
>
> (Miyoshi and Harootunian 1989: 271; 1993b: 51–52)

Consequently, he insists that no matter how postmodern Japan looks from a Western point of view, the current situation in Japan has resulted from its own historical tradition and cannot be easily compared with the Western idea of postmodernism.

As Karatani warns us, we surely have to take the cultural and traditional differences between the West and Japan into consideration. But, at the same time, it is also necessary to see a common something that underlies global modernisation in the form of power structures. Karatani sees in postmodernism the critique of rationality and the death of a teleological concept of history – the death of the 'spirit' that surveys history in terms of its end or goal (Miyoshi and Harootunian 1989: 260). But it seems that he does not pay sufficient attention to the connection between postmodernism (the critique of modernism) and the criticism of power structures and discrimination evident in modernism. However, it is not that he is not concerned with them, since he specifically deals with power structures in a different context in his second English book *Architecture as Metaphor: Language, Number, Money* (1995b). In this book he presents his unique concept of the 'Other'.

Philosophy of the Other/exteriority

Karatani's concept of the 'Other' derives from the realisation that we have to avoid solipsism, which, for him, means we have to create a philosophy beyond philosophy. In other words, the legitimacy of philosophy can only be judged from outside the enclosures of philosophy. Karatani says that 'it is impossible to determine the "sense" of philosophy within philosophy, since it can only be determined outside philosophy and outside form' (Karatani 1995b: 105). If the 'sense' of philosophy is determined solely within philosophy, then this results in solipsism. Karatani warns us that solipsism not only acknowledges and, in fact, privileges the existence of the self, but it also asserts that what is true of the self must be universally true. And, in order for this to be possible, the Other must already have been interiorised in the self (Karatani 1995b: 133). Karatani sees violence as the by-product of the discrimination that occurs in this process of interiorisation of the 'Other' under the aegis of universal truth. In order to avoid solipsism in Karatani's sense, therefore, we have always to attempt to encounter the 'Other'.

In the process of encountering the 'Other', Karatani first cautions us against taking two obvious courses. One is to presuppose that exteriority (Other) exists as something positive or substantial, since, he says, exteriority, which is apprehended by the interiority already, belongs to the latter. The second course is the tendency to indulge in a facile romanticism or to narrate the exteriority poetically (Karatani 1988: 314–315). Karatani argues that in the attempt to overcome rationality's monologic communication we must be cautious not to take refuge in the realm of romanticism. Romanticism may be opposed to rationality, but, as we have seen, it is an empathic identification, and certainly not a relation between others in Karatani's sense. At this point it is necessary to remind ourselves that in Chapter 1 romance and fantasy were distinguished: the latter being taken as a potential for postmodernism. Romanticism however, paired as it is with rationalism, is one of the typical features of modernism.

For Karatani, who has avoided taking either of the above two courses, there remains one way to meet the 'Other': and that is to overthrow the self. Karatani is, in this sense, attempting to subvert the formal system of interiority, what, in the 1970s he termed 'consciousness', in order to encounter the 'Other' in exteriority (outside philosophy) or, what he calls 'nature'. Namely, he tries to break down the sense of interiority so as to encounter the 'Other' in the exteriority. Karatani, of course, is not the first to attempt this but has been preceded by others who have attempted to subvert interiority through revealing its inconsistency.

Among these, Karatani first introduces Kurt Gödel and his incompleteness theorem into his own discussion. Here I refer to Solomon Feferman who summarises Gödel's incompleteness theorem as follows:

> Any formal system S in which a certain amount of theoretical arithmetic can be developed and which satisfies some minimal consistency conditions is *incomplete*: one can construct an elementary arithmetical statement A such that neither A nor its negation is provable in S. In fact, the statement so constructed is true, since it expresses its own unprovability in S via a representation of the syntax of S in arithmetic. Furthermore, one can construct a statement C which expresses the consistency of S in arithmetic, and C is not provable in S if S is consistent.
>
> (Feferman 1986: 6; emphasis in the original)

Gödel's incompleteness theorem, which was presented as a mathematical model in 1931, is in many ways similar to Karatani's philosophical formulation that it is impossible to determine the 'sense' of philosophy within philosophy, since this sense can only be determined outside philosophy. Referring to Derrida's deconstruction and Gödel's incompleteness theorem, Karatani remarks that although both of them at first sight seem to follow formalism, in actuality they are attempts to prove incompleteness within a formal system (Karatani 1985a: 25–26). Since Karatani asserts that the exterior only appears as an inconsistency within the formal system (Karatani 1988: 137; 1993a: 14), it is crucial for him to analyse and subvert the notion of the interior within the formal system (Karatani 1988: 314–315).

As Karatani points out, his method is further related to self-referential contradictions (Karatani 1988: 122–127; 1995b: 47–57). The origin of self-referential contradictions can be traced back to Cantor and Burali-Forti's paradoxes of the greatest cardinal and ordinal numbers, and further to the well-known paradox of Epimenides: '"All Cretans always lie", said a Cretan'. These paradoxes are further related to Russell's contradiction of the class of all classes that are not members of themselves. Russell says:

> Let *w* be the class of all those classes that are not members of themselves. Then, whatever class *x* may be, '*x* is a *w*' is equivalent to '*x* is not an *x*'. Hence, giving to *x* the value *w*, '*w* is a *w*' is equivalent to '*w* is not a *w*'.
>
> (Whitehead and Russell 1910 I: 63)

Russell's argument runs as follows: The class 'animal', for instance, consists of lions, rabbits and so on, but does not include the term 'animal' itself. The paradox resides in the question whether the class of all those classes that are not members of themselves is a member of itself or not. If it were to be, then it would mean that it was not a member of itself. If it were not, then it would mean that it was one of those classes that were not members of themselves and therefore it was a member of itself (Garciadiego

1992: 108). These paradoxes are similar to statements such as 'There is nothing true in this world'. If the sentence is true, it negates itself, and if the sentence is false, it turns out to be true.

Russell discerns a common characteristic in these contradictions, which may be described as self-reference or reflexiveness. He says that in these contradictions 'something is said about *all* cases of some kind, and from what is said a new case seems to be generated, which both is and is not of the same kind as the cases of which *all* were concerned in what was said' (Whitehead and Russell 1910 I: 64–65). In order to avoid these illegitimate totalities, Russell introduces the vicious-circle principle which states that whatever involves all of a collection must not itself be of the collection (Whitehead and Russell 1910 I: 40).

He explains that 'this is the characteristic of illegitimate totalities, as we defined them in stating the vicious-circle principle. Hence all our contradictions are illustrations of vicious-circle fallacies. It only remains to show, therefore, that the illegitimate totalities involved are excluded by the hierarchy of types which we have constructed' (Whitehead and Russell 1910 I: 65). He continues: thus,

> if p is a proposition of nth order, a proposition in which p occurs as an apparent variable is not of the nth order, but of a higher order. Hence the kind of truth or falsehood that can belong to the statement 'there is a proposition p which I am affirming and which has falsehood of the nth order' is truth or falsehood of a higher order than the nth. Hence the statement of Epimenides does not fall within its own scope, and therefore no contradiction emerges.
>
> (Whitehead and Russell 1910 I: 65)

In contrast to this solution of paradox offered by Russell, Alfred Tarski, the advocate of the concept of meta-language, considers that value judgement – the definition of truth – exists exterior to the logical system. Thus, he differentiates between 'object-language' (the propositional system that becomes the object of value judgement) and 'meta-language' (the system that contains value judgement itself). He says:

> [W]hen we investigate the language of a formalized deductive science, we must always distinguish clearly between the language *about* which we speak and the language *in* which we speak, as well as between the science which is the object of our investigation and the science in which the investigation is carried out. The names of the expressions of the first language, and of the relations between them, belong to the second language, called the *meta-language* (which may contain the first as a part).
>
> (Tarski 1956: 167; emphasis in the original)

Neither the Russellian or Tarskian ways of solving the paradox seem very different – they both argue that we should distinguish between a class and its members, the nth order and the higher order, and object-language and meta-language.

Charles Parsons mentions that this kind of hierarchical approach has been rejected in later literature on semantic paradoxes that argues that the sentences involved are semantically deficient, or at least become so in the contexts in which they are used (Parsons 1984: 9–10). Furthermore, it seems that in the field of LISP computer language,[4] computer scientists are also attempting to solve the self-referential paradox in a different manner (See Asada Akira's remarks in Karatani ed. 1989: 157). More recently, the Tarskian schema has been defended in the so-called revision theory of truth which insists that the semantic status of each sentence is determined by its Tarskian biconditional, once a totality of nonsemantic facts and an initial extension of the truth predicate are posited (Yaqūb 1993: 4).

It remains to be seen whether specialist logicians or computer scientists can solve the problem of paradox. Yet, it seems doubtless that by using self-reflexive or self-referential language we can subvert the identity of subjectivity that posits the 'truth' of itself as object. By using self-referential language, or meta-language in Tarski's terminology, we can go beyond the class to which we have so far belonged, or we can change the meaning of 'all'. For instance, once a Cretan says 'All Cretans always lie', if her assertion is correct, then she is no longer a Cretan, or otherwise, she has changed the meaning of 'all Cretans'. To state that nothing is true in this world, if this statement is correct, is to step outside the world. To suppose a universal set and objectify it is to inevitably transcend it.

The cause of these paradoxes, including Zenon's paradoxes, seems to be, as pointed out by Bergson as early as the beginning of the twentieth century (Bergson 1910: 113), the inconsistency which arises between a moving, becoming or expanding existence and a static understanding. In Russell's terms, once a statement is made about all cases of a kind, the speaker appears to be unavoidably separated from all these cases. Empathy is, as we have seen, an unconscious identification in which the interiority is still not clearly differentiated from the exteriority, and knowledge is, as we have also seen, founded on the distinction between interiority and exteriority. In contrast, self-reference serves to produce or invite the exteriority into the interiority.

Hence, in this way, the current dilemma can be subverted by means of self-referential or self-reflexive language that offers the potential to go beyond the present enclosure. For instance, we can create the following paradox: it is always possible to show the object of discrimination beyond the object of unification, since unification only appears as a reaction against discrimination, and vice versa. Now, if 'universal unification' or 'global unification' is considered, that is the unification of all the objects, then, a contradiction clearly arises. So, by disclosing this contradiction, the contrast between unification and discrimination, which appears as 'object-language' or the problem on the *n*th level, can be problematised from the perspective of 'meta-language' or from the level higher than the *n*th. Thus, we can then go beyond the enclosure of the contrast between unification and discrimination, and reach a point from which both of them can be evaluated. As a matter of fact, the self-reflexive language has something in common with the concept of deconstruction, in the sense that deconstruction also attempts to resolve opposing concepts, not by taking one of them, but by shifting the boundary between the two.

There is a further connection between the subversion of formality or interiority and the deconstruction of desire, which has so far been outlined in this book. We have seen how Murakami Haruki's and Yoshimoto Banana's stories transgress the boundaries between cultural, gender and sexual otherness and familiarity, in order to subvert the distinction between heterogeneity and homogeneity as it exists in many different aspects of human society. We have also noticed in these stories the reformation of emotional romantic love, sexual desire, the desire to do violence, exogamous rivalry and vital, energetic and triangular movements of evolution on the one hand, and incestuous autism, and a calm, quiet and narcissistic circular repetition on the other.

Furthermore, as a methodological possibility, we have discerned the potential to subvert the binary oppositions between the emotionally identical *philia* expressed towards the homogeneous family/friend and the *eros*/violence felt towards the heterogeneous Other. This is achieved both through psychological incest and homosexuality, and also through conceiving nostalgia towards heterogeneous opponents. By exchanging family with strangers and vice-versa, friends with lovers and vice-versa, or the same-sex/gender opponent with opposite-sex/gender opponent and vice-versa, we have created the potential for new human relations. It is clear that these attempts have much in common with Karatani's endeavour to subvert the interior in order to meet the exterior through using self-referential language.

Karatani, however, in his afterword to *Researches I* (*Tankyū I*) declares that he has abandoned this method of analysing and subverting the interior through inviting in it the exterior. He outlines a new strategy to directly experience the 'Other' outside the formal system (Karatani 1992b: 254–255; Shindō 1995a, 1995b). Azuma Hiroki insists that the reason behind Karatani's change in method is that he became aware that even if he succeeded in subverting the interiority, the exteriority could only be represented negatively. Thus, Karatani's new approach can be regarded as a movement from negatively describing the exteriority through the subversion of the formal system (interiority) to directly describing the exteriority (Azuma 1995: 74–77).[5] How then can exteriority be described in positive language? Who is the 'Other'? If, as Karatani insists, the 'Other' is one who does not follow a common set of rules with members of a community, and if an exteriority conceptually grasped as something positive or substantial is no longer exteriority, where then, is the 'Other' located?

Avoiding romantic and empathic identification, as well as rationalistic monologue, Karatani finds a relationship with others in teaching–learning and selling–buying activities. Karatani follows Wittgenstein who, in his *Philosophical Investigations*, attempted to introduce the Other that could no longer be interiorised, that is, the otherness of the Other. In the course of this project Wittgenstein reintroduced the notion of teaching in the form of teaching language to foreigners or children that Plato had discarded (Karatani 1995b: 113). To communicate with foreigners or children is, for Karatani, to teach those who do not share a common set of rules. Karatani calls this communication with the Other 'intercourse'. Thus, one could say that the 'intercourse' with the Other, the one who does not share a common set of rules, invariably takes the form of a teaching–learning relationship (Karatani 1995b: 116).

Thus, following Wittgenstein, Karatani consequently finds the 'Other' directly experienced outside the formal system in children and foreigners. He remarks that by singling out children and foreigners as Others who do not follow a common set of rules, Wittgenstein discovered a kind of exchange between communities, as opposed to the exchange within one community in which communication is governed by a single set of rules (Karatani 1995b: 115–116, 143; 2001: 104–105). Though the supposedly strong or authoritarian position of the teacher may raise concern, Karatani insists that, contrary to expectation, the teacher is not authoritarian, but in fact the weaker partner in the relationship, because the teacher is subordinated to the student's acquisition of knowledge. This inferiority might be likened to the selling position in the buyer–seller relation. Citing Marx, Karatani argues that because the selling position is subordinate to the will of the buyer (to the owner of money), the selling–buying relationship, too, is asymmetrical (Karatani 1995b: 117). Thus, we can see in Karatani's change of method a shift from Gödel's incompleteness theorem of subverting interiority to Wittgenstein's idea of foreigner/child as the 'Other' of exteriority.

On the basis of this distinction between those who follow the same rules in a community and those who do not, Karatani differentiates between monologue and dialogue, and community and sociality. For Karatani, those who are 'Other' cannot share a set of rules between each other, and communication between them must not take the form of monologue but of dialogue (Karatani 1995b: 113, 133). The group, which consists of people who share common rules based upon monologic communication, is called a 'community', whereas communication between communities that do not share a common set of rules is called 'sociality'. Karatani says that 'the language spoken to the Other will become social, dialogic, and polyphonic only if the Other is an outsider to the community where a common set of rules is shared; the dialogue within a "community" is merely a monologue' (Karatani 1995b: 140).

From this point of view, Karatani attacks the Western community, saying that it was built on the basis of the monologue of rationality (Karatani

1995b: 112).[6] This criticism of Western rationality can be found elsewhere, too, in Karatani's writings. As we have noted, it can be found even in Karatani's early essays on Sōseki and Ōgai. In his later essays, Karatani, in relation to the lack of dialogue in Descartes, introduces Nicholas Rescher, who criticises the egocentric perspective of modern epistemology since Descartes. But Karatani writes that the key terms such as Rescher's dialogue, and Jürgen Habermas's communicative rationality too, 'cannot be equated with the dialogue in the social field as long as they are set within a community where a common rule is shared. Rather, they function as exclusionary to the non-Western "Other"' (Karatani 1995b: 153).

Singularity and proper name

As Sabu Kohso points out in his Translator's Remarks in Karatani's book, singularity is a key term that stands out in Karatani's philosophy (Karatani 1995b: xxii), and his concept of the 'Other' can be said to relate closely to his notion of singularity (*tandokusei*). Karatani's *Researches II* opens with an essay entitled 'Singularity and Particularity', in which he remarks:

> I am not special. I know how common I am and yet 'this I' feels 'am not anyone else'. What is at stake here is the 'this' in 'this I' and not the consciousness….For instance, when I say 'this dog', it does not indicate a particular one among the genus *Canis* (in general). The 'this'-ness of this dog named Taro has nothing to do with its features and characteristics. It is simply 'this dog'.
>
> I will call the 'this'-ness of 'this I' or 'this dog' *singularity*, to distinguish it from *particularity*. *Singularity*, as explained later, does not mean that a thing is only one. Singularity, as opposed to particularity – that is, an individuality seen from a position of generality – is an individuality no longer able to belong to the realm of generality. We must distinguish (1) 'I am' from (2) 'this I am': the 'I' in (1) is one (a particular) of the I's in general, pertinent to any one of the I's, but the 'I' in (2) is *singular*, irreplaceable by any other I.
> (Karatani 1994: 10–11; trans. Sabu Kohso in Karatani 1995b: xxii–xxiii)

Karatani discerns the origin of this distinction made between singularity/universality and particularity/generality in Descartes' philosophy. According to an interpretation made by Karatani, Descartes observed that the proof offered by his *cogito* was sufficient for himself only, and not for others. While in conventional introspective thought the self is understood as a particular case of the general self, the Cartesian *cogito* proved to be the discovery of a *singular self*, totally disconnected from the circuit of particular/general selves. That is to say, in place of the particularity/generality circuit, Descartes introduced singularity/universality.

This aspect of Cartesianism has, however, been ignored by later philosophers such as Kant, Hegel, Husserl, Heidegger and so forth. According to Karatani, all invariably returned to the circuit of particularity/generality (Karatani 1995b: 150–151). Hence, Karatani's criticism of Western philosophy is really two-fold. First, he opposes its monological rationalism, and second he criticises its lack of a notion of singularity in the particularity/generality circuit. Underlying both of the above two criticisms is Western philosophy's lack of the 'Other' in Karatani's sense.

Karatani's emphasis on the concept of singularity is closely related to his notion of 'difference'. In a dialogue with Nakagami Kenji, Karatani explains how the concept of 'difference' is important for him.

> Simply speaking, there are in the world no two things that are exactly the same. But, the existence of number indicates that we suppose an identity between different things. The same can be said of money. Number and monetary value can exist because we find identity between completely distinct things. And so, every commodity seems to have an inherent value. It is so in the case of human identity, too. To promote identity means to progress. Thus, Marxism is nothing but bourgeois thought. Bourgeois thought can also be discovered in egalitarianism.
>
> Since I am attempting to subvert the metaphysics of identity, the concept of 'difference' is important for me.
>
> (Karatani 1987a: 171; my translation)

All things are different and unique and two things that are exactly the same cannot exist. It seems that by insisting on 'difference', Karatani is taking a position very close to the modernist idea of existentialism. But the point Karatani is attempting to raise here is neither the preciousness of individual uniqueness, nor the burden this brings; Karatani's notion of 'difference' is, instead, related to his concept of the 'Other' which is an attempt to subvert the interiority that includes Western logic, a logic based upon abstraction that inevitably neglects singularity.

Thus, Karatani's concepts of 'difference', 'Other' and 'singularity' can be understood as tools in his attempt to provide a genealogy of logic. In order to think logically, it is necessary to find something that various unique objects have in common such as number, language and monetary value. It may be assumed that one plus one equals two for all people; but this only works as a mathematical abstraction. Once this principle is applied to the real world, there is no situation in which it really works out. For instance, if you put one apple on a table and place another beside it, and in so doing say that one apple plus one apple equals two apples, then, you are guilty of generalising 'apple': you have supposed that the two apples are the same. In actuality, there exists only apple A and apple B: A plus B by no means equals two. Nonetheless, we generalise situations like this all the time without doubting the function of abstraction.

What is the mechanism underlying this abstraction? Karatani, in his book *Marx: The Centre of His Possibilities* (*Marx sono kanōsei no chūshin*, 1985b), draws our attention to the following remarks made by Marx:

> Men do not therefore bring the products of their labour into relation with each other as values because they see these objects merely as the material integuments of homogeneous human labour. The reverse is true: by equating their different products to each other in exchange as values, they equate their different kinds of labour as human labour. They do this without being aware of it.
>
> (Marx 1990–1992 I: 166–167; Karatani 1985b: 35–36)

As Hiromatsu Wataru has pointed out, what interests Karatani here is the fact that it is not a product's inherent value that makes exchange possible, but rather that it is the process of exchange itself which makes something appear valuable (Karatani 1987a: 252). This value is, as Karatani mentions, the same as the commonality underlying language, monetary value and number. Following Karatani's logic here, we can argue that it is not any inherent common feature shared among ourselves that enables us to understand each other through the exchange of language, money or number, but rather it is the activity of exchange or the intention to communicate that makes an intersubject appear to have value.

'Language, number, money', is the subtitle of Karatani's book *Architecture as Metaphor* and these three abstracts show how our commonality has emerged through the practice of exchange. It is clear that the practice of exchange or the intention to communicate or have 'intercourse' with the Other is both the source and the result of unification and discrimination. However, it seems impossible that our intention to exchange, communicate or 'intercourse' with each other could ever be discarded, despite the fact that it results in discrimination, as well as unification.

In previous chapters we have noted the future potential in solipsism, autism, incestuous nostalgia and desire for eternal repetition (Amaterasu circle) to overcome discrimination and unification (Oedipal triangle). Yet, at the same time, we have confirmed that if we lose the intention to exchange, communicate or 'intercourse' with the Other without changing the current form of desire formulated in the self/family/stranger human relations, we cannot keep on living any longer. Therefore, the problem which remains to be solved is how to reformulate the relations between the intention to exchange and that to enclose, between uniqueness and commonality, and furthermore between violent discrimination and forceful unification. Karatani's concept of 'singularity' is one way in which a door may be opened to this new horizon.

Karatani understands the singularity of a distinct individual to be manifested in a proper name, for, as he says 'a singularity – as distinct from particularity – cannot be reduced to any bundle of sets, to any generality'. Karatani continues: 'Singularity, contrary to the nuances it may convey, has nothing to do with bourgeois individualism; paradoxically enough, singularity is inseparable from society, from being "in between" communities' (Karatani 1995b: 152). Thus, the link between Karatani's concept of singularity and Saul Kripke's notion of proper name, to which he refers, is clear.

With regard to Kripke's theory of proper name, a label, which in every possible world designates the same object, is referred to as a *rigid designator*. Taking the former US President Richard Nixon as an example, Kripke explains: '"President of the U.S. in 1970" designates a certain man, Nixon; but someone else (e.g., Humphrey) might have been the President in 1970, and Nixon might not have; so this designator [President of the U.S. in 1970] is not rigid'. In contrast, Kripke continues, 'although the man (Nixon) might not have been the President, it is not the case that he might not have been Nixon (though he might not have been called "Nixon")'. Thus, for Kripke, the proper name 'Nixon' must be a *rigid designator* (Kripke 1972: 49). What does this 'rigid designator' exactly mean? Referring to Kripke, Karatani discovers his concept of the 'Other' in the ideas of singularity and proper name. He writes:

> Linguists, for example, exclude proper names from their objects of analysis not only because proper names reinforce the illusion of the direct link between words and things, but also because proper names, being untranslatable into any other language, cannot be interiorized by any of the systems of *langue*. Does not this externality of proper names that resists being interiorized within any *langue* or community indicate that the names are themselves 'social'? Proper names involve an otherness or contingency that can never be interiorized by a self or a community. This can be understood simply by examining the communicative relation between Kripke's giver and receiver of the name; the relationship is that of teaching–learning, where a common rule has not yet been established. Therefore, it is with the proper name, which linguists ignore, that the sociality in communication is fully exposed.
>
> (Karatani 1995b: 152)

Kripke writes that in order to understand the relationship between a proper name and its reference, an initial 'baptism' must take place:

> Here the object may be named by ostension,[7] or the reference of the name may be fixed by a description. When the name is 'passed from link to link', the receiver of the name must, I think, intend when he learns it to use it with the same reference as the man from whom he heard it. If I hear the name 'Napoleon' and decide it would be a nice name for my pet aardvark, I do not satisfy this condition.
>
> (Kripke 1972: 96)

This process can be applied specifically to Wittgenstein's teaching–learning relation between adult native-speakers and foreigners or children. That is, the proper name brings into everyday life the relation with the 'Others' which otherwise can only be experienced when communicating with children and foreigners. Whenever we apprehend the meaning of a proper name through an initial baptism, we are repeating the process through which we acquired our native language as children, or when we acquire a second language as foreigners. Furthermore, by emphasising the distinct character-istic of the proper name, Kripke is attempting to oppose descriptions theory. That is, by insisting that the proper name cannot be reduced to a set of descriptions, Kripke is bringing the idea of singularity in Karatani's sense into the world of particularity/generality expressed through common nouns.

It is clear, then, that Karatani has focused on two aspects of Kripke's theory of proper name. First, he argues that the proper name can be repre-sentative of the singularity that in Karatani's sense represents the idea of the 'Other' in the exterior. And second, he notes that the process through which we acquire the meaning of a proper name (initial baptism) is analogical to the teaching–learning relation which is a relation between 'Others', that is between the interior and the exterior.

Apart from the above two points, I want now to focus on an aspect of proper name which has so far been neglected by Kripke and Karatani: while the common noun can indicate both the specific member and the generic in one word, the proper name lacks this function. The word 'computer', for instance, can indicate both the particular computer on which I am writing this book and the generic term for a category of machine. I can say that this computer is the best computer, or even that this computer is not the computer – in both cases, the former 'computer' is the name of a particular computer, whereas the latter 'computer' refers to the generic class. In this formula partic-ularity is confronted with generality, to use Karatani's term. Or, this particular, specific and unique thing before my eyes is inevitably compared with the normal, ideal, general and universal class in which it is placed.

In so comparing, we are unconsciously doing two things. First, we set up a contrast between the real and the ideal and second, by looking at an object as a mere member of its class, we deprive a unique object of its singularity. It is out of the conflict between these two functions of common nouns that typically modern binary ideas such as uniqueness/particularity versus universality/generality, reality versus ideality, and autism versus rivalry, necessarily appear. Or, rather, it is from our inclination to long for ideals, progress, development and so forth, as opposed to particularity in the present state, that the use of a common noun to indicate a particular object and its generic in the same term has emerged. Thus, we can say that the use of the common noun is typically modern.

Obviously, however, this is not the case with the proper name, which has no reference beyond itself. I am perhaps neither a normal person, nor a good teacher, nor an ideal researcher, etc. As a person, as a teacher and as a researcher, I can be compared with and included in a group of some other persons, teachers and researchers. It might be supposed that, for instance, there are numbers of persons, some are teachers and some others are researchers here, including Ms A, Mr B, Ms C,...and myself. And it might further be said that Ms A is the most normal person, Mr B is the best teacher and Ms C is the ideal researcher. In this case, I am treated like an expendable object, just like the apple, which can be added or subtracted from the pile on the table. But, indeed, this is not the case with the proper name. When described by my proper name, I cannot be added to a group of people who also share that name; I can only be included in a group as a distinct individual.

Perhaps the proper name is not only a rigid designator (something which cannot be substituted or replaced by some other thing in any possible world), but also something whose ideal state cannot be imagined. We cannot evaluate, esteem and judge with the proper name, since though I can be a good person, I cannot be a good 'I'. To evaluate, to esteem or to judge means to contrast the attributes of a thing in terms of particularity/generality, specificity/normality, or uniqueness/universality. Taking the US President as an example again, though the ideal 'President' can be imagined, the ideal 'Nixon' cannot. Just as Nixon today is not the 'real' Nixon, the proper name might also have flexibility of meaning. But, the extent or scope of the flexibility is not comparable with that of the common noun. If you still insist that you can imagine the ideal Nixon, I would argue that in that case you are looking at Nixon not from the perspective of a proper name, but from some other point of view such as a person, son, father, US President, and so on. Nixon as a proper name *per se* cannot be idealised.

All things which can be included in a category of common noun, are necessarily situated in the contrast between particularity, specificity and uniqueness on the one hand, and normality, ideality, generality and universality on the other. Only the proper name has the potential to transcend the contrast. From this point of view we can argue that although Karatani presents the contrast between particularity/generality and singularity/universality, the concept of 'singularity' cannot be paired with anything. For, if 'singularity' is analogous to the proper name, it must exist beyond the comparison. Since the proper name is free from ideality, which produces the desire of rivalry represented in the inverted Oedipal triangle, we can suppose that it is beyond power structures. While Karatani has found an analogy for singularity and teaching–learning/selling–buying relations in the proper name, it can also be argued that, in addition, the proper name represents a postmodern situation. Here people cannot compete, cannot even be compared with each other and cannot force each other to follow a particular ideal. This must be the basis of the concept of 'difference'.

Karatani's understanding of 'proper name' appears to have a potential to go beyond the current enclosure of binarism between individuality and totality, particularity and generality, and so on. In his recent book

Transcritique (2001 (J), 2003 (E)) however, Karatani explores his new idea of 'Other' and finds it in Kant's writings. Karatani first finds the concept of 'Other' in Kant's idea of 'universality', because it, Karatani insists, necessarily goes beyond 'community'. Kant's idea of 'universality' for Karatani must be applicable even to outsiders of the community; those who do not share common rules based upon monologic communication. From this point of view, Karatani claims that Kant's concept of universal law of morality presented in his *Critique of Practical Reason* is the morality applicable to the 'Other'. 'Other' in this case, therefore, besides foreigners and children, includes the dead that is 'Other' in the past and the unborn, or 'Other' in the future (Karatani 2001: 81, 186 (J); 52–53, 127 (E)). Karatani mentions that when Kant says 'the human being (and with him every rational being) is an end in itself, that is, can never be used merely as a means by anyone (not even by God)' (Kant 1997b: 109), he attempts to regard the 'Other' as a free agent (Karatani 2001: 171 (J); 119 (E)).

Universality, universal law and the human being as a free agent, that is individuality, all these concepts are what we have in this book called into question as modern ideology which brought about the forceful progress in one direction. But Karatani's argument here reminds us of the fact that these ideas functioned in the past when they were born as self-reflexive language and helped people to go beyond enclosure and encounter the 'Other'. What is needed for us now to confirm is thus not just to criticise the ideologies currently working forcefully, stagnantly and discriminately, even if in the past they were emancipative, but also to be continuously calling the current ideas of emancipation into question, by using self-reflexive language.

In the latter half of *Transcritique*, Karatani presents four different forms of exchange (Karatani 2001: 30–31, 301–304, 405–407 (J); 12–13, 201–204, 275–277 (E); see also Karatani ed. 2000b: 41–44, 88–92). First is the reciprocal exchange on the basis of gifts and the obligation to return the gifts (within an agricultural community). This is of mutual aid, but exclusive and totalitarian. The second form is the usurpation, or raids and plunder on the basis of power relations (feudal state). Karatani considers this also as a form of exchange, because in order to continuously usurp, one must protect the object of usurpation from other usurpers. This is, for Karatani, the prototype of state. In order to continuously raid and plunder, the state guarantees the reproduction of labour force by means of redistribution, and attempts to increase the agricultural productivity by conducting the public enterprise such as irrigation. People in this form of exchange are obliged to repay this protection of the nation-state in the form of tax. Therefore, this is, in Karatani's sense, also a type of exchange.

Karatani introduces Marx's concept of exchange of commodities as the third form of exchange. It is based on neither the relationship of mutual aid, nor that of usurpation. The basis of exchange of commodities is the juridical relation, whose form is a contract that produces surplus value

(Marx 1990–1992 I: 178). Though tacitly the Marxist in general considers that the surplus value is produced by exploitation in the process of production, Karatani claims that it is produced in between the different value systems (Karatani 2001: 27–28 (J); 9–10 (E)). Citing Marx's words in his *Capital* that the exchange of commodities begins where communities have their boundaries, at their points of contact with other communities, or with members of the latter (Marx 1990–1992 I: 182), Karatani argues that in Marx's theory the surplus value appears in the exchange between different communities, that is in Karatani's term between 'Others'.

In the modern period, the third form of exchange (exchange of commodities) widely expands and overpowers the other two forms of exchange. But, Karatani insists that it cannot or should not be universal, because it presupposes the nation-state, which violently guarantees the execution of the contract, and it cannot dissolve community (Karatani 2001: 303–304 (J); 203–204 (E)). By criticising possibility of violence in the power relations between others, Karatani is now searching for something different. That is explored in the fourth type of exchange.

As the fourth type of exchange Karatani introduces the concept of 'association' or 'federation'. The idea of association (federation) is initiated by Pierre-Joseph Proudhon, a nineteenth-century French socialist. Proudhon defines 'federation' by saying:

> FEDERATION, from the Latin *fœdus*, gen. *fœderis*, that is to say pact, contract, treaty, convention, alliance, etc., is an agreement by which one or several heads of a family, one or several communes, one or several groups of communes or states, bind themselves by mutual and equal agreements for one or several determinate aims, for which the responsibility falls specifically and exclusively on the members of the federation.
>
> (Proudhon 1969: 106)

He also mentions elsewhere that free association is the only possible, the only just and the only true form of society, and that the government of man by man, under whatever name it is disguised, is oppression (Proudhon 1994: 215–216).

The difference between nation/state and association (federation) is, Karatani defines, an association that is, like a gift, of mutual aid, but their reciprocity is, unlike a gift, neither obligatory nor xenophobic in nature, but self-generating and open to the exterior. Moreover, it is, unlike state and capital, not exploitative (Karatani 2001: 31, 303, 406 (J);13, 204, 276 (E)). Karatani finds the same character of Proudhon's concept of association in Marx's idea of 'united co-operative society'.

> [I]f united co-operative societies are to regulate national production upon a common plan, thus taking it under their own control, and putting an end to the constant anarchy and periodical convulsions

which are the fatality of Capitalist production – what else, gentlemen, would it be but Communism, 'possible' Communism?

(Marx 1975– XXII: 335)

Citing the above, Karatani says that communism for Marx means in actuality 'association' (Karatani ed. 2000a: 9; Karatani 2001: 241–242, 417, 433 (J); 165–166, 283–284, 297 (E)). Karatani mentions that the movement of capital accumulation, M (Money) – C (Commodity) – M′ (Money + Surplus Value), will stop only when surplus value is not produced. In order to stop producing surplus value, then, it is necessary to establish a new form of consumption and production outside the relation between money and commodity. Karatani finds its possibility in 'association'. In June 2000 based on this theory Karatani established NAM (New Associationist Movement) aimed at resisting capital and the nation-state.[8]

Karatani considers that in the process of M–C–M′ there are two critical moments for capital to obtain surplus value. One is when commodified labour power is purchased and the second is when the products are sold back to the workers. If a failure occurs in either moment, capital is unable to obtain surplus value. This indicates that workers can counteract capital at either of these two moments. In the first instance, they can adopt the strategy of not-to-work, and in the second occasion, they can take the strategy of not-to-buy. But in order to make it possible for these workers-as-consumers to take actions not-to-work and not-to-buy, it is necessary for them to have an alternative place where they can work and buy. The aim of NAM is to provide them with this alternative.

As practical schemes for this movement, Karatani introduces three systems. One is a new local money system LETS (Local Exchange Trading System).[9] In this LETS everyone has an account, and each new account starts at zero. For instance, I can issue money from my account and give it to you for your goods and services and you can spend it elsewhere in the system. LETS money exists only for exchange on the basis of members' consent and there can be no profit and no interest in storing it. Negative balances mean nothing but you have received more goods and services than you have given out. Even if someone goes away from the system leaving a negative balance, it just means that they have taken more goods and services from the system than they have given. They are regarded basically as a dead loss.

The second scheme is a lottery. Karatani considers that the system to prevent the rise of entrenched power is not an election, but a lottery. For Karatani, a lottery is supposed to make power struggle useless and meaningless (Karatani ed. 2000b: 100–103; Karatani 2002a, 2002b). In particular, Karatani proposes to select three candidates by ballot, and then make the final selection from among them by lottery. Because the final stage in the process is ruled entirely by chance, the power struggle by means of rationality or whatever would be pointless. Karatani says that someone who has won by virtue of chance has no grounds for boasting of their personal power, just as those candidates who were not chosen by lottery have no reason to refuse to cooperate with the chosen representative.

The third system is the system of multiple affiliations for each member. Karatani writes that most organisations to date have formed around only one interest or around the amorphous image of a 'citizen' or 'consumer' from which all concrete reality has been abstracted away. As a result, because all other dimensions (social relations) are abstracted away, the group's perspective and interests are narrowly limited. Consequently, the organisation ends up being either closed off in exclusionary isolation, or it splinters, or it simply collapses. The 'essence' of the individual is, Karatani insists, nothing more than the ensemble of various social relations. Thus, we should not abstract away the diverse social relations to which each individual belongs. These are to be respected in the various interest sections. Therefore in NAM each individual is free to simultaneously affiliate with multiple interest and regional sections, according to his or her wish. Moreover, one can add or drop affiliations at any time.

Karatani assumes neither that 'human nature' and the will to power should change, nor that diversity and individual differences of ability will or should be abolished. 'Principles of the New Associationist Movement (NAM)' in the NAM website says:

> A movement of resistance against the state and capital should therefore be organized around a system that introduces an element of chance into those parts of its organization where power is concentrated. Otherwise, that movement will come to resemble the very thing it hopes to resist...NAM does not simply aim at the realization of participatory democracy as a future goal; it must actualize this in its own movement structure...NAM must be a real movement that in its own organization realizes communism....To realize this, as is clear in the planks in the NAM organizational principles, NAM has adopted three distinct systems: the selection of representatives by lottery, the system of multiple affiliations for each member, and LETS.[10]

Towards the place where the violence of unification/discrimination is overcome

Having followed Karatani's philosophy thus far, from the subversion of formality (interiority) through direct contact with the 'Other' (exteriority) through interacting with foreigners and children represented by the proper name in teaching–learning/selling–buying activities to the formation of association, at least three problems can be discerned. First, there appear to be two distinct modes of behaviour. On the one hand is solipsism, and on the other is the attempt to interiorise the 'Other' within the self through asserting that what is true of the self must be universally true. As we have noted, Karatani insists that solipsism not only acknowledges but in fact privileges the existence of the self, and in so doing asserts that what is true of the self must be universally true, and he also argues that in order for the latter to be possible, the Other must already have been interiorised in the self (Karatani 1995b:133). It seems to me however that solipsism and the assertion that what is true of the self must be universally true are rather different issues.

For instance, to analyse Karatani's position in the terms of our present discussion, it can be argued that the legitimacy of such groups as gender, sexuality, family, etc. cannot be judged in terms of those groups. In order to determine the 'sense' of any group to which we belong, it is necessary to refer to some perspective outside the group, or otherwise go beyond the enclosure of the group. This involves either inviting in or becoming the 'Other' in Karatani's sense. I do not see any problem so far. However, I take issue with Karatani to the extent that although I might be comfortable being myself, I do not necessarily need to persuade or force others to be like me.

Hence, when Karatani insists that no matter how deeply we analyse the mechanisms of discrimination within a community, discrimination cannot be avoided because discrimination is an inherent factor in the formation of a sense of community (Karatani and Hasumi 1988: 182), I see the same misconception at work. My argument is that even if we exist as part of a community, we are not necessarily discriminatory. Karatani explains that the concept of the 'Other' (inter-community) in his sense is different from that of 'stranger' (intra-community) (Karatani 1991: 123, 238–239, 297). His notion of 'stranger' is, at least partly based upon René Girard's theory of violence and the sacred. As we have seen in previous chapters, community in Girard's sense consists of identity and distinction among family members and strangers. Once equality is achieved in a community based on a shared identity, that is to say, once everybody in a community becomes family, people inevitably seek to find an 'Other' in the form of a stranger (scapegoat), in order to release the energy of violence. In this sense, the desire to do violence is fundamental to the evolution of a community. Therefore, through subverting this system, Karatani seeks to discover the 'Other' rather than the 'stranger'.

In order to do violence to someone, this someone must be one's rival – a person with whom we are in competition. To this extent, this someone should not be the 'Other', but the 'stranger' in Karatani's sense. Hence, what is in need of repudiation is the binary opposition between family/stranger, and not the 'Other' in Karatani's sense. So far we have been using the two terms 'stranger' and the 'Other' without any clear distinction. Following Karatani, however, the four terms 'self/family/stranger/Other' should be set out in order, from 'close to' to 'distant from' the self.

Karatani attempts to avoid being caught up in the community system in which the dichotomic separation between family and stranger inevitably arises. In this system, the 'Other' in Karatani's sense tends to be regarded either as stranger or as family; in the former case, Karatani discerns the tendency towards discrimination and in the latter case, fascistic identification. Hence, as has been noted, he rejects the description of the 'Other' as something positive or substantial in terms of the domain of family/stranger, and presents the concept of the 'Other' in order to escape from this dichotomic system of family/stranger.

Yet Girard's theory might only be applicable to capitalist and modernist societies in which people are encouraged to progress in order to produce profit on the basis of the difference that appears in the family/stranger binarism. That is to say, it may not be viable in either premodern or postmodern societies. So far in this book we have been looking at ways of precipitating society from a modernist to a postmodernist condition in which people no longer appear as rivals with other members of their own community, albeit at the expense of deep, empathic and romantic emotions that are expressed in terms of modernist love. That is to say, in postmodern society, to be solipsistic does not necessarily mean to be violent, even if it is beyond the ability of solipsism to determine its 'sense' in the solipsistic sphere. Or in other words, we can conceive of a society that transcends the contrast between unification and differentiation.

The notion of pre/postmodern society is, as we have seen in Chapter 1, deeply related to an antipathy to progress. Karatani also mentions that an uncivilised society is not the same as a primitive society. So-called uncivilised societies are communities that, at certain historical stages of their development, have withdrawn from 'intercourse' with other societies. In such communities, the encounter with an exteriority (otherness) that would challenge their self-sufficiency is perceived as threatening (Karatani 1995b: 147). If an uncivilised society is defined in terms of its avoidance of intercourse with other societies, then it is not very different from the definition of a pre/postmodern society. For, to renounce the 'intercourse' with other societies means to prohibit the erotic desire felt towards strangers. Yet, it can at the same time be argued that people in uncivilised societies obviously do not assert that what is true of themselves must be universally true. We can be uncivilised in this sense; hence, I am saying that we can be solipsists without asserting that our sense is universal. Although, as has been cautioned many times, we should not forget that, without deconstructing the self/family/stranger distinction, to be content in autism means a one-way road to stagnant isolation.

A second problem that I discern in Karatani's philosophy concerns his formulation of teaching–learning/selling–buying relations. At first sight, it seems as though power struggles or discrimination occur only between members of the same community, for only they share the same benefits or the same rules. In contrast, power struggles between the 'Others' in different communities who encounter each other in teaching–learning or selling–buying relations seem less likely since they do not share common interests. But, what would happen if both sides attempted to teach or sell? Which party would teach its language? Suppose a situation in which an English woman and a Japanese woman meet together and discuss an issue.

Who teaches her native language to her opponent is of crucial importance in structuring the power relations between them (if they regard power structures as fundamentally crucial, that is, if they are modernists). In this case it can easily be imagined how they might struggle for mastery. It has been common throughout history for stronger societies to teach their language to the weaker, seldom the other way round. Once we begin to regard the other as our counterpart in a teaching–learning or selling–buying relationship, the other is no longer the 'Other' in Karatani's sense; it is either family or a stranger.

Moreover, in contrast, the complete 'Others' do not fight and compete for mastery. Yet, at the same time, they do not even attempt to understand each other. They neither embark on teaching/selling nor care about learning/buying: they are indifferent. In this case, we must admit that no matter what we take, we cannot invite the 'Other' into our community, for while individuals remain in the position of the Other, they have nothing to do with us. But, once they are brought into some kind of relationship with us, they are no longer the Others. Though, as we have noted, Karatani's concept of the 'Other' as represented by 'proper name' has a potential to undermine binarism between individuality and totality, particularity and generality, and so on, the 'Other' as a foreigner or a child seems to be a less useful idea. It seems to be impossible to invite in a complete 'Other' from the exterior. Rather, I find a potential to incessantly subvert interiority to make the 'Other' appear inside the interiority.

Also, it seems that Karatani's attempt to find the 'Other' in foreigners is doomed to fail from another point of view. Since, due to the current explosion in worldwide communications technology, we are going to increasingly lose the idea of 'foreigners' inhabiting 'foreign' countries. Although we have to do our very best to preserve indigenous perceptions in order to avoid being colonised by the strongest ideology, in the sphere beyond the present horizon of *multi*culturalism, a gradual vision of a global monolithic culturalism is emerging. Foreigners will soon no longer be the 'Other': objects beyond one's understanding. Children might still have the potential to fulfil the role of the Other, although they will increasingly be treated as subjects for training in a meritocratic world, following the decline of humanism. But, it seems certain that we will soon inevitably lose the concept of foreigners as the Other.

If we look at the 'stranger' in foreigners, then from the viewpoint of violence of discrimination, the disappearance of foreigners as objects of discrimination is not necessarily bad news. But if we attempt to find the 'Other' in foreigners, that possibility will be lost. It is true that innumerable people are now fighting for the benefit of their ethnicity, country, nation-state, religion, etc. with so-called foreigners. Yet, I still believe that the foreigners are in the process of disappearing.

In the future we should not try to find the 'Other' in exteriority, but attempt to find the 'Other' in interiority, in ourselves and among familiar persons. At the same time we need to recognise ourselves in unfamiliar persons.[11] By finding the 'Other' in ourselves, in our families, in our countries, and so forth, by means of self-referential or self-reflexive language, we can continue moving. This movement differs from that of dialectic, will to power, *élan vital*, historical materialism, *projet*, reflexive modernisation based on the idea of progress and so on, in the sense that it is not oriented in a specific direction. Schizophrenic movement is in this sense very close to the idea of moving to find the 'Other' in ourselves. As we have noted, the circular movement termed the Amaterasu circle revolving around the desire for nostalgia should be added to the schizophrenic movement.

The 'Other' in this sense, therefore, must not be projected on to strange, uncanny or weird persons. For example, while same-sex partners must appear as 'Others' to heterosexual people in terms of their erotic desires, their opposite-sex partners appear as 'Others' to homosexual people in this regard. Another instance might be an old friend from childhood who appears as the 'Other' in terms of one's present career, since he or she has nothing to do with one's current business. Thus, what is important is not to invite or reject the 'Other' in the family/stranger system, but to find out a new way of dealing with family/strangers in various aspects of human characteristics in a specific situation. By so doing, we may be able to incessantly undermine the binary distinction and devise a way of dealing with the 'Others' that involves pleasure and enjoyment in relations with them. Rather than the dichotomous interaction that currently exists between family/stranger, monologue/dialogue and community/society, an approach that involves the unceasing interrogation and negotiation of borderlines is necessary.

The third problem is in NAM. Does this new association work well? I have two reservations. First, though Karatani insists that we should not assume that the 'human nature' which seeks power can change, or we should not imagine that difference and variation of individual ability disappear (Karatani 2001: 272 (J); 184 (E)), the idea of LETS seems to presuppose them. If there appears someone who does not care about debt and people start thinking a punishment is necessary to clear off the debt, the situation is not improved. If we can do well with LETS, we could do well with the current money system. Karatani and Nishibe Makoto insist that the LETS would play the role of anti-cancer cells (Karatani ed. 2000a: 30, 187, 2000b: 135, 137). But it might turn out that anti-cancer can become real cancer when the real cancer disappears.

A second point is where can we find the 'Other' in NAM? The concept of the 'Other' played a very important role in Karatani's thought. In Karatani's recent book *Transcritique*, the 'Other' specifically means one's other party, with whom one conducts the selling–buying activity in a system of exchange of commodities at the boundaries of communities. But, where is the 'Other' located in the system of NAM? Without the 'Other', is it not that the system is enclosed? Did Karatani give up the strategy of directly experiencing the 'Other' outside the formal system, and return to his old method of analysing and subverting the interior through inviting into it the exterior? Perhaps, it is still too early to evaluate the movement now, since it started no more than four years ago. Having registered my reservations, I would like to keep a close watch on what will happen in the movement in the future.

Conclusion

In this book I have analysed the literary works of four contemporary Japanese writers: Murakami Haruki, Yoshimoto Banana, Yoshimoto Takaaki and Karatani Kōjin, from the perspectives of postmodernism, feminism, queer studies and postcolonial studies. In so doing, I have placed special emphasis on the critique of rationalism, emotionalism, utopian/dystopian worlds, the distinction between family and strangers, power systems, the structure of discrimination and the concept of the 'Other'.

In Murakami Haruki's novels two typically modern ideologies were discovered: 'strong-is-good' and 'love-is-beautiful', both of which over-value progress and romantic love. Although in the modern period these ideologies have long been highly regarded, in late capitalist society their negative effects have increasingly become apparent. Apart from the obvious ecological pollution that modernist developments have caused, the concept of rational progress inevitably requires that everyone progress in the same direction. Furthermore, apart from the empathic identification that exists between loving people, love also causes discrimination against the 'stranger'.

Highly sensitive to these negative aspects, many of Murakami Haruki's narrators and characters in his early stories experience emotional and rational detachment both from themselves and from the events taking place around them. These characters display a paradigm shift from modernism to postmodernism, from an obsession with evolution and love to an indifferent egalitarianism based on fairness or justice without force. Murakami's recent characters, however, start realising the importance of the deep love of prejudice. They begin to abandon detachment in favour of a commitment to love and the mirror aspect of love – the desire to do violence. They are now struggling with the problem of what to do about that violence.

In Yoshimoto Banana's stories we have discovered the modernist family/stranger binarism in which the erotically charged desire to do violence against the stranger (Oedipal triangle) and the gentle but autistic emotion experienced in relation to the family (Amaterasu circle) are contrasted. In modernist society, the desire for food and nostalgic feelings function to confirm human unity within the family whereas erotic attraction or violent hostility is experienced toward heterogeneous strangers. However, Banana's characters eat with strangers, experience erotic desire towards familiar persons and feel nostalgia with heterogeneous people. By so doing, they attempt to subvert the modernist binary opposition between the family (homogeneity) and the stranger (heterogeneity) and so create something new.

In Banana's fiction, this attempt opens up a new dimension that embraces both incest and homosexuality. In both the incestuous and homogeneous erotic desires in Banana's stories there exists a desire to go back to the pre-castrative setting in which the distinction between masculinity and femininity or phallic authority and envious obedience have not yet been articulated. This is the original stage of fusion in which heterosexual/power oriented desires and bisexual/incestuous desires co-exist without being distinguished. Consequently, Banana's stories attempt to transgress the borderlines between cultural, gender and sexual otherness and familiarity, and subvert the distinction between *eros* and *philia*. They merge the triangular movements characteristic of heterogeneity with the incestuous and narcissistic circular repetitions characteristic of homogeneity. Banana's stories suggest that these binary oppositions can be transcended through psychological incest, homosexuality, and in conceiving nostalgia towards heterogeneous opponents.

Both Murakami Haruki and Yoshimoto Banana attempt to deconstruct the polarised oppositions between fascistic totalitarianism and violent discrimination that are based on the distinction made between homogeneous family and heterogeneous strangers. Murakami first tries to keep his distance from both homogeneity and heterogeneity as, in the town of *The End of the World*, he created a place where people are released from the obsession for progress and love. He then rather faces the modernist binary desire and attempts to deal with the deep love of homogeneous people and the desire to do violence to 'Others'. In contrast, Banana attempts to discover heterogeneity within the family and homogeneity among strangers. She does this by eating with and conceiving nostalgia towards strangers, and at the same time by acknowledging erotic desire among family members.

Yoshimoto Takaaki's scholarly work, however, attempts to resist the elite's suppression of the subaltern or the stronger culture's colonisation of the weaker. Yoshimoto contrasts the logocentric West and the pre- and/or post-modern East, and suggests that logic or theories derived from Western cultures are not suitable for analysing the situation of other cultures in other regions. He is concerned with the disparity between Western logic and non-Western situations, and expresses doubts about the validity of the standard by which the former evaluates the latter. He opposes colonisation by the intellectual/strong/logos of people who are weak/pre- and post-logos in the form of the Enlightenment project. By so doing, he attempts to preserve the indigenous perception of the indigenous situation that cannot be articulated in terms of a foreign ideology. For Yoshimoto, to preserve multiple perspectives is necessary in order to prevent everybody in the world from being colonised by a monolithic global culture. Unless we attempt to protect indigenous experiences, some day everything will be subsumed under the strongest ideological logic, producing a single global culture without boundaries.

Yoshimoto distinguishes the *eros* that exists without violence in the family from the power relations that operate in society. He regards social relations as being rooted in power structures, whereas he considers the family a utopian sphere in which people can engage in erotic relations without the desire to do violence. Yoshimoto regards erotic relations within a homogeneous group in the sphere of 'family' as calm and comfortable experiences in which an individual can lose the sense of self without being alienated or appropriated. However, he considers the 'culturally' and 'socially' homogeneous relations to have been formed by a compelling force structured by power relations. Although there is the danger of falling into ethnocentrism, there might also be potential in Yoshimoto's concept of *eros* without violence among homogeneous people to deconstruct the modernist binary opposition between self/family/stranger. In this regard, it is possible to argue that his daughter, Yoshimoto Banana is attempting to avoid the risk her father Takaaki runs in inviting *eros* into the homogeneous family sphere, leaving violence in the heterogeneous stranger's domain, by means of conceiving *philia* or nostalgia (*natsukashisa*) towards heterogeneous strangers.

An analysis of these three writers has shown how there can be a reformulation of desire, so as to refigure the 'Other' and overcome the violence of exclusion. We have found that the modernist is torn between two extremely polarised axes, individual differentiation and totalitarian identification. In order to overcome this conflict, it is necessary to deconstruct desire and find out new pleasures or ways of enjoyment. Since we understand that *eros* and violence, unification and discrimination, or longing and disdain select the 'Other' as their object, in order to reform desire, we need to transgress the boundary between self and the 'Other'. To achieve this, the concept of kinship or family, set in between the self and the 'Other', must play an important role.

Finally, Karatani Kōjin focuses on the notions of interiority and exteriority. For Karatani, human relations within interiority result in either violent discrimination or fascistic identification. Hence, we need 'intercourse' with the 'Other' in exteriority. Karatani reformulates the distinction between self and others as self/stranger/Other. In our terminology the stranger is the object of erotic desire or violent discrimination, whereas the 'Others' are indifferent to each other. Hence, in order to avoid the 'stranger' and engage with the 'Other', Karatani first attempts to subvert interiority, since the concept of interiority replaces the 'Other' in exteriority with the 'stranger' in interiority. But, finding this approach to be futile, he then attempts to establish direct contact with the 'Other' as represented by foreigners and children in situations that involve teaching–learning and/or selling–buying.

Furthermore he tries to express the concept of the 'Other' using Kripke's idea of 'proper name'. For Karatani the relationship between people who do not share anything in common (exteriority) is analogous to a proper name. Finally, in order to overcome the violence appearing from the current system of exchange of commodities, Karatani formed a New Associationist Movement in 2000. In analysing Karatani's thought we have reached the conclusion that rather than attempting to find the 'Other' in foreigners and children in teaching–learning and/or selling–buying relations, it would be better to attempt to find the 'Other' in interiority, by means of self-referential or self-reflexive language. Concerning the NAM, we would like to keep a close eye on the movement with some reservations.

The work of these four contemporary Japanese writers has brought up two main issues. First, to analyse the relationship between the desire for progress and the desire to do violence, and to discriminate is not sufficient; the connection between the desire for progress and erotic desire must also be critiqued. People who have given up the desire for evolution and violence feel comfortable in distancing themselves from extreme rationalisation, emotionalisation, totalisation and individualisation, favouring instead indifference and detachment. In such a society, people will lose both the energy to progress and the desire to unify. That is, if we prefer to renounce development and progress in order to avoid arrogant colonisation and exploitation, we have also to give up or at least diminish feelings of love and respect. In this sense, we cannot optimistically expect in a postmodern society the bright future envisaged in modernism. What we see is rather the dismal future represented by the town of *The End of the World* in Murakami Haruki's novel. It is a world in which people lack polarised emotions such as love/hate, longing/disdain and respect/contempt. No one harms anyone else there; everyone is equal. The people enjoy their work purely for the sake of the work, not for the goals it achieves. Yet, at the same time, they cannot love and respect each other. For, in the modernist mode the desire to progress is closely connected with the romantic desire felt towards strangers, which includes both *eros* and violence.

Second, in order to create a society without modernist binary emotions, we need to deconstruct desire by refiguring the relations between family, stranger and the 'Other'. It is dangerous to strive to realise society without discrimination within the sphere of modernist desires in which the desire for discrimination is inseparably tied to the desire for progress and erotic desire. Thus we have to emancipate the 'desire' that so far has been encapsulated into the binary opposition between familiar solidarity and violent discrimination. Beyond the existing horizon of modernist desire we should ceaselessly deconstruct and reform the relations between family/stranger/Other among ourselves.

In the process of reading these writers, one obvious aim of this book has been to analyse and appreciate their literary work as a literary critical study. Furthermore, through introducing the work of these Japanese intellectuals, I have attempted to bring out two points. First, how Japanese thinkers can contribute to the current Euro-American debate about postmodernism, feminism and postcolonialism and second, how Japanese writers can be analysed from a Euro-American viewpoint. I have thus attempted to create a dialogue between Japanese and Euro-American thought. Obviously, the work of Japanese novelists and literary critics is understood differently when it is read in the context of indigenous Japanese studies than when it is read in the context of Euro-American ideas. I have thus attempted to critique Japanese ideas by reading them in terms of western notions but, at the same time, I have also attempted to critique Western notions using Japanese ideas. In so doing, I have not attempted to simply relativise both positions but to deconstruct them. I hope that through this meeting of two distinct 'Others', the boundaries which restrict both Japanese and Western modes of analysis can be challenged and transcended. It is through this 'intercourse with the Other' in Karatani's sense, that we can become conscious of the constraints limiting our understanding. Through such encounters we can become more self-reflexive, more conscious of individual difference and consequently better able to subvert the modernist trend towards a single monolithic culture.

Notes

Introduction

1 Susan J. Napier has traced the collapse of the ideology 'outsiders-are-evil versus insiders-are-good' in the Japanese panic films from *Godzilla* through *Nihon chinbotsu* to *Akira* (Napier 1993).
2 Concerning this issue, see the aforementioned Weber's study (1991: 333–334), and also Habermas 1984–1987 II: 1; and Habermas 1993: vii.
3 Zygmunt Bauman considers that the traditional and emotional heterophobia (resentment of the different) played but an auxiliary role in the initiation and perpetuation of the Holocaust. He says that the possibility of the Holocaust was rooted in certain universal features of modern civilisation (Bauman 1989: 81–82). But, as I will discuss later, heterophobia itself is, in my view, one of the universal features of modernism.
4 Simon Malpas also says: 'There is a tendency to differentiate between postmodernism as an artistic movement and postmodernity as the general social condition that is studied in these disciplines [the humanities such as history, sociology, politics, philosophy and anthropology: F. Murakami]' (Malpas 2001: 3).
5 See also McGuigan 1999: Chapter 6.
6 Being slightly distinct from these fields of study, the concept of globalisation is, as Best and Kellner comment, 'extremely complex and ambiguous' (Best and Kellner 2001: 207). See also Ashcroft *et al.* 1998: 110–114. Although some anticipate that globalisation will bring cultural hybridisation rather than cultural homogeneity (Beynon and Dunkerley 2000: 26–27), or a multi-polar system rather than a unipolar one (Huntington 2000: 3–13), the theorists of globalisation in general approve of the law of the jungle in a borderless world. They regard effectiveness, efficiency, meritocracy and competitiveness as essential elements in a climate of equal opportunity. I share the uneasiness of Doreen Massey that, in spite of its potential, globalisation is similar to the modernist story of progress, and integral to its achievement is the mobilisation of a powerful geographical imagination of the world (Massey 1999: 33–40).
7 In the 1980s and 1990s, while Isozaki Arata and Kurokawa Kisho were the leading figures in postmodern architecture in Japan (Isozaki *et al.* 1985; Isozaki 1991; Kurokawa 1994), Kuma Kengo, an architect of the younger generation declared the end of postmodernism in his book *Guddobai posutomodan: 11 nin no Amerika kenchikuka (Good-bye Post-modern: Eleven American Architects)* (1989).
8 It seems inappropriate to group books about postmodernism in Japanese with postmodern treatments of Japan in English. As Karatani Kōjin points out, and as we will discover later, it is possible to find postmodern ideas even in nineteenth-century Japan (Karatani 1989b: 269). But, as I have mentioned, I do not

separate them and in what follows are listed some of books on Japanese post-modernism published in Japanese.

Posutomodan feminizumu (*Postmodern Feminism*) (Kanai 1989) and *Posutomodan to esunikku* (*Postmodern and Ethnic*) (Okabayashi 1991) were published in the late 1980s and in the early 1990s. They were followed by the publication in the journal *Hihyōkūkan* (*Critical Space*) of a round-table discussion between Asada Akira, Karatani Kōjin and Fredric Jameson which took place in 1991, entitled 'After the Gulf War: The Third Stage of Imperialism and Postmodernism'. It originally appeared in 1992 and was later included in a compilation entitled *Shinpojiumu I* (*Symposium I*), edited by Karatani in 1994. A journal *Studia Semiotica* (*Journal of the Japanese Association for Semiotic Studies*) published its twelfth issue entitled *A Postmodern Turn in Semiotics: Information and Icon* in 1992, which includes papers presented in the workshop 'Postmodern Space of Information' held in 1991 (Nihon kigō gakkai 1992). In the middle to late 1990s some more books on postmodernism appeared in Japan. *Modan to posutomodan: Gendai shakaigaku kara no sekkin* (*The Modern and the Postmodern: Approach from Contemporary Sociology*) introduces Euro-American academic studies on postmodernism in its first and last chapters (Sengoku 1994). A 1996 edition of the journal *Daikōkai* features a reconsideration of postmodernism (*Daikōkai*, no. 10, 1996). Also, some other books, *Posutomodan no rinrigaku* (*Postmodern Ethics*) (Aoki 1997), *Posutomodan no seiji to shūkyō* (*Postmodern Politics and Religion*) (Tsuchiya 1998) and *Posutomodan keieigaku* (*Postmodern Business Administration*) (Enta 2001) appeared. Most recently the journal *Gendai shisō* (*Contemporary Thought*) featured postmodernism in its November 2001 issue entitled 'What was the Postmodern?' ('Posutomodan to wa nan datta noka').

9 Concerning postmodern Japanese literature in general, see Kodama and Inoue 1997.

10 The May 1993 issue of *Eureka*, featured 'Gay Culture' and the November 1996 issue featured 'Queer Readings'. *Imago* featured 'Lesbian' in August 1991 and 'Gay Liberation' in its November 1995 issue. A *Gendai shisō* (*Contemporary Thought*), special issue, featuring 'Lesbian/Gay Studies' appeared in May 1997. Concerning the publication of gay and lesbian studies in Japan, see Vincent *et al.* 1997, the journal *Queer Japan* published from 1999 by Keisō shobō, Fushimi 1997 and Fushimi *et al.* 2000.

11 It originally appeared in the journal *Hihyōkūkan* (*Critical Space*) in October 1996 and was later included in a compilation entitled *Shinpojiumu III* (*Symposium III*), edited by Karatani in 1998.

12 See also Eliade 1954 and Gould 1987: 10–16.

13 After completing this book in 2003 I found Leith Morton's *Modern Japanese Culture: The Insider View.* In Chapter 3 he introduces Yoshimoto Takaaki (Morton 2003).

1　Murakami Haruki's postmodern world

1 For a commentary and criticism of Murakami Haruki's works, see Miyoshi 1991; Rubin J. 1992, 1999, 2003; Iwamoto Yoshio 1993; Matsuoka 1993, 2002; Ellis 1995; Napier 1996; Laughman 1997; Walley 1997; Strecher's three journal articles and two books (1998a, 1998b, 1999, 2002a, 2002b); Fisher 2000; Cassegard 2001 and Kawakami 2002.

2 Concerning the various interpretations of what the sheep symbolises, see Imai 1990: 180–185.

3 The page number of citation from Murakami Haruki's works is, unless otherwise mentioned, or unless there is no English translation, from the English translated version.

4 A military rebellion took place in Tokyo between 26 and 29 February 1936. After killing several key political figures, the rebel junior army officers demanded that the government carry out political reforms to ensure the supremacy of the Emperor Hirohito to whom they declared absolute loyalty. However, faced with the emperor's outraged reaction, the rebels were swiftly suppressed and sentenced to death.

5 See Imai 1990: 180–185.

6 Another attempted *coup d'état* was by young ultra-nationalist and ultra-rightist naval officers on 15 May 1932.

7 Susan J. Napier also points out that the Japanese Empire's pre-war activities in Manchuria and the post-war collusion between government, industry and the right wing underlie the story of *A Wild Sheep Chase*. See Napier 1996: 208–209.

8 Kawamoto Saburō sees in the Rat's final decision to kill the sheep and himself the story of death and rebirth after the corruption of individualism (Kawamoto 1988: 116).

9 In this regard, we can also refer to Inoue Yoshio's interpretation that Murakami Haruki prefers the natural environment in small towns and suburbs to the lack of nature in cities (Inoue 1999: 188).

10 Concerning 'self-reflexive language', see Chapter 4, 'Philosophy of the Other/exteriority'.

11 In actuality, the protagonist 'I' in *The End of the World* decides to live in the woods located between the two worlds.

12 See also Takeda Seiji 1998: 142 and Yoshida Haruo 1997: 81.

13 We will discuss the terminology of universality/generality versus originality/particularity in Chapter 4 as it relates to the concept of singularity.

14 We will discuss this kind of paradox in Chapter 4.

15 Anthony Giddens forms a different understanding of romantic love, by distinguishing it from amour passion. See Giddens 1992: 44.

16 Concerning other definitions of fantasy, see Irwin 1976: 4; Jackson 1981: 13–37 and Napier 1996: 5–11. Napier herself argues, based on Kathryn Hume's definition (Hume 1984: 21), that 'fantasy is any *conscious* departure from consensus reality' (emphasis in the original). The 'departure from consensus reality' pointed out by Hume and Napier also suggests a relation between fantasy and postmodernism. Freudian or Lacanian concepts of fantasy and Yoshimoto Takaaki's concept of *'gensō* (fantasy)' will be dealt with later separately. Concerning the relation between fantasy and postmodernism/feminism, see Walker 1990: 29–30; Attebery 1992: 14–17, 36–37 and Monnet 1996: 407–408.

17 See Rubin, J. 2003: 160–161, endnote 272.

18 Kuroko Kazuo, like the writer, supposes that these six skeletons are Dick North, Gotanda, Rat, Kiki, Mei and the protagonist writer's own old self. His interpretation is that the writer is reborn when he starts a new life with Yumiyoshi (Kuroko 1993: 99–101).

19 Jay Rubin associates this coldness with the coldness of the chicken warehouse in *Pinball, 1973*, as well as the coldness in *The End of the World* (Rubin, J. 2003: 51, 126). In *Pinball, 1973*, when the protagonist 'I' found the pinball machine, three-flipper 'Spaceship', in a warehouse that used to be the cold storage for a chicken farm, it was very cold. If the three-flipper 'Spaceship' is the substitution of dead Naoko, as Kobayashi Masaaki suggests (Kobayashi 1998: 57), this coldness most probably represents the world of the dead. See also Yoshida 1997: 102–103.

20 Murakami Haruki (1995) also mentions that *South of the Border, West of the Sun* is basically a story of a man possessed by a spirit.

21 Concerning this change, see also Yoshida 1997.

22 Concerning the violent action in *The Wind-Up Bird Chronicle*, see Kuritsubo and Tsuge 1999 IV, and regarding the relationship between violence and sexuality, see Strecher 2002b: 53–56.

23 This paragraph is omitted from Jay Rubin's English translation. See Rubin, J. 2003: 273–282.
24 In this regard, Yoshida Haruo's interpretation that Wataya Noboru is the protagonist Okada Toru's alter ego is important in understanding this work. See Yoshida 1997: 189–194. See also Strecher 2002b: 26, 51–52.
25 Besides '*naihei*' (autistic), the similar term '*jiheiteki*' is often used for describing Murakami Haruki's work. Matthew Strecher says that rather than the medical term 'autistic', the meaning of '*jiheiteki*' is closer to the expression 'self-absorbed' or 'self-centred' (Strecher 2002a: 19, 99). I will use the term 'autistic' or 'autism' as indicating the human inclination to retreat from the outer world by means of being enclosed only in familiar relations, and to lose the energy to progress towards the future and foreign places.
26 Kobayashi Masaaki interprets that the well ('*ido*' in Japanese) in Murakami's work is the Freudian term 'id' (Kobayashi 1998: 20–25).
27 Murakami Haruki repeatedly mentions that *Kafka on the Shore* is based on the Greek myth story *Oedipus the King*, but not on the Freudian concept of the Oedipal complex (Murakami 2003: 320, 326). But we can say that Oedipal desire underlies both of them.

2   Yoshimoto Banana's feminine family

1 For a feminist criticism of Yoshimoto Banana's works, see Kanai 1991.
2 The page number of citation from Yoshimoto Banana's works is, unless otherwise mentioned (unless there is no English translation), from the English translated version. In some cases 'J' indicates the Japanese original version, and 'E' the English translation.
3 In the Japanese original version the name of the place where Yuichi is staying is not specified.
4 The theme of incest and kinship is also discussed in Judith Butler's recent book (2000).
5 Concerning Banana's incest theme, see also Heung 2002.
6 René Girard also regards the Oedipal triangle as a model, not of fundamental human desire, but of modern capitalist society which is based on a philosophy of rivalry, progress, evolution, dynamic movement, competition, and fighting (Girard 1977: 190). This idea is supported, if unconsciously, by many modern theorists – Hegel's 'dialectic', Nietzsche's 'will to power', Bergson's '*élan vital*', Marx's 'historical materialism', Sartre's '*projet*' – all suggest that the Oedipal triangle is a fundamental metaphor which explains the structure of modern society.
7 *Kojiki* is considered to be Japan's first literary work and consists of myths, history, songs, legends, genealogies, and so forth. It was compiled in 712 by ï no Yasumaro and translated into English by Donald Philippi in 1969.
8 I refer to René Girard's study in this discussion, too. See Girard 1977.
9 None of the above however should be read as suggesting a fundamental difference between the Western and Japanese myths. For in the Kojiki the Oedipal type of incest is also found in many stories, and the desire for rebirth discerned in Amaterasu is surely not limited to Japan.
   For instance, the Oedipal type of incest is found in the relations between Prince and Princess Sao, and between Prince and Princess Karu, in *Kojiki* Books 2 and 3, respectively. Their incestuous desires are depicted with strong tension and rivalry: the rivalry between Prince Sao and his sister Princess Sao's husband (Emperor Suinin) in the former story and that between Prince Karu and his brother Prince Anaho (the later Emperor Ankō) in the latter. They are narrated

as romantic stories involving erotic desire and power struggles and finally both of the couples kill themselves. Their incestuous desires are fundamentally very similar to the story of Oedipus.

Furthermore, other than Princes and Princesses Sao and Karu, the Oedipal triangle is well attested in classical Japanese culture, too, as can be seen in the triangular relation between father Emperor Kiritsubo, his wife Lady Fujitsubo and Hikaru in *The Tale of Genji*. The rivalry is also found in *The Tale of the Heike* (*Heike monogatari*, c.1219), *The Record of the Great Peace* (*Taiheiki*, 1372), and many other works whose topic is the civil wars in thirteenth- to four-teenth-century Japan.

Also, the desire to be reborn recurs in many literary works. These include: in Japanese fiction Nō theatre of the Muromachi period; *The Biographies of Eight Dogs* (*Nansō Satomi hakkenden*, 1814–1842) of the Edo period; in Western discourse, for example, Christ's resurrection, Nietzsche's 'eternal recurrence', and Marcel Proust's *A la recherche du temps perdu*. An interesting point here is that the incest stories in the *Kojiki* well reflect the transition from the desire for rebirth to that of rivalry which can be observed in various other cultures.

Consequently, as Mircea Eliade points out, there can be found at least two types of desire – triangular and circular – in human culture. The former is directed towards hope, future, rivalry, individuality, and evolution, whereas the latter focuses on the past, the return to the original totality, and nostalgia. Concerning the 'linear progress of history' and 'eternal repetition', see Eliade 1954: 17–21, 73–92, 112–130, 141–162.

10 Further related to this kind of cyclic desire, Wole Soyinka points out the cyclic consciousness of time or cyclic reality which exists in Africa in contrast to the linear conception of time prevalent in the West (Soyinka 1990: 2, 10). Julia Kristeva also remarks on the existence of 'women's time', which essentially retains repetition and eternity, or cycles, gestation, the eternal recurrence of a biological rhythm, and has little to do with masculine linear time (Kristeva 1991: 445). Stephen Jay Gould explains the phrase 'time's arrow' as follows: 'history is an irreversible sequence of unrepeatable events, each moment occupies its own distinct position in a temporal series, and all moments, considered in proper sequence, tell a story of linked events moving in a direction'. He defines 'time's cycle' as 'events (that) have no meaning as distinct episodes with causal impact upon a contingent history' (Gould 1987:11).

11 Eliade considers that people in the past in cyclic time could endure such 'terror of history' as wars, social injustice and massacres, because they accorded the historical event no value in itself. In contrast, modern people living in linear time, as exemplified by the philosophies of Hegel and Marx, endure the terror of history by means of hoping for the future realisation of an ideal society. Finally, Eliade introduces the viewpoint of historicism, which asserts that every historical event finds its full and only meaning in its realisation alone, and poses the question of how the 'terror of history' can be tolerated (Eliade 1954: 141–162). The question can be interpreted in our terms, as the way in which traditional people living in cyclic time can tolerate the terror of history in their trans-historical position by returning back to the original ideal, while modern people living in linear time can endure it by hoping for an ideal future. But how can people like postmodernists who have lost these two positions endure the terror?

12 Eliade says: 'religious valuation of ritual death finally led to conquest of the fear of *real* death, and to belief in the possibility of a purely spiritual survival for the human being' (Eliade 1958:132). For Eliade, initiatory death and rebirth signifies the end of the natural, noncultural man, and passage to a new modality of exis-tence – that of a being 'born to spirit', that is, a being that does not live solely in a immediate reality (Eliade 1958:132).

13 The concept of nostalgia has attracted attention in a postmodern context from Fredric Jameson (1991: 279–296), Kathleen Stewart (1988), Susan Stewart (1984), Bryan S. Turner (1987), and others. Nostalgia in Japan has also been discussed by Treat (1993) and Marilyn Ivy (1995), and in Japan Kamata Tōji (1989, 1991) and Hasumi Shigehiko (1994: 229–234) have also analysed nostalgia in Banana's and Ōe's literary works respectively. Using their analyses as a starting point, in what follows I would like to present a new aspect of nostalgia focusing on its relationship with the Amaterasu circle and also with psychoanalytical concepts.

14 Although the idea of resurrection in the West differs from rebirth in the East, the same nostalgic desire underlies both. This nostalgic desire to recover the past is not limited to fiction alone but occurs in everyday activities such as the purchase of souvenirs which have no value or use other than to satisfy the demand for nostalgia, as Susan Stewart has pointed out (Stewart, S. 1984: 135). Moreover, taking souvenir pictures when travelling is a worldwide phenomenon.

15 The Japanese original expression 'zotto suru hodo natsukashii' (so nostalgic that it makes me shake) (Yoshimoto Banana 1989b: 167 (J)) is translated into English as 'so familiar and so terribly dear to me that it made me shake' (63–64 (E)).

16 One may find here support for Baudrillard's claim that in the postmodern world the boundary between image or simulation and reality implodes, and together with it, the experience and ground of 'the real' disappears. See Baudrillard 1983.

17 See Freud's 'The Dissolution of the Oedipus Complex' and 'Female Sexuality'. And also Lacan 1977b: 287–288.

18 Besides the death drive that desires to go back to the pre-birth stage, and the desire for mastery of the future, there is one more desire for repetition as a result of fantasy, that is the yearning to go back to the pre-castrative stage. As we will see soon, nostalgia's longing ensues typically from the third type of repetition. There must certainly be a delight in the phantasmic repetition. We can find a fantasy yearning repeatedly to see and hear a nostalgic object in many children's games such as the Freudian *fort/da* game, peekaboo, hide-and-seek and the *inai-inai-baa* of Japanese children. And furthermore, as pointed out by Freud in his *Beyond the Pleasure Principle*, children who never tire of asking an adult to repeat the same game or who insist on hearing the same story over and over again are also longing for a nostalgic object. They play these games for the enjoyment they feel when they recognise a nostalgic figure again and again. The desire for repetition must not always be the death drive which leads one to go back before birth by means of killing oneself, or for digesting or mastering mechanisms for the future growth. Refer to Kaja Silverman's study which differentiates the Freudian death drive from other types of repetition which result from unconscious fantasies and lead to mastery (Silverman 1992: 58).

19 Concerning these two types of castration, see also Slavoj Žižek (1994: 201–203).

20 Mircea Eliade sees in the primitives' tendency toward purification, that is, their attempt to return to a state of innocence by periodically confessing their faults, the possibility of their nostalgic desire for the lost paradise of animality, because, as Hegel wrote, only the animal is truly innocent. But in the final analysis, Eliade rejects this idea and, on the contrary, he sees in their nostalgia a desire to attain the image of an ideal humanity enjoying a beatitude and spiritual plenitude forever unrealisable in the present state of 'fallen man' (Eliade 1954: 90–91). Carl Olson in his study of Eliade regards this nostalgia as a nostalgic wish to a return to what Eliade calls cosmic Christianity (Olson, C. 1992: 153). Putting the relationship between ideal humanity and Christianity aside, what Eliade points out here might be similar to humanity in the pre-castrative stage of indiscrimination without power struggle.

From a similar but significantly different point of view, Judith Butler argues that heterosexuality is cultivated through prohibitions of homosexuality, or homosexuality is foreclosed from the start, and the loss of homosexuality creates 'melancholy' (Butler 1990: 57–65; 1997b: 132–140). The difference between her and my points is that I suppose an original stage of fusion in which heterosexual/power-oriented desires and bisexual/incestuous-autistic desires co-exist without being distinguished. I call the desire to return to that position 'nostalgia', whereas Butler supposes homosexuality first, and argues that its loss ensues 'melancholy'.

21 See 'Q & A' in Yoshimoto Banana's Official Website at http://www.yoshimoto-banana.com/index.html (as of June 2004). Also see Awaya and Phillips 1996; Sherif 1999 and Yoshimoto 2002a.

22 Concerning feminism and postmodernism, see also Singer 1992.

23 Against this point, Ann Ferguson argues that Calhoun's insistence is not convincing because gender and sexual outlaws are, for Ferguson, if separable in some points, in some other points overlapping. See Ferguson 2001: 219.

24 Concerning the concept of scapegoat, see Girand 1997.

3 Yoshimoto Takaaki and the subaltern

1 Although Yoshimoto has conducted discussions with other European scholars, his discussion with Foucault is of most interest here. See Yoshimoto T. and Baudrillard 1995 and Yoshimoto T. 1987.

2 Hereafter the *Complete Works of Yoshimoto Takaaki* (*Yoshimoto Takaaki zen chosaku shū*, 1968–1975, Keisō shobō) is abbreviated as (Yoshimoto, volume: page).

3 Maruyama's analytical method can be found in his three widely known and highly regarded books – *Studies in the Intellectual History of Tokugawa Japan* (*Nihon seiji shisō shi kenkyū*; original 1952), *Thought and Behavior in Modern Japanese Politics* (*Gendai seiji no shisō to kōdō*; original 1956) and *Japanese Thought* (*Nihon no shisō*; original 1961).

4 Yoshimoto's article was first published in *Hitotsubashi News* (*Hitotsubashi shinbun*) from 15 January 1962 to 15 February 1963.

5 Concerning the relation between postmodernism and postcolonialism, Ato Quayson's precise summary is useful. See Quayson 2000.

6 The English translation of part of this quotation can also be found in Miyoshi and Harootunian 1989: 269–270.

7 Excerpts from 'An Essay on the Gospel According to Matthew' ('Machiu sho shiron') were published in 1954. The whole piece appeared in 1959 compiled in Yoshimoto's book *The Artistic Resistance and Setback* (*Geijutsu-teki teikō to zasetsu*).

8 I have amended Kenneth G. Henshall's translation. See Tayama 1981: 164.

9 Takamura Kōtarō, while in his twenties, studied sculpture in the USA and Europe from 1906 to 1909. He was one of the elite in the early period of Japan's Westernisation together with Mori Ōgai, Natsume Sōseki, and Nagai Kafū. However, unlike Kafū who secluded himself in artistic decadence during the China–Japan and Pacific Wars, Kōtarō enthusiastically co-operated with the military imperialists and vigorously encouraged the Japanese to fight with Western countries.

10 Ueno Chizuko recalls the excitement with which she first read *A Theory of Collective Fantasy*. She points out two reasons why she considers Yoshimoto's work epoch-making: 1) he revealed that 'nation', 'society' and even 'self' were the product of fantasy, and 2) he introduced the third category (conjugal and sexual fantasy) in between the traditional binary opposition of self and society (Ueno 1986: 2).

11 Later Yoshimoto mentions that the African system is the general basis of human culture from which Asian and European systems develop (Yoshimoto T. 1998a: 80).

12 Though I discuss African and Asian consciousnesses separately, in order to avoid unnecessary confusion, I do not highlight the distinction between them in Yoshimoto's theory. Instead I focus on the difference between European consciousness and African/Asian consciousness.

13 As cultures which construct the self in social context rather than as an individual psychological core, T. Len Holdstock lists as: 'African, Balinese, Cheyenee, Chewong of Malaysia, Chinese, Filipino, Gahuku-Gama of New Guinea, Indian, Inuit (Eskimo), Islamic, Japanese, Javanese, Lohorung of eastern Nepal, Maori, Moroccan, Ojibwa Indian of North America, and the Zapotec of Mexico' (Holdstock 2000: 103).

14 Concerning Yanagita Kunio's methodology, see also Kawada (1993), especially Chapter 5 ('On the Methodology of Yanagita Kunio') and Chapter 6 ('Problems Concerning the Idea of Communality in the Writings of Yanagita') and Chapter 2 of Morton (2003).

15 Orikuchi Shinobu (1887–1953) was a scholar of Japanese literature and folklore. He was also a well-known tanka poet who wrote under the pen name Shaku no Chōkū.

16 Okakura Tenshin (1862–1913) was an art critic, philosopher and one of the founders of Japan's first official art academy, Tokyo Bijutsu Gakkō (now Tokyo University of Fine Arts and Music). He is widely known as the writer of *The Ideals of the East* (1903), *The Awakening of Japan* (1904) and *The Book of Tea* (1906).

17 Nitobe Inazō (1862–1933) was an educator, known for his book *Bushidō: The Soul of Japan* (1899).

18 Suzuki Daisetsu (1870–1966) was a Buddhist philosopher who introduced Zen thought to Western countries in his *Essays in Zen Buddhism* (1927–1934) and other works.

19 See also Introduction, 'Postmodernism, feminism, postcolonialism and Japan'.

20 Yoshimoto uses the word *muishiki* (unconscious), which can be interpreted as meaning 'inherent' or 'intrinsic', because both are beyond the subject's recognition.

21 Karatani Kōjin also mentions the same story from Yanagita Kunio's *Mountain Life* (*Yama no jinsei*). See Karatani 1989a: 248–252.

4   Karatani Kōjin and the intercourse with the other

1 The Naturalists were a group of authors including Kunikida Doppo (1871–1908), Tayama Katai (1871–1930) and Shimazaki Tōson (1872–1943) who were influenced by French Naturalism and believed it was important to write about their own lives just as they were.

2 The term *junshi* is applied to the suicide of a *samurai* for the purpose of following his lord into death. It was considered the ultimate expression of loyalty and gratitude for favours received. The retainers who were allowed to commit *junshi* suicide were honoured by being buried beside their lord and having their families well provided for (from *Kodansha Encyclopedia of Japan*, 1983).

3 We can refer here to Nietzsche's argument against causality compiled in 'Section 8: Against Causalism' in Book Three of *The Will to Power*. Especially the following passage:

> There is no such thing as 'cause'; some cases in which it seems to be given us, and in which we have projected it out of ourselves in order to understand an event, have been shown to be self-deceptions. Our 'understanding of an event' has consisted in our inventing a subject which was made responsible

for something that happens and for how it happens. We have combined our feeling of will, our feeling of 'freedom', our feeling of responsibility and our intention to perform an act, into the concept 'cause': *causa efficiens* and *causa finalis* are fundamentally one.

We believed that an effect was explained when a condition was detected in which the effect was already inherent. In fact, we invent all causes after the schema of the effect: the latter is known to us – Conversely, we are not in a position to predict of any thing what it will 'effect'.

(Nietzsche 1968: 295–296; emphasis in the original)

4 LISP (List Processing) is a computer language that can be used to manipulate symbols and lists rather than numerical data. It is often used in artificial-intelligence applications.

5 More recently Karatani has cited the following passage from Kant's *Critique of Pure Reason* on three separate occasions in his *Researches III* (*Tankyū III*), May 1995 and March 1996, and in his essay 'Death and Nationalism' ('Shi to nashionarizum') (Karatani 1993–1996; 1998). See also Morimura 1998: 59.

Human reason has the peculiar fate in one species of its cognitions that it is burdened with questions which it cannot dismiss, since they are given to it as problems by the nature of reason itself, but which it also cannot answer, since they transcend every capacity of human reason.

(Kant 1997a: 99)

Through repeatedly referring to this quotation from Kant, it would seem that Karatani is still struggling with the problem of self-referential language.

6 See also Young 1990: 12–15.
7 'An ostensive definition' is 'one which points to individual instances: e.g. of *chair* by pointing out one or more individual chairs, or of *cut* by performing the action of cutting' (*Oxford Concise Dictionary of Linguistics*).
8 Concerning NAM, see Karatani ed. 2000b and NAM Students 2001.
9 LETS is originated in LETSystem designed and developed by Michael Linton and Angus Soutar in Canada. See http: //www.gmlets.u-net.com/ (as of June 2004)
10 NAM web site is now closed and Karatani's official web site does not have this document, either (as of June 2004).
11 As well as Yoshimoto Banana, Livia Monnet also points out that the 'other' exists inside oneself (Karatani and Monnet 1998: 19; Monnet 1998: 136).

Bibliography

Abe Kōbō (1967a) *Suna no onna* (*The Woman in the Dunes*), trans. E. Dale Saunders, Tokyo: Tuttle. English original version was published by Knopf in 1964. Japanese original was published by Shinchōsha in 1962.

—— (1967b) *Tanin no kao* (*The Face of Another*), trans. E. Dale Saunders, Tokyo: Tuttle. English original version was published by Knopf in 1966. Japanese original was published by Kōdansha in 1964.

—— (1970) *Moetsukita chizu* (*The Ruined Map*), trans. E. Dale Saunders, Tokyo: Tuttle. English original version was published by Knopf in 1969. Japanese original was published by Shinchōsha in 1967.

Abelove, Henry, Barale, Michèle Aina and Haplerin, David M. (eds) (1993) *Lesbian and Gay Studies Reader*, New York and London: Routledge.

Althusser, Louis (1984) *Essays on Ideology*, London and New York: Verso.

Anderson, Benedict (1983) *Imagined Communities: Reflections on the Origin and Spread of Nationalism*, London and New York: Verso.

Anderson, Perry (1974) *Lineages of the Absolutist State*, London and New York: Verso.

Aoki Katsuhito (1997) *Posutomodan no rinrigaku* (*Postmodern Ethics*), Hiroshima: Keisuisha.

Arens, W. (1986) *The Original Sin: Incest and Its Meaning*, New York and Oxford: Oxford University Press.

Arnason, Johann P. and Sugimoto Yoshio (eds) (1995) *Japanese Encounters with Postmodernity*, London and New York: Kegan Paul International.

Asada Akira (1983) *Kōzō to chikara* (*The Structure and the Power*), Tokyo: Keisō shobō.

Ashcroft, Bill, Griffiths, Gareth, and Tiffin, Helen (1989) *The Empire Writes Back*, London and New York: Routledge.

—— (1995) *The Post-Colonial Studies Reader*, London and New York: Routledge.

—— (1998) *The Key Concepts in Post-Colonial Studies*, London and New York: Routledge.

Attebery, Brian (1992) *Strategies of Fantasy*, Bloomington and Indianapolis: Indiana University Press.

Awaya Nobuko and Phillips, P. David (1996) 'Popular Reading: The Literary World of the Japanese Woman' in Imamura, Anne E (ed.) *Re-Imaging Japanese Women*, Berkeley, Los Angeles and London: University of California Press, 244–270.

Azuma Hiroki (1995) 'Jacques Derrida to Karatani Kōjin' ('Jacques Derrida and Karatani Kōjin') in Sekii Mitsuo (ed.) *Karatani Kōjin*, Tokyo: Shibundō, 71–78.

—— (2000) 'Posutomodan saikō' ('The Postmodern Reconsidered') *Asuteion* (*Asteion*) number 54, cited from Azuma Hiroki's website http://www.hiroki-azuma.com/ (as of February 2002).

—— (2001) *Dōbutsuka suru posutomodan* (*The Animalised Postmodernism*), Tokyo: Kōdansha gendai shinsho.

Bataille, Georges (1986) *Erotism: Death & Sensuality*, trans. Mary Dalwood, San Francisco: City Lights.

Baudrillard, Jean (1983) *Simulations*, New York: Semiotext(e).

—— (1984) 'On Nihilism' *On the Beach*, 6 (Spring).

Bauman, Zygmunt (1989) *Modernity and the Holocaust*, Cambridge, UK: Polity Press.

Beck, Ulrich, Giddens, Anthony and Lash, Scott (1994) *Reflexive Modernization: Politics, Tradition, and Aesthetics in the Modern Social Order*, Cambridge, UK: Polity Press.

Bergson, Henri (1910) *Time and Free Will: An Essay on the Immediate Data of Consciousness*, trans. F. L. Pogson, London: George Allen & Unwin Ltd.

—— (1920) *Creative Evolution*, trans. Arthur Mitchell, London: Macmillan.

Bernier, Bernard (1985) 'Yanagita Kunio's "About Our Ancestors": Is It a Model for an Indigenous Social Science?' in Koschmann, J. Victor, Ōiwa Keibō and Yamashita Shinji (eds) *International Perspectives on Yanagita Kunio and Japanese Folklore Studies*, Cornell University East Asia Papers, number 37, East Asia Program, Ithaca, New York: Cornell University, 65–95.

Bernstein, Richard J. (ed.) (1985) *Habermas and Modernity*, Cambridge, UK: Polity Press.

Bertens, Hans and Fokkema, Douwe (eds) (1997) *International Postmodernism: Theory and Literary Practice*, Amsterdam and Philadelphia: John Benjamins Publishing Company.

Best, Steven and Kellner, Douglas (1991) *Postmodern Theory*, New York: Guilford Press.

—— (2001) *The Postmodern Adventure*, London: Routledge.

Beynon, John and Dunkerley, David (2000) *Globalization: The Reader*, London: Athlone Press.

Bhabha, Homi K. (1994) *The Location of Culture*, London and New York: Routledge.

Boswell, John (1980) *Christianity, Social Tolerance, and Homosexuality*, Chicago and London: University of Chicago Press.

Brah, Avtar, Hickman, Mary J. and Mac an Ghaill, Máirtín (eds) (1999) *Global Futures: Migration, Environment, and Globalizatioon*, Basingstoke, Hampshire: Macmillan; New York: St Martin's Press.

Bronfen, Elisabeth and Kavka, Misha (eds) (2001) *Feminist Consequences: Theory for the New Century*, New York: Columbia University Press.

Brodzki, Bella and Schenck, Celeste (eds) (1988) *Life/Lines: Theorizing Women's Autobiography*, Ithaca and London: Cornell University Press.

Burgin, Victor, Donald, James and Kaplan, Cora (eds) (1986) *Formations of Fantasy*, London and New York: Methuen.

Buruma, Ian (1996) 'Becoming Japanese' *The New Yorker*, special fiction issue, December 23 and 30.

Butler, Judith (1987) *Subjects of Desire: Hegelian Reflections in Twentieth-Century France*, New York: Columbia University Press.

—— (1990) *Gender Trouble: Feminism and the Subversion of Identity*, New York and London: Routledge.

—— (1993) *Bodies That Matter: On the Discursive Limits of 'Sex'*, New York and London: Routledge.

—— (1997a) *Excitable Speech: A Politics of the Performative*, New York and London: Routledge.

—— (1997b) *Psychic Life of Power: Theories in Subjection*, Stanford: Stanford University Press.

—— (2000) *Antigone's Claim: Kinship between Life and Death*, New York: Columbia University Press.

—— (2001) 'The End of Sexual Difference?' in Bronfen, Elisabeth and Kavka, Misha (eds) *Feminist Consequences: Theory for the New Century*, New York: Columbia University Press, 414–434.

Butler, Judith and Scott, Joan W. (eds) (1992) *Feminists Theorize the Political*, New York and London: Routledge.

Calhoun, Cheshire (2000) *Feminism, the Family, and the Politics of the Closet: Lesbian and Gay Displacement*, Oxford and New York: Oxford University Press.

Cassegard, Carl (2001) 'Murakami Haruki and the Naturalization of Modernity' *International Journal of Japanese Sociology*, vol. 10: 80–92.

Cornell, Drucilla (1992a) *The Philosophy of the Limit*, New York and London: Routledge.

—— (1992b) 'Gender, Sex and Equivalent Rights' in Butler, Judith and Scott, Joan W. (eds) *Feminists Theorize the Political*, New York and London: Routledge, 280–296.

Deleuze, Gilles and Guattari, Félix (1984) *Anti-Oedipus*, trans. Robert Hurley, Mark Seem, and Helen R. Lane, London: Athlone Press.

—— (1988) *A Thousands Plateaus*, trans. Brian Massumi, London: Athlone Press.

Denoon, Donald *et al.* (ed.) (1996) *Multicultural Japan: Palaeolithic to Postmodern*, Cambridge, UK, New York and Melbourne: Cambridge University Press.

Diamonstein, Barbaralee (1980) *American Architecture Now*, New York: Rizzoli.

Dreyfus, Hubert L. and Rabinow, Paul (1983) *Michel Foucault: Beyond Structuralism and Hermeneutics,* 2nd edn with an afterword by and an interview with Michel Foucault, Chicago: University of Chicago Press.

Eagleton, Terry (1996) *The Illusions of Postmodernism*, Oxford, UK and Malden, MA: Blackwell.

Egusa Mitsuko and Urushida Kazuyo (eds) (1992) *Onna ga yomu Nihon kindai bungaku: Feminizumu hihyō no kokoromi* (*Readings by Women of Modern Japanese Literature: An Attempt at Feminist Critique*), Tokyo: Shin'yōsha.

Ehara Yumiko (1988) *Feminizumu to kenryokusayō (shinsōban)* (*Feminism and Power Function: A New Binding Version*), Tokyo: Keisō shobō.

—— (2001) *Jendā chitsujo* (*Gender Order*), Tokyo: Keisō shobō.

Eisenberg, Nancy and Strayer, Janet (eds) (1987) *Empathy and its Development*, Cambridge, UK, New York and Melbourne: Cambridge University Press.

Ekpo, Denis (1995) 'Towards a Post-Africanism: Contemporary African Thought and Postmodernism' *Textual Practice*, 9 (1): 121–135.

Eliade, Mircea (1954) *The Myth of the Eternal Return or, Cosmos and History*, trans. Willard R. Trask, Princeton, NJ: Princeton University Press.

—— (1958) *Birth and Rebirth: The Religious Meanings of Initiation in Human Culture*, trans. Willard R. Trask, New York: Harper and Brothers Publishers.

Eliot, T. S. (1976) *Selected Essays*, London: Faber and Faber.

Ellis, Toshiko (1995) 'Literature: Questioning Modernism and Postmodernism in Japanese Literature' in Arnason, Johann P. and Sugimoto Yoshio (eds) *Japanese Encounters with Postmodernity*, London and New York: Kegan Paul International, 133–153.

Enta Yūshi (2001) *Posutomodan keieigaku* (*Postmodern Business Administration*), Tokyo: Bunshindō.

Feferman, Solomon (1986) 'Gödel's life and work' in Gödel, Kurt *Collected Works*, 3 vols, Oxford: Clarendon Press; New York: Oxford University Press, vol. I: 1–36.

Ferguson, Ann (2001) 'Cheshire Calhoun's Project of Separating Lesbian Theory from Feminist Theory' *Hypatta*, 13 (1) (Winter).

Fisher, Susan (2000) 'An Allegory of Return: Murakami Haruki's *The Wind-Up Bird Chronicle*' *Comparative Literature Studies*, 37 (2): 155–170.

Fixico, Donald L. (1996) 'The Struggle for Our Homes: Indian and White Values and Tribal Lands' in Weaver, Jace (ed.) *Defending Mother Earth: Native American Perspectives on Environmental Justice*, Maryknoll, New York: Orbis Books, 29–46.

—— (1998) *The Invasion of Indian Country in the Twentieth Century: American Capitalism and Tribal Natural Resources*, Niwot, CO: University Press of Colorado.

Foucault, Michel (1978–1986) *The History of Sexuality*, 3 vols, London, New York, Ringwood, Toronto and Auckland: Penguin.

—— (1983) 'Why Study Power: The Question of the Subject' in Dreyfus, Hubert L. and Rabinow, Paul *Michel Foucault: Beyond Structuralism and Hermeneutics*, Chicago: University of Chicago Press, 208–216.

—— (1984) *The Foucault Reader*, ed. Paul Rabinow, London, New York, Ringwood, Toronto and Auckland: Penguin.

—— (1994) *The Order of Things: An Archaeology of the Human Sciences*, New York: Vintage Book. Original English version was published by Random House in 1970.

Freud, Sigmund (1964) *The Standard Edition of the Complete Psychological Works of Sigmund Freud*, vol. XXIII, London: Hogarth Press.

—— (1991) *The Penguin Freud Library*, vol. 11, London, New York, Ringwood, Toronto and Auckland: Penguin.

Frye, Northrop (1976) *The Secular Scripture*, Cambridge, MA and London: Harvard University Press.

Fukami Haruka (1990) *Murakami Haruki no uta* (*Murakami Haruki's Song*), Tokyo: Seikyūsha.

Furuhashi Nobuyoshi (1990) *Yoshimoto Banana to Tawara Machi* (*Yoshimoto Banana and Tawara Machi*), Tokyo: Chikuma shobō.

Fushimi Noriaki (1997) *<Sei> no misuterī;* (*Mystery of <Sex>*), Tokyo: Kōdansha gendai shinsho.

Fushimi Noriaki et al. (2000) *Sei no rinrigaku* (*Ethics on Sex*), Tokyo: Asahi shinbunsha.

Futabatei Shimei (1965) *Japan's First Modern Nobel: Ukigumo of Futabatei Shimei*, trans., Marleigh Grayer Ryan, New York: Columbia University Press.

Garciadiego, Alejandro R. (1992) *Bertrand Russell and the Origins of the Set-theoretic 'Paradoxes'*, Basel, Boston and Berlin: Birkhäuser Verlag.

Garrison, Deborah (1993) 'Day-O!' *The New Yorker*, 25 January.

Gaylin, Willard (1986) *Rediscovering Love*, New York: Viking.

Giddens, Anthony (1990) *The Consequences of Modernity*, Stanford: Stanford University Press.

—— (1991) *Modernity and Self-Identity: Self and Society in the Late Modern Age*, Stanford: Stanford University Press.

—— (1992) *The Transformation of Intimacy: Sexuality, Love and Eroticism in Modern Societies*, Stanford: Stanford University Press.

Girard, René (1977) *Violence and the Sacred*, trans. Patrick Gregory, Baltimore: Johns Hopkins University Press.

Gödel, Kurt (1986–1995) *Collected Works*, 3 vols, ed. Solomon Feferman et al., Oxford: Clarendon Press; New York: Oxford University Press.

Goldberg, David Theo (2000) 'Heterogeneity and Hybridity: Colonial Legacy, Post-colonial Heresy' in Schwarz, Henry and Ray, Sangeeta (eds) *A Companion to Postcolonial Studies*, Malden, MA and Oxford: Blackwell, 72–86.

—— (ed.) (1994) *Multiculturalism: A Critical Reader*, Oxford, UK and Cambridge, MA: Blackwell.

Gould, Stephen Jay (1987) *Time's Arrow, Time's Cycle: Myth and Metaphor in the Discovery of Geological Time*, Cambridge, MA and London, England: Harvard University Press.

Guha, Ranajit (ed.) (1982) *Subaltern Studies I: Writings of South Asian History and Society*, Delhi: Oxford University Press.

Habermas, Jürgen (1984–1987) *The Theory of Communicative Action*, trans. Thomas McCarthy, Cambridge, UK: Polity Press.

—— (1993) *The Philosophical Discourse of Modernity*, trans. Frederick G. Lawrence, Cambridge, MA: MIT Press.

Hakutani Yoshinobu (ed.) (2002) *Postmodernity and Cross-Culturalism*, Madison, NJ: Fairleigh Dickinson University Press; London: Associated University Press.

Hall, Stuart (1996) 'Who Needs Identity?' in Hall, Stuart and Du Gay, Paul, (eds) (1996) *Questions of Cultural Identity*, London, Thousand Oaks and New Delhi: Sage Publications, 1–17.

Hall, Stuart and Du Gay, Paul, (eds) (1996) *Questions of Cultural Identity*, London, Thousand Oaks and New Delhi: Sage Publications.

Halperin, David, M. (1995) *Saint Foucault: Towards a Gay Hagiography*, New York and Oxford: Oxford University Press.

Harvey, David (1989) *The Condition of Postmodernity*, Cambridge, MA and Oxford, UK: Blackwell.

Hastings, James (ed.) (1909) *Encyclopædia of Religion and Ethics*, vol. 2, Edinburgh: T. & T. Clark.

Hasegawa Izumi (ed.) (1991) *Josei sakka no shinryū* (*A New Current of Women Writers*), Tokyo: Shibundō.

Hasumi Shigehiko (1994) *Shōsetsu kara tōku hanarete* (*Far from the Novel*), Tokyo: Kawade bunko. Originally appeared in the journal *Kaien*, March 1987–September 1988, and was published as a hardcover book by Nihonbungeisha in 1989.

Hegel, G. W. Friedrich (1900) *The Philosophy of History*, trans. J. Sibree, New York: Colonial Press.

Heung, Jimmy (2002) 'Yoshimoto Banana *N.P.* ni okeru kinshin sōkan' ('Incest in Yoshimoto Banana's *N.P.*') *Nihon gakkan* (*Japanese Studies*), Society of Japanese Language Education, Hong Kong, number 6, 96–112.

Hirakawa Sukehiro (1976) *Wakon yōsai no keifu* (*Genealogy of Wakon Yōsai*), Tokyo: Kawade shobō.

Hirsch, Marianne and Keller, Evelyn Fox (eds) (1990) *Conflicts in Feminism*, New York and London: Routledge.

Holdstock, T. Len (2000) *Re-Examining Psychology: Critical Perspectives and African Insights*, London and Philadelphia: Routledge.

Horkheimer, Max and Adorno, Theodor W. (1973) *Dialectic of Enlightenment*, trans. John Cumming, London: Allen Lane.

Hume, Kathryn (1984) *Fantasy and Mimesis: Responses to Reality in Western Literature*, New York and London: Methuen.

Huntington, Samuel P. (2000) 'Culture, Power, and Democracy' in Plattner, Marc F. and Smolar Aleksander (eds) *Globalization, Power, and Democracy*, Baltimore and London: Johns Hopkins University Press, 3–13.

Huyssen, Andreas (1990) 'Mapping the Postmodern' in Nicholson, Linda J. (ed.) *Feminism/Postmodernism*, New York and London: Routledge. Originally published in *New German Critique*, vol. 33, Fall 1984.

Ikegami Yoshihiko (ed.) (1998) *Gendai shisō rinji zōkan gō: Sōtokushū Karatani Kōjin* (*An Extra Issue of Contemporary Thought: A Special Edition for Karatani Kōjin*), 26 (9) July, Tokyo: Seidosha.

Imai Kiyoto (1990) *Murakami Haruki – Off no kankaku* (*Murakami Haruki: A Sense of Switching Off*), Tokyo: Kokken shuppan.

—— (1999) '*Murakami Haruki ron* (A Study of Murakami Haruki)' in Kuritsubo Yoshiki and Tsuge Teruhiko (eds) *Murakami Haruki sutadeizu* (*Murakami Haruki Studies*), Tokyo: Wakakusa shobō,V: 99–123. Originally published *Kokubungaku kaishaku to kanshō bessatsu*, January 1995.

Imamura, Anne E (ed.) (1996) *Re-Imaging Japanese Women*, Berkeley, Los Angeles and London: University of California Press.

Inoue Teruko, Ueno Chizuko and Ehara Yumiko (eds) (1994–1995) *Nihon no feminizumu* (*Feminism in Japan*), 7 vols and 1 additional vol., Tokyo: Iwanami.

Inoue Yoshio (1999) *Murakami Haruki to Nihon no 'kioku'* (*Murakami Haruki and Japan's 'Memory'*), Tokyo: Shinchōsha.

Irwin, William Robert (1976) *The Game of the Impossible: A Rhetoric of Fantasy*, Urbana, Chicago and London: University of Illinois Press.

Isoda Kōichi (1990) '"Machiu sho shiron" no mondai (zoku) ('The Problems of "An Essay on the Gospel According to Matthew": Continued') in *Isoda Kōichi chosaku shū* (*Collected Works of Isoda Kōichi*), vol. 2, Tokyo: Ozawa shoten.

Isozaki Arata (1991) *Arata Isozaki*, criticism by Kenneth Frampton, ed. and photographed by Yukio Futagawa, Tokyo: A.D.A. Edita.

Isozaki Arata *et al* (1985) *Posuto-modan no jidai to kenchiku* (*Postmodern Age and its Architecture*), Tokyo: Kashima shuppan kai.

Ivy, Marilyn (1995) *Discourses of the Vanishing: Modernity, Phantasm, Japan*, Chicago and London: University of Chicago Press.

Iwabuchi Hiroko, Kitada Sachie and Kōra Rumiko (eds) (1995) *Feminizumu hihyō e no shōtai: Kindai josei bungaku o yomu* (*Invitation for Feminist Criticism: Reading Modern Female Literature*), Tokyo: Gakugei shorin.

Iwamoto Yoshio (1993) 'A Voice of Postmodern Japan: Haruki Murakami' *World Literature Today*, 67 (2).

Iwamoto Yoshiteru (1992) *Yanagita minzokugaku to tennōsei* (*The Yanagita Folklore and the Emperor System*), Tokyo: Yoshikawa kōbunkan.

Izenberg, Gerald N. (1992) *Impossible Individuality*, Princeton, NJ and Oxford: Princeton University Press.

Jackson, Rosemary (1981) *Fantasy: The Literature of Subversion*, London and New York: Methuen.

Jameson, Fredric (1981) *The Political Unconscious*, Ithaca, New York: Cornell University Press.
—— (1991) *Postmodernism, Or, The Cultural Logic Of Late Capitalism*, Durham: Duke University Press.
—— (1998) *The Cultural Turn: Selected Writings on the Postmodern 1983–1998*, London and New York: Verso.
Jencks, Charles (1988) *Architecture Today*, New York: Harry N. Abrams, Inc..
Kamata Tōji (1989) 'Kazoku no shōzō: *Kitchin*' ('A Portrait of the Family: *Kitchen*') in *Shūkan dokushojin* (*Weekly Dokushojin*), June 5. The article was later compiled in Kamata Tōji *Oi to shi no fōkuroa* (*The Folklore of the Aging and Death*), Tokyo: Shin'yōsha, 1990, 395–402.
—— (1990) *Oi to shi no fōkuroa* (*The Folklore of the Aging and Death*), Tokyo: Shin'yōsha.
—— (1991) '"Atogaki" to "natsukashisa" ("Afterword" and "Nostalgia"') in Hasegawa Izumi (ed.) *Josei sakka no shinryū* (*A New Current of Women Writers*), Tokyo: Shibundō, 278–290.
Kanai Yoshiko (1989) *Posutomodan feminizumu* (*Postmodern Feminism*), Tokyo: Keisō shobō.
—— (1991) 'Feminizumu no me de "Banana genshō" o yomeba ('If We Read "Banana Phenomenon" From the Feminist Viewpoint') in Hasegawa Izumi (ed.) *Josei sakka no shinryū* (*A New Current of Women Writers*), Tokyo: Shibundō, 265–277.
Kant, Immanuel (1997a) *Critique of Pure Reason*, trans. and ed. Paul Guyer, Cambridge, New York and Melbourne: Cambridge University Press.
—— (1997b) *Critique of Practical Reason*, trans. and ed. Mary Gregor, Cambridge, New York and Melbourne: Cambridge University Press.
Kanth, Rajani Kannepalli (1997) *Against Economics: Rethinking Political Economy*, Aldershot, Hants and Brookfield, VT: Ashgate.
Karatani Kōjin (1979a) *Ifu suru ningen (shinsōban)* (*Man Who Has a Feeling of Awe: New Version*), Tokyo: Tōjusha.
—— (1979b) *Han bungaku ron* (*Anti-Literature Theory*), Tokyo: Tōjusha.
—— (1980) *Nihon kindai bungaku no kigen*, Tokyo: Kōdansha. English translation *Origins of Modern Japanese Literature* (1993) trans. Brett de Bary et al., Durham and London: Duke University Press.
—— (1985a) *Hihyō to posutomodan* (*Criticism and Postmodernism*), Tokyo: Fukutake.
—— (1985b) *Marx sono kanōsei no chūshin* (*Marx: The Centre of His Possibilities*), Tokyo: Kōdansha bunko.
—— (1987a) *Daiarōgu I* (*Dialogue I*), Tokyo: Dai san bunmeisha.
—— (1987b) *Daiarōgu III* (*Dialogue III*), Tokyo: Dai san bunmeisha.
—— (1988) *Naisei to sokō* (*Introspection and Retrospection*), Tokyo: Kōdansha gakujutsu bunko.
—— (1989a) *Imi to iu yamai* (*Disease Called Meaning*), Tokyo: Kōdansha bungei bunko.
—— (1989b) 'One Spirit, Two Nineteenth Centuries' in Miyoshi Masao and Harootunian, H. D. (eds) *Postmodernism and Japan*, Durham and London: Duke University Press.
—— (1990) *Daiarōgu II* (*Dialogue II*), Tokyo: Dai san bunmeisha.
—— (1991) *Daiarōgu IV* (*Dialogue IV*), Tokyo: Dai san bunmeisha.

—— (1992a) *Sōseki ron shūsei* (*Collected Essays on Sōseki*), Tokyo: Dai san bunmeisha.

—— (1992b) *Tankyū I* (*Researches I*), Tokyo: Kōdansha gakujutsu bunko.

—— (1993a) *Kotoba to higeki* (*Words and Tragedy*), Tokyo: Kōdansha gakujutsu bunko.

—— (1993b) *Hyūmoa to shite no yuibutsuron* (*Materialism as Humour*), Tokyo: Chikuma shobō.

—— (1993c) *Origins of Modern Japanese Literature*, trans. Brett de Bary et al., Durham and London: Duke University Press. Original Japanese version *Nihon kindai bungaku no kigen* (1980), Tokyo: Kōdansha.

—— (1993–1996) *Tankyū III* (*Researches III*), published intermittently in literary journal *Gunzō* from the January 1993 issue to the September 1996 issue.

—— (1994) *Tankyū II* (*Researches II*), Tokyo: Kōdansha gakujutsu bunko.

—— (1995a) *Shūen o megutte* (*On the End*), Tokyo: Kōdansha gakujutsu bunko.

—— (1995b) *Architecture as Metaphor: Language, Number, Money*, trans. Sabu Kohso, ed. Michael Speaks, Cambridge, MA: MIT Press.

—— (1998a) 'Shi to nashonarizumu' ('Death and Nationalism') *Hihyōkūkan* (*Critical Space*), 2 (16) Tokyo: Ōta shuppan.

—— (2000) *Rinri 21* (*Ethics 21*), Tokyo: Heibonsha.

—— (2001) *Toransukuritēku – Kant to Marx*, Tokyo: Hihyōkūkan. English translation *Transcritique: On Kant and Marx* (2003), trans. Sabu Kohso, Cambridge, MA and London: MIT Press.

—— (2002a) 'Irefuda to kujibiki' ('Voting and Lottery') *Bungakukai*, January and February issues, Tokyo: Bungei shunjūsha.

—— (2002b) *Nihon seishin bunseki* (*Japanese Psychoanalysis/Analysis of Japanese Psychology*), Tokyo: Bungei shunjūsha.

—— (2003) *Transcritique: On Kant and Marx*, trans. Sabu Kohso, Cambridge, MA and London: MIT Press. Original Japanese version *Toransukuritēku – Kant to Marx* (2001), Tokyo: Hihyōkūkan.

Karatani Kōjin (ed.) (1989) *Shinpojiumu* (*Symposium*), Tokyo: Shichōsha.

—— (1994) *Shinpojiumu I* (*Symposium I*), Tokyo: Ōta shuppan.

—— (1998) *Shinpojiumu III* (*Symposium III*), Tokyo: Ōta shuppan.

—— (2000a) *Kanōnaru komyunizumu* (*Possible Communism*), Tokyo: Ōta shuppan.

—— (2000b) *Genri* (*Principle*), Tokyo: Ōta shuppan.

Karatani Kōjin and Hasumi Shigehiko (1988) *Tōsō no echika* (*Ethica of Struggle*), Tokyo: Kawade shobō shinsha.

Karatani Kōjin and Monnet, Livia (1998) 'Mirai to shite no tasha' ('The Other as the Future') in Ikegami Yoshihiko (ed.) *Gendai shisō rinji zōkan gō: Sōtokushū Karatani Kōjin* (*An Extra Issue of Contemporary Thought: A Special Edition for Karatani Kōjin*), 26 (9) July, Tokyo: Seidosha, 8–21.

Kasai Kiyoshi (1999) 'Toshi kankaku to iu inpei – Murakami Haruki' ('Something Hidden Behind Urbanised Sensibility') in Kuritsubo Yoshiki and Tsuge Teruhiko (eds) *Murakami Haruki sutadeizu* (*Murakami Haruki Studies*), Tokyo: Wakakusa shobō, I: 207–233. Originally published in *Gensō bungaku*, Autumn 1987.

Katō Kōichi (1983) 'Shisha tachi no okurimono – Murakami Haruki ron' ('The Gift from the Dead: A Study of Murakami Haruki') *Gunzō*, August, Tokyo: Kōdansha, 202–212.

—— (1999) 'Ishō no mori o aruku – Murakami Haruki ron' ('Walking in the Wood of Different Phenomenon: A Study of Murakami Haruki') in Kuritsubo Yoshiki and Tsuge Teruhiko (eds) *Murakami Haruki sutadeizu* (*Murakami Haruki Studies*), Tokyo: Wakakusa shobō, III: 108–133.

Katō Norihiro (1988) '"Masaka" to "yareyare" ("Masaka" and "Yareyare"') *Gunzō*, July, Tokyo: Kōdansha, 104–128.

Katō Norihiro (ed.) (1996) *Murakami Haruki Yellow Page*, Tokyo: Kōchi shuppansha.

Katō Norihiro et al. (1997) *Gunzō Nihon no sakka 26: Murakami Haruki*, Tokyo: Shōgakukan.

Kauffman, Linda S. (ed.) (1993) *American Feminist Thought at Century's End: A Reader,* Cambridge, MA and Oxford, UK: Blackwell.

Kawada Minoru (1993) *The Origin of Ethnography in Japan: Yanagita Kunio and His Times*, London and New York: Kegan Paul International.

Kawakami Chiyoko (2002) 'The Unfinished Cartography: Murakami Haruki and the Postmodern Cognitive Map' *Monumenta Nipponica*, 57 (3).

Kawamoto Saburō (1988) *Toshi no kanjusei* (*The Sensibilities of Metropolis*), Tokyo: Chikuma bunko.

Kearney, Michael (1984) *World View*, Novato, CA: Chandler & Sharp Publishers.

Kellner, Douglas (1989) *Jean Baudrillard: From Marxism to Postmodernism and Beyond*, Cambridge, UK: Polity Press.

Kimata Satoshi (1995) 'Murakami Haruki ni shōjita aru "rinri"' ('A Certain "Ethics" Appearing in Murakami Haruki') *Shūkan dokushojin* (*Weekly Dokushojin*), December 22.

Kimata Satoshi (ed.) (1998) *Murakami Haruki: Nihon bungaku kenkyū ronbun shūsei* (*Murakami Haruki: Collection of Research Papers on Japanese Literature*), vol. 46, Tokyo: Wakakusa shobō.

Kitada Sachie (1991) 'Feminizumu bungaku hihyō no "genzai" (Nihon-hen) ('"The Present Time" of Feminist Literary Criticism (Japan)') in Mizuta Noriko (ed.) (1991) *New Feminism Review*, Tokyo: Gakuyoshobo. Expanded and revised version is in Kitada Sachie, 'Nihon no feminizumu bungaku hihyō no "genzai"' ("The Present Time" of Feminist Literary Criticism in Japan') *Nichi-bei josei jānaru* (*U.S.-Japan Women's Journal*), number 16, May 1994, 41–61. English translation of expanded and revised version is in Kitada Sachie, 'Contemporary Japanese Feminist Literary Criticism', trans. Miya E. M. Lippit, *U.S.-Japan Women's Journal*, English Supplement, number 7, 1994, 72–97.

Kobayashi Masaaki (1995) '"Kokkyō no minami, taiyō no nishi" ron' ('On *South of the Border, West of the Sun*') *Kokubungaku*, 40 (4) March, Tokyo: Gakutōsha.

—— (1998) *Murakami Haruki: Tō to umi no kanata ni* (*Murakami Haruki: Beyond the Tower and the Sea*), Tokyo: Shinwasha.

Kodama Sanehide and Inoue Ken (1997) 'Postmodernism in Japan' in Bertens, Hans and Fokkema, Douwe (eds) *International Postmodernism: Theory and Literary Practice*, Amsterdam and Philadelphia: John Benjamins Publishing Company, 511–515.

Kodansha (1983) *Kodansha Encyclopedia of Japan* (Tokyo: Kodansha)

Kohama Itsuo (1999) *Yoshimoto Takaaki*, Tokyo: Chikuma shobō.

Komashaku Kimi (1984) *Majo no ronri – Zōho kaitei ban* (*The Witches' Logic: Enlarged and Revised Version*), Tokyo: Fuji shuppan. The original version was published by Ebona shuppan in 1978.

—— (1987) *Sōseki to iu hito* (*A Man Called Sōseki*), Tokyo: Shisō no kagaku sha.

—— (1991) *Murasaki Shikibu no messēji* (*Murasaki Shikibu's Message*), Tokyo: Asahi shinbunsha.

—— (1992) *Takamura Kōtarō no feminizumu* (*Feminism of Takamura Kōtarō*), Tokyo: Asahi bunko. The original version was published by Kōdansha in 1980.

Komori Yōichi (2001) *Posutokoroniaru* (*Postcolonial*), Tokyo: Iwanami.

Koschmann, J. Victor, Ōiwa Keibō and Yamashita Shinji (eds) (1985) *International Perspectives on Yanagita Kunio and Japanese Folklore Studies*, Cornell University East Asia Papers, number 37, East Asia Program, Ithaca, New York: Cornell University.

Kripke, Saul (1972) *Naming and Necessity*, Cambridge, MA: Harvard University Press.

Kristeva, Julia (1991) 'Women's Time' in Warhol, Robyn R. and Herndl, Diane Price (eds) *Feminisms: An Anthology of Literary Theory and Criticism*, New Brunswick, NJ: Rutgers University Press. Originally published in *Sings* 7 (1) (1981).

Kuma Kengo (1989) *Guddobai posutomodan: 11 nin no Amerika kenchikuka* (*Goodbye Post-Modern: Eleven American Architects*), Tokyo: Kashima shuppan kai.

Kuritsubo Yoshiki and Tsuge Teruhiko (eds) (1999) *Murakami Haruki sutadeizu* (*Murakami Haruki Studies*), 5 vols, Tokyo: Wakakusa shobō.

Kurokawa Kisho (1994) *The Philosophy of Symbiosis*, trans. Jeffrey Hunter, London: Academy Editions.

Kuroko Kazuo (1993) *Murakami Haruki: Za rosuto wārudo* (*Murakami Haruki: The Lost World*), Tokyo: Dai san shokan.

Kurosawa Ariko (1990) 'Yume no kitchin' ('A Dreamy Kitchen') in Ueno Chizuko (ed.) *New Feminism Review*, vol. 1, Tokyo: Gakuyoshobo, 134–151.

Lacan, Jacques (1977a) *The Four Fundamental Concepts of Psycho-Analysis*, ed. Jacques-Alain Miller, trans. Alan Sheridan, London: Hogarth Press.

—— (1977b) *Écrits*, trans. Alan Sheridan, London: Tavistock.

Laplanche, Jean and Pontalis, Jean-Bertrand (1973) *The Language of Psycho-Analysis*, trans. Donald Nicholson-Smith, New York: W. W. Norton & Company. Inc.

—— (1986) 'Fantasy and the Origins of Sexuality' in Burgin, Victor, Donald, James and Kaplan, Cora (eds) *Formations of Fantasy*, London and New York: Methuen..

Laughman, Celeste (1997) 'No place I was meant to be: Contemporary Japan in the short fiction of Haruki Murakami' *World Literature Today*, 71 (1), Winter. The article was later compiled in Hakutani Yoshinobu (ed.) (2002) *Postmodernity and Cross-Culturalism*, Madison, NJ: Fairleigh Dickinson University Press; London: Associated University Press, 17–30.

Lenin, V. I. (1964) *V. I. Lenin: Collected Works*, vol. 21 (August 1914-December 1915), Moscow: Progress Publisher.

Li Jun (1996) *Chinese Civilization in the Making, 1766–221 BC*, London: Macmillan; New York: St Martin's Press.

Lyotard, Jean-François (1979) *The Postmodern Condition*, trans. Geoff Bennington and Brian Massumi, Minneapolis: University of Minnesota Press.

—— (1985) *Just Gaming*, trans. Wlad Godzich, Minneapolis: University of Minnesota Press.

Malinowski, Bronislaw (1961) *Sex and Repression in Savage Society*, London: Routledge & Kegan Paul.

Malpas, Simon (ed.) (2001) *Postmodern Debates*, Basingstoke, Hampshire and New York: Palgrave.

Marder, Tod A. (ed.) (1985) *The Critical Edge*, Cambridge, MA and London, UK: MIT Press.

Martin, Biddy (1988) 'Lesbian Identity and Autobiographical Difference[s]' in Brodzki, Bella and Schenck, Celeste (eds) *Life/Lines: Theorizing Women's Autobiography*, Ithaca and London: Cornell University Press, 77–103. The chapter is also compiled in Abelove, Henry, Barale, Michèle Aina and Haplerin, David M. (eds) *Lesbian and Gay Studies Reader*, New York and London: Routledge, 274–293.

Martin, L. Robert (ed.) (1984) *Recent Essays on Truth and the Liar Paradox*, Oxford: Clarendon Press; New York: Oxford University Press.

Maruyama Keizaburō (1981) *Soshūru no shisō* (*The Thought of Saussure*), Tokyo: Iwanami.

Maruyama Masao (1960) '8.15 to 5.19' ('15 August and 19 May') *Chūō kōron*, August, 44–54.

—— (1961) *Nihon no shisō* (*Japanese Thought*), Tokyo: Iwanami shinsho.

—— (1974) *Studies in the Intellectual History of Tokugawa Japan*, trans. Mikiso Hane, Princeton, NJ: Princeton University Press; Tokyo: University of Tokyo Press. Japanese original *Nihon seiji shisō shi kenkyū* (1952), Tokyo: University of Tokyo Press.

—— (1979) *Thought and Behavior in Modern Japanese Politics*, ed. Ivan Morris, Tokyo, Oxford and New York: Oxford University Press. Japanese original *Gendai seiji no shisō to kōdō* (1956), Tokyo: Miraisha.

Marx, Karl (1970) *A Contribution to the Critique of Political Economy*, with an introduction by Maurice Dobb, trans. S. W. Ryazanskaya, ed. Maurice Dobb, New York: International Publishers.

—— (1975–) *Karl Marx, Frederick Engels Collected Works*, London: Lawrence & Wishart.

—— (1990–1992) *Capital*, 3 vols, London, New York, Ringwood, Toronto and Auckland: Penguin.

Massey, Doreen (1999) 'Imagining Globalization: Power-Geometries of Time–Space' in Brah, Avtar, Hickman, Mary J. and Mac an Ghaill, Máirtín (eds) *Global Futures: Migration, Environment, and Globalizatioon*, Basingstoke, Hampshire: Macmillan; New York: St Martin's Press, 27–44.

Matsumura Takeo (1954–1958) *Nihon shinwa no kenkyū* (*A Study of the Japanese Myth*), 4 vols, Tokyo: Baifūkan.

Matsuoka Naomi (1993) 'Murakami Haruki and Raymond Carver: The American Scene' *Comparative Literature Studies*, 30 (4): 423–438.

—— (2002) 'Murakami Haruki and Anna Deavere Smith: Truth by Interview' *Comparative Literature Studies*, 39 (4): 305–313.

Matthews, P.H. (1997) *Oxford Concise Dictionary of Linguistics* (Oxford, U.K.: Oxford University Press

May, Stephen (ed.) (1999) *Critical Multiculturalism: Rethinking Multicultural and Antiracist Education*, London and Philadelphia: Falmer Press.

McGowan, John (1991) *Postmodernism and Its Critics*, Ithaca and London: Cornell University Press.

McGuigan, Jim (1999) *Modernity and Postmodern Culture*, Buckingham and Philadelphia: Open University Press.

McHale, Brian (1987) *Postmodernist Fiction*, New York and London: Methuen.

Merck, Mandy, Segal, Naomi and Wright, Elizabeth (eds) (1998) *Coming out of Feminism?*, Oxford, UK and Malden, MA: Blackwell.

Merleau-Ponty, Maurice (1962) *Phenomenology of Perception*, trans. Colin Smith, London and New York: Routledge & Kegan Paul.

Min, Tu-ki (1989) *National Polity and Local Power: The Transformation of Late Imperial China*, ed. Philip A. Kuhn and Timothy Brook, The Council on East Asian Studies/Harvard University and The Harvard-Yenching Institute, Cambridge, MA and London: Harvard University Press.

Mitchell, Juliet (1984) *Women: The Longest Revolution*, London: Virago Press.

Mitsui Takayuki and Washida Koyata (1989) *Yoshimoto Banana shinwa (A Yoshimoto Banana Myth)*, Tokyo: Seikyūsha.

Miura Masashi (1997) 'Murakami Haruki to kono jidai no rinri' ('Murakami Haruki and the Current Ethics') in Katō Norihiro et al. *Gunzō Nihon no sakka 26: Murakami Haruki*, Tokyo: Shōgakukan, 30–46.

Miyoshi Masao (1991) *Off Center*, Cambridge, MA and London, England: Harvard University Press.

Miyoshi Masao and Harootunian, H. D. (eds) (1989) *Postmodernism and Japan*, Durham and London: Duke University Press.

Mizuta Noriko (1982) *Hiroin kara hīrō e (From Heroine to Hero)*, Tokyo: Tabata shoten.

—— (1991) *Feminizumu no kanata: Josei hyōgen no shinsō (Beyond Feminism: The Deep Structure of Woman's Expression)*, Tokyo: Kōdansha.

—— (1993) *Monogatari to hanmonogatari no fūkei (Landscape of Monogatari and Anti-monogatari)*, Tokyo: Tabata shoten.

—— (2003) *20-seiki no josei hyōgen (The Woman's Expression in the 20th Century)*, Tokyo: Gakugei shorin.

—— (2004) *Joseigaku to no deai (An Encounter with Women's Studies)*, Tokyo: Shūeisha shinsho.

Mizuta Noriko (ed.) (1991) *New Feminism Review*, vol. 2, Tokyo: Gakuyoshobo.

Monnet, Livia (1996) 'Connaissance délicieuse, or the Science of Jealousy: Tsushima Yūko's "The Chrysanthemum Beetle"' in Schalow, Paul Gordon and Walker, Janet A. (eds) *The Woman's Hand: Gender and Theory in Japanese Women's Writing*, Stanford: Stanford University Press, 383–424.

—— (1998) 'Haha=tasha to shite no geijutsuka no serufu-pōtoreito' ('A Self-Portrait of the Artist as a Mother=Other') in Ikegami Yoshihiko (ed.) *Gendai shisō rinji zōkan gō: Sōtokushū Karatani Kōjin (An Extra Issue of Contemporary Thought: A Special Edition for Karatani Kōjin)*, 26 (9) July, Tokyo: Seidosha, 112–144.

Moore-Gilbert, Bart (2000) 'Spivak and Bhabha' in Schwarz, Henry and Ray, Sangeeta (eds) *A Companion to Postcolonial Studies*, Malden, MA and Oxford: Blackwell, 451–466.

Mori Ōgai (1977) *The Historical Literature of Mori Ōgai*, 2 vols, ed. David Dilworth and J. Thomas Rimer, Honolulu: University Press of Hawaii.

Morimura Osamu (1998) '*Risei no unmei*' ('The Fate of Reason') in Ikegami Yoshihiko (ed.) *Gendai shisō rinji zōkan gō: Sōtokushū Karatani Kōjin (An Extra Issue of Contemporary Thought: A Special Edition for Karatani Kōjin)*, 26 (9) July, Tokyo: Seidosha, 59–85.

Morton, Leith (2003) *Modern Japanese Culture: The Insider View*, South Melbourne: Oxford University Press.

Motoori Norinaga (1968) *Motoori Norinaga zenshū (Complete Works of Motoori Norinaga)*, vol. 1, Tokyo: Chikuma shobō.

Mukai Satoshi (1993) 'Shudai ni shūshite monogatari o ushinau: Murakami Haruki *Kokkyō no minami, taiyō no nishi*' ('Murakami Haruki Lost the Story by Sticking to the Theme: *South of the Border, West of the Sun*') *Bungakukai*, January, 300–303.

Murai Osamu (1995) *Zōho kaitei: Nantō ideorogī no hassei (The Birth of Southern Islands Ideology: An Enlarged and Revised Edition)*, Tokyo: Ōta shuppan.

Murakami Fuminobu (1988) 'Incest and Rebirth in *Kojiki*' *Monumenta Nipponica*, 43 (4): 455–463.

—— (1996) *Ideology and Narrative in Modern Japanese Literature*, Assen, Netherlands: Van Gorcum.

—— (2002a) 'Murakami Haruki's Postmodern World' *Japan Forum*, 14 (1): 127–141.

—— (2002b) 'Yoshimoto Takaaki and Globalisation' in *Proceedings of the International Conference on the East Asian Society and Culture in the Changing Period*, Tianjin, China: Tianjin People's Press, 140–150 (in Chinese).

Murakami Haruki (1979) *Kaze no uta o kike*, Tokyo: Kōdansha. Kōdansha bunko (1982). English translation *Hear the Wind Sing* (1987), trans. Alfred Birnbaum, Tokyo: Kodansha English Library.

—— (1980) *1973-nen no pinbōru*, Tokyo: Kōdansha. Kōdansha bunko (1983). English translation *Pinball, 1973* (1985), trans. Alfred Birnbaum, Tokyo: Kodansha English Library.

—— (1982) *Hitsuji o meguru bōken*, Tokyo: Kōdansha. Kōdansha bunko (1985). English translation *A Wild Sheep Chase* (1989), trans. Alfred Birnbaum, Tokyo: Kodansha English Library.

—— (1985) *Sekai no owari to hādoboirudo-wandārando*, Tokyo: Shinchōsha. Shinchō bunko (1988). English translation *The Hard-Boiled Wonderland and the End of the World* (1992), trans. Alfred Birnbaum, London, New York, Ringwood, Toronto and Auckland: Penguin.

—— (1987) *Noruwei no mori*, Tokyo: Kōdansha. Kōdansha bunko (1991). English translation *Norwegian Wood* (1989), trans. Alfred Birnbaum, Tokyo: Kodansha English Library.

—— (1988) *Dansu dansu dansu*, Tokyo: Kōdansha. Kōdansha bunko (1991). English translation *Dance Dance Dance* (1995), trans. Alfred Birnbaum, London, New York, Ringwood, Toronto and Auckland: Penguin.

—— (1990–1991) *Murakami Haruki zensakuhin 1979–1989* (*Complete Works of Murakami Haruki 1979–1989*), 8 vols, Tokyo: Kōdansha.

—— (1992) *Kokkyō no minami, taiyō no nishi*, Tokyo: Kōdansha. Kōdansha bunko (1995). English translation *South of the Border, West of the Sun* (1999), trans. Philip Gabriel, London: Harvill Press.

—— (1994–1995) *Nejimakidori kuronikuru*, Tokyo: Shinchōsha. English translation *The Wind-Up Bird Chronicle* (1997), trans. Jay Rubin, Knopf. Cited from the Panther paperback edition by Harvill Press (London).

—— (1995) 'Meikingu obu *Nejimakidori kuronikuru*' ('Making of *The Wind-Up Bird Chronicle*') *Shinchō*, November.

—— (1996a) 'Hon'yaku suru koto to, hon'yaku sareru koto' ('To Translate and To Be Translated') *Kokusai kōryū*, number 73, Tokyo: Japan Foundation.

—— (1999) *Supūtoniku no koibito*, Tokyo: Kōdansha. English translation *Sputnik Sweetheart* (2001), trans. Philip Gabriel, London: Harvill Press.

—— (2002) *Umibe no Kafuka* (*Kafka on the Shore*), 2 vols, Tokyo: Shinchōsha.

—— (2003) *Shōnen Kafuka* (*A Boy Kafka*), Tokyo: Shinchōsha.

Murakami Haruki and Kawai Hayao (1996) *Murakami Haruki, Kawai Hayao ni ai ni iku* (*Murakami Haruki Goes To See Kawai Hayao*), Tokyo: Iwanami.

Murakami Haruki and Kawamoto Saburō (1985) '"Monogatari" no tame no bōken' ('An Adventure for the sake of "Monogatari"') *Bungakukai*, August, 34–86, Tokyo: Bungei shunjūsha.

Murakami Haruki and Shibata Motoyuki (1989) 'Yagi san yūbin mitai ni meiroka shita sekai no naka de' ('In the Labyrinthine World of the Goat Postmen') *Eureka*, 21 (8) Tokyo: Seidosha.

Nakagami Kenji (1977) *Kareki nada* (*The Sea of Kareki*), Tokyo: Kawade shobō shinsha.

NAM Students (ed.) (2001) *NAM seisei* (*NAM Formation*), Tokyo: Ōta shuppan.

Napier, Susan Jolliffe (1991) *Escape from the Wasteland: Romanticism and Realism in the Fiction of Mishima Yukio and Ōe Kenzaburō*, Cambridge, MA: Harvard-Yenching Institute monograph series, number 33.

—— (1993) 'Panic Sites: The Japanese Imagination of Disaster from *Godzilla* to *Akira*' *Journal of Japanese Studies*, 19 (2).

—— (1996) *The Fantastic in Modern Japanese Literature: The Subversion of Modernity*, London and New York: Routledge.

Nelson, Cary and Grossberg, Lawrence (eds) (1988) *Marxism and the Interpretation of Culture*, Urbana and Chicago: University of Illinois Press.

Nicholson, Linda J. (ed.) (1990) *Feminism/Postmodernism*, New York and London: Routledge.

Nietzsche, Friedrich (1967) *On the Genealogy of Morals and Ecce Homo*, trans. Walter Kaufmann and R. J. Hollingdale, New York: Vintage Books.

—— (1968) *The Will to Power*, trans. Walter Kaufmann and R. J. Hollingdale, New York: Vintage Books.

Nihon kigō gakkai (Japanese Association for Semiotic Studies) (ed.) (1992) *Kigōgaku kenkyū* (*Studia Semiotica*), number 12, Tokyo: Tokai University Press.

Nishida Kitarō (1988) 'Watashi to nanji' ('I and You') in *Nishida Kitarō zenshū* (*Complete Works of Nishida Kitarō*), vol. 6, 341–427, Tokyo: Iwanami. Originally published in 1932.

Oda Motoko (1988) *Feminizumu hihyō: Rironka o mezashite* (*Feminist Criticism: For Theorisation*), Tokyo: Keisō shobō.

Ōe Kenzaburō (1971) *The Silent Cry*, Tokyo:Kodansha International.

——(1984) *Dōjidai gēmu* (*The Game of Contemporaneity*), Tokyo: Shinchō bunko. Originally published by Shinchōsha in 1979.

—— (1989) 'Japan's Dual Identity: A Writer's Dilemma' in Miyoshi Masao and Harootunian, H. D. (eds) *Postmodernism and Japan*, Durham and London: Duke University Press, 189–213.

Okabayashi Hiroshi (ed.) (1991) *Posutomodan to esunikku* (*Postmodern and Ethnic*), Tokyo: Keisō shobō.

Okakura Tenshin (1903) *Ideals of the East* (London: Murray, 1903)

—— (1904) *The Awaking of Japan* (New York: Century, 1904)

—— (1906) *The Book of Tea* (New York: Fox, Duffield)

Oketani Hideaki (1992) *Shōwa seishin shi* (*A Spiritual History of Shōwa*), Tokyo: Bungei shunjūsha. Bunshun bunko (1996).

—— (2000) *Shōwa seishin shi: Sengo hen* (*A Spiritual History of Shōwa: Postwar Period*), Tokyo: Bungei shunjūsha. Bunshun bunko (2003).

O'Leary, Brendan (1989) *The Asiatic Mode of Production: Oriental Despotism, Historical Materialism and Indian History*, Oxford, UK and Cambridge, MA: Basil Blackwell.

Olson, Carl (1992) *The Theology and Philosophy of Eliade: A Search for the Centre*, Basingstoke, Hampshire: Macmillan.

Olson, Lawrence (1978) 'Intellectuals and "The People": On Yoshimoto Takaaki' *Journal of Japanese Studies*, 4 (2).

Ōtsuka Eiji (1990) *Kodomo ryūritan* (*A Story of Wandering Children*), Tokyo: Shin'yōsha.

Parsons, Charles (1984) 'The Liar Paradox' in Martin, L. Robert (ed.) *Recent Essays on Truth and the Liar Paradox*, Oxford: Clarendon Press; New York: Oxford University Press, 9–45.

Philippi, Donald L. (trans.) (1968) *Kojiki*, Tokyo: University of Tokyo Press.

Plattner, Marc F. and Smolar Aleksander (eds) (2000) *Globalization, Power, and Democracy*, Baltimore and London: Johns Hopkins University Press.

Proudhon, Pierre-Joseph (1969) *Selected Writings of Pierre-Joseph Proudhon*, ed. with intro Stewart Edwards, trans. Elizabeth Fraser, London: Macmillan.

—— (1994) *What is Property?*, ed. and trans. Donald R. Kelley and Bonnie G. Smith, Cambridge, New York and Oakleigh: Cambridge University Press.

Quayson, Ato (2000) 'Postcolonialism and Postmodernism' in Schwarz, Henry and Ray, Sangeeta (eds) *A Companion to Postcolonial Studies*, Malden, MA and Oxford: Blackwell, 87–111.

Raffel, Stanley (1992) *Habermas, Lyotard and the Concept of Justice*, Basingstoke, Hampshire: Macmillan.

Rattansi, Ali (1999) 'Racism, "Postmodernism" and Reflexive Multiculturalism' in May, Stephen (ed.) *Critical Multiculturalism: Rethinking Multicultural and Antiracist Education*, London and Philadelphia: Falmer Press, 77–112.

Reiter, Rayna R. (ed.) (1975) *Toward an Anthropology of Women*, New York and London: Monthly Review Press.

Rich, Adrienne (1980) 'Compulsory Heterosexuality and Lesbian Existence' *Signs*, Summer, 5: 631–660. The article was later compiled in Rich, Adrienne (1986) *Blood, Bread(,) and Poetry: Selected Prose 1978–1985*, London: Virago Press, 23–75 and also in Abelove, Henry, Barale, Michèle Aina and Haplerin, David M. (eds) (1993) *Lesbian and Gay Studies Reader*, New York and London: Routledge, 227–254.

—— (1986) *Blood, Bread(,) and Poetry: Selected Prose 1978–1985*, London: Virago Press.

Rorty, Richard (1989) *Contingency, Irony, and Solidarity*, Cambridge: Cambridge University Press.

Rubin, Gayle (1975) 'The Traffic in Women: Notes on the "Political Economy" of Sex' in Reiter, Rayna R. (ed.) *Toward an Anthropology of Women*, New York and London: Monthly Review Press, 157–210.

—— (1984) 'Thinking Sex: Notes for a Radical Theory of the Politics of Sexuality' in Vance, Carole S. (ed.) *Pleasure and Danger: Exploring Female Sexuality*, Boston, London, Melbourne and Henley-on-Thames: Routledge & Kegan Paul, 267–319. This paper was later reprinted in Kauffman, Linda S. (ed.) (1993) *American Feminist Thought at Century's End: A Reader*, Cambridge, MA and Oxford, UK: Blackwell, 3–64; and in Abelove, Henry, Barale, Michèle Aina and Haplerin, David M. (eds) (1993) *Lesbian and Gay Studies Reader*, New York and London: Routledge, 3–44.

Rubin, Gayle with Judith Butler (1998) 'Sexual Traffic' in Merck, Mandy, Segal, Naomi and Wright, Elizabeth (eds) *Coming out of Feminism?*, Oxford, UK and Malden, MA: Blackwell, 36–73. First appeared in *differences*, 6 (2)–(3), Summer–Fall, 1994.

Rubin, Jay (1992) 'The Other World of Murakami Haruki' *Japan Quarterly* 39 (4): 490–500.

—— (1999) 'Murakami Haruki's Two Poor Aunts Tell Everything They Know about Sheep, Wells, Unicorns, Proust, Elephants, and Magpies' in Snyder, Stephen and Gabriel, Philip (eds) *Ōe and Beyond*, Honolulu: University of Hawaii Press, 177–197.

—— (2003) *Haruki Murakami and the Music of Words*, London: Harvill Press.

Saegusa Kazuko (1991) *Ren'ai shōsetsu no kansei* (*Trap of Love Story*), Tokyo: Seidosha.

Saitō Eiji (1993) 'Gendai no gōsuto sutōrī – Murakami Haruki *Kokkyō no minami, taiyō no nishi*' ('The Contemporary Ghost Story: Murakami Haruki *South of the Border, West of the Sun*') *Shinchō*, February, Tokyo: Shinchōsha.

Sakai Naoki (1991) *Voices of the Past: The Status of Language in Eighteenth-Century Japanese Discourse*, Ithaca and London: Cornell University Press.

—— (1997) *Nihon shisō to iu mondai: Hon'yaku to shutai* (*The Problem of Japanese Thoughts: Translation and Subjectivity*), Tokyo: Iwanami. English version *Translation and Subjectivity: On Japan and Cultural Nationalism* (1997), Minneapolis and London: University of Minnesota Press.

Sardar, Ziauddin (1998) *Postmodernism and the Other: The New Imperialism of Western Culture*, London and Sterling, Virginia: Pluto Press.

Schalow, Paul Gordon and Walker, Janet A. (eds) (1996) *The Woman's Hand: Gender and Theory in Japanese Women's Writing*, Stanford: Stanford University Press.

Schwarz, Henry and Ray, Sangeeta (eds) (2000) *A Companion to Postcolonial Studies*, Malden, MA and Oxford: Blackwell.

Scott, Joan W. (1990) 'Deconstructing Equality-Versus-Difference: Or, the Uses of Poststructuralist Theory for Feminism' in Hirsch, Marianne and Keller, Evelyn Fox (eds) *Conflicts in Feminism*, New York and London: Routledge.

Sedgwick, Eve Kosofsky (1985) *Between Men*, New York: Columbia University Press.

—— (1991) *Epistemology of the Closet*, Hertfordshire: Harvester Wheatsheaf.

Sekii Mitsuo (ed.) (1995) *Karatani Kōjin*, Tokyo: Shibundō.

Sengoku Yoshirō (ed.) (1994) *Modan to posutomodan: Gendai shakaigaku kara no sekkin* (*The Modern and the Postmodern: Approach from Contemporary Sociology*), Kyoto: Hōritsubunkasha.

Sherif, Ann (1999) 'Japanese Without Apology: Yoshimoto Banana and Healing' in Snyder, Stephen and Gabriel, Philip (eds) *Ōe and Beyond*, Honolulu: University of Hawaii Press, 278–301.

Shindō Masahiro (1995a) 'Gaibu/Naibu' ('Outside/Inside') in Sekii Mitsuo (ed.) *Karatani Kōjin*, Tokyo: Shibundō, 168.

—— (1995b) '*Taido no henkō* (The Change of Attitude)' in Sekii Mitsuo (ed.) *Karatani Kōjin*, Tokyo: Shibundō, 183.

Silverman, Kaja (1992) *Male Subjectivity at the Margins*, New York and London: Routledge.

Simmel, Georg (1971) *On Individuality and Social Forms: Selected Writings*, ed. Donald N. Levine, Chicago: University of Chicago Press.

Singer, Linda (1992) 'Feminism and Postmodernism' in Butler, Judith and Scott, Joan W. (eds) *Feminists Theorize the Political*, New York and London: Routledge, 464–475.

Skov, Lise and Moeran, Brian (eds) (1995) *Women, Media and Consumption in Japan*, Richmond, Surrey: Curzon Press.

Snyder, Stephen and Gabriel, Philip (eds) (1999) *Ōe and Beyond*, Honolulu: University of Hawaii Press.

Sokal, Alan and Bricmont, Jean (1998) *Fashionable Nonsense: Postmodern Intellectuals' Abuse of Science*, New York: Picador.

Sone Hiroyoshi (1991) 'Kaisetsu' ('Explanatory Notes') in Yoshimoto Banana, *Kitchin*, Fukutake bunko.

Soyinka, Wole (1990; original 1976) *Myth, Literature and the African World*, Cambridge, New York and Oakleigh: Cambridge University Press.

Spivak, Gayatri Chakravorty (1987) *In Other Worlds: Essay in Cultural Politics*, New York and London: Methuen.

—— (1988) 'Can the Subaltern Speak?' in Nelson, Cary and Grossberg, Lawrence (eds) *Marxism and the Interpretation of Culture*, Urbana and Chicago: University of Illinois Press.

—— (1990) *The Post-Colonial Critic: Interviews, Strategies, Dialogues*, ed. Sarah Harasym, New York and London: Routledge.

—— (1999) *A Critique of Postcolonial Reason: Toward a History of the Vanishing Present*, Cambridge, MA: Harvard University Press.

Stewart, Kathleen (1988) 'Nostalgia – A Polemic' *Cultural Anthropology*, 3 (3): 227–240.

Stewart, Susan (1984) *On Longing: Narratives of the Miniature, the Gigantic, the Souvenir, the Collection*, Baltimore and London: Johns Hopkins University Press.

Strecher, Matthew C. (1998a) 'Murakami Haruki: Japan's Coolest Writer Heats Up' *Japan Quarterly*, 45 (1).

—— (1998b) 'Beyond "Pure" Literature: Mimesis, Formula, and the Postmodern in the Fiction of Murakami Haruki' *Journal of Asian Studies*, 57 (2).

—— (1999) 'Magical Realism and the Search for Identity in the Fiction of Murakami Haruki' *Journal of Japanese Studies*, 25 (2).

—— (2002a) *Dances With Sheep: The Quest for Identity in the Fiction of Murakami Haruki*, Ann Arbor: University of Michigan Press.

—— (2002b) *Haruki Murakami's The Wind-Up Bird Chronicle*, New York and London: Continuum International Publishing Group Inc.

Suzuki Tomi (1996) *Narrating the Self*, Stanford: Stanford University Press.

Takeda Seiji (1996) *Sekai to iu hairi* (*Irrationality Called the World*), Tokyo: Kōdansha gakujutsu bunko. Originally published by Kawade shobō shinsha in 1988.

—— (1998) '"Ren'ai shōsetsu" no kūkan' ('Space of "Love Novel"') in Kimata Satoshi (ed.) (1998) *Murakami Haruki: Nihon bungaku kenkyū ronbun shūsei* (*Murakami Haruki: Collection of Research Papers on Japanese Literature*), vol. 46, Tokyo: Wakakusa shobō. Originally published in *Gunzō*, March 1988.

Takemura Kazuko (1996) '<Genjitsukai> wa hirekishiteki ni seika sarete iruka? –feminizumu to Žižek' ('Is <Reality> Non-historically Sexualised?: Feminism and Žižek') *Gendai shisō* (*Contemporary Thought*), 24 (15) December, Tokyo: Seidosha.

—— (2000) *Feminizumu* (*Feminism*), Tokyo: Iwanami.

—— (2002) *Ai ni tsuite: Aidentitī to yokubō no seijigaku* (*On Love: Identity, Desire, and Politics*), Tokyo: Iwanami.

Tarski, Alfred (1956) *Logic, Semantics, Metamathematics: Papers From 1923 to 1938*, trans. J. H. Woodger, London: Oxford University Press.

Tayama Katai (1981) *The Quilt and Other Stories by Tayama Katai*, trans. Kenneth G. Henshall, Tokyo: University of Tokyo Press.

Todorov, Tzvetan (1973) *The Fantastic*, trans. Richard Howard, Cleveland, OH: Press of Case Western Reserve University.

Treat, John Whittier (1993) 'Yoshimoto Banana Writes Home: *Shōjo* Culture and the Nostalgic Subject' *Journal of Japanese Studies*, 19 (2).

—— (1995) 'Yoshimoto Banana's *Kitchen*, or the Cultural Logic of Japanese Consumerism' in Skov, Lise and Moeran, Brian (eds) *Women, Media and Consumption in Japan*, Richmond, Surrey: Curzon Press.

Tsuchiya Keiichirō (1998) *Posutomodan no seiji to shūkyō* (*Postmodern Politics and Religion*), Tokyo: Iwanami.

Tsuge Teruhiko (1999) 'Enkan/Takai/Media – *Supūtoniku no koibito* kara no tenbō' ('Circle/Other World/Media: A Prospect from *Sputnik Sweetheart*') in Kuritsubo Yoshiki and Tsuge Teruhiko (eds) *Murakami Haruki sutadeizu* (*Murakami Haruki Studies*), Tokyo: Wakakusa shobō, vol. V: 5–37.

Turner, Bryan S. (1987) 'A Note on Nostalgia' *Theory Culture & Society*, 4 (1) February.

Tymn, Marshall B., Zahorski, Kenneth J., and Boyer, Robert H. (1979) *Fantasy Literature*, New York and London: R. R. Bowker Company.

Ueno Chizuko (1986) *Onna to iu kairaku* (*The Pleasure to be a Woman*), Tokyo: Keisō shobō.

—— (1989) *Sukāto no shita no gekijō* (*Theatre in the Skirt*), Tokyo: Kawade shobō shinsha.

—— (1990a) *Kafuchōsei to shihonsei: Marx shugi to feminizumu no chihei* (*The Patriarchy and Capitalism: Horizon of Marxism and Feminism*), Tokyo: Iwanami.

—— (1990b) *Middonaito kōru* (*Midnight Call*), Tokyo: Asahi shinbunsha.

—— (1994) *Kindai kazoku no seiritsu to shūen* (*The Birth and Death of Modern Family*), Tokyo: Iwanami.

—— (1998a) *Hatsujō sōchi: Erosu no shinario* (*The Erotic Apparatus: Scenario of Eros*), Tokyo: Chikuma shobō.

—— (1998b) *Nashonarizumu to jendā* (*Engendering Nationalism*), Tokyo: Seidosha.

—— (2000) *Ueno Chizuko ga bungaku o shakaigaku suru* (*Ueno Chizuko Studies Literature from a Sociological Perspective*), Tokyo: Asahi shinbunsha.

—— (2002) *Sai no seijigaku* (*Politics of Difference*), Tokyo: Iwanami.

Ueno Chizuko (ed.) (1990) *New Feminism Review*, vol. 1, Tokyo: Gakuyoshobo.

Ueno Chizuko and Ogura Chikako (2002) *Za feminizumu* (*The Feminism*), Tokyo: Chikuma shobō.

Ueno Chizuko, Ogura Chikako and Tomioka Taeko (1992) *Danryū bungaku ron* (*On Men Writers*), Tokyo: Chikuma shobō.

Urushida Kazuyo (1987) 'Joseigaku-teki bungaku kenkyū no chihei' ('The Horizon of Literary Studies From the Viewpoint of Women's Studies') in *Kōza joseigaku* (*Women's Studies Lecture Series*), vol. 4, Tokyo: Keisō shobō.

Vance, Carole S. (ed.) (1984) *Pleasure and Danger: Exploring Female Sexuality*, Boston, London, Melbourne and Henley-on-Thames: Routledge & Kegan Paul.

Vincent, Keith, Kazama Takashi and Kawaguchi Kazuya (1997) *Gei sutadeizu* (*Gay Studies*), Tokyo: Seidosha.

Walker, Nancy A. (1990) *Feminist Alternatives: Irony and Fantasy in the Contemporary Novel by Women*, Jackson and London: University Press of Mississippi.

Walley, Glynne (1997) 'Two Murakamis and Their American Influence' *Japan Quarterly*, 44 (1): 41–50.

Warhol, Robyn R. and Herndl, Diane Price (eds) (1991) *Feminisms: An Anthology of Literary Theory and Criticism*, New Brunswick, NJ: Rutgers University Press.

Washida Koyata (1992) *Zōho Yoshimoto Takaaki ron* (*On Yoshimoto Takaaki: An Enlarged Edition*), Tokyo: San'ichi shobō.

Watanabe Kazuko (1993) *Feminizumu shōsetsu ron* (*Feminist Theory of Novel*), Tokyo: Tsuge shobō.

Watsuji Tetsurō (1934) *Ningen no gaku to shite no rinrigaku* (*Ethics as a Study of Man*), Tokyo: Iwanami zensho.

Weaver, Jace (1997) *That the People Might Live: Native American Literatures and Native American Community*, New York and Oxford: Oxford University Press.

—— (2000) 'Indigenousness and Indigeneity' in Schwarz, Henry and Ray, Sangeeta (eds) *A Companion to Postcolonial Studies*, Malden, MA and Oxford: Blackwell, 221–235.

Weaver, Jace (ed.) (1996) *Defending Mother Earth: Native American Perspectives on Environmental Justice*, Maryknoll, NY: Orbis Books.

Weber, Max (1991) *From Max Weber: Essays in Sociology*, trans. and ed. with intro H. H. Gerth and C. Wright Mills, London: Routledge.

Westermarck, Edward (1968) *A Short History of Marriage*, New York: Humanities Press.

Whitehead, Alfred North and Russell, Bertrand (1910) *Principia Mathematica*, 3 vols, Cambridge: Cambridge University Press.

Wittgenstein, Ludwig (1958) *Philosophical Investigations*, 2nd edn, trans. G. E. M. Anscombe, Oxford, UK and Cambridge, MA: Blackwell.

Wittig, Monique (1992) *The Straight Mind and Other Essays*, New York, London, Toronto, Sydney, Tokyo and Singapore: Harvester Wheatsheaf.

Yamagata Kazumi (ed.) (1997) *Sai to dōitsuka: Posutokoroniaru bungaku ron* (*Difference and Identification: Postcolonial Literary Theory*), Tokyo: Kenkyūsha.

Yanagita Kunio (1960) 'Meiji Taishō shi: Sesō hen' ('A Meiji and Taishō History: Part of Aspects of Life') in *Teihon Yanagita Kunio shū* (*The Standard Edition of Collected Works of Yanagita Kunio*), vol. 24, Tokyo: Chikuma shobō. Originally published by Asahi shinbunsha (Tokyo) in 1931.

Yaqūb, Aladdin Mahmud (1993) *The Liar Speaks the Truth: A Defense of the Revision Theory of Truth*, New York and Oxford: Oxford University Press.

Yokoo Kazuhiro (1994) *Murakami Haruki x 90 nendai* (*Murakami Haruki x 1990s*), Tokyo: Daisan shokan.

Yonaha Keiko (1986) *Gendai joryū sakka ron* (*On Contemporary Women Writers*), Tokyo: Shinbisha.

Yoshida Haruo (1997) *Murakami Haruki, tenkan suru* (*Murakami Haruki, Changing*), Tokyo: Sairyūsha.

Yoshimoto Banana (1988a) *Kitchin*, Tokyo: Fukutake. Fukutake bunko (1991). English translation *Kitchen* (1993), trans. Megan Backus, New York, London, Toronto, Sydney, Tokyo and Singapore: Washington Square Press.

—— (1988b) *Utakata/Sankuchuari* (*Fleeting Bubbles/Sanctuary*), Tokyo: Fukutake. Fukutake bunko (1991).

—— (1988c) *Kanashii yokan* (*A Sad Premonition*), Tokyo: Kadokawa. Kadokawa bunko (1991).

—— (1989a) *Tugumi*, Tokyo: Chūō kōron shinsha. Chūkō bunko (1992). English translation *Goodbye Tsugumi* (2002), trans. Michael Emmerich, New York: Grove Press.

—— (1989b) *Shirakawa yofune*, Tokyo: Fukutake. Fukutake bunko (1992). English translation *Asleep* (2000), trans. Michael Emmerich, London: faber and faber.

—— (1990) *N.P.*, Tokyo: Kadokawa. Kadokawa bunko (1992). English translation *N.P.* (1994), trans. Ann Sherif, London and Boston: faber and faber.

—— (1993) *Tokage*, Tokyo: Shinchōsha. Shinchō bunko (1993), English translation *Lizard* (1995), trans. Ann Sherif, New York, London, Toronto, Sydney, Tokyo and Singapore: Pocket Books (Simon & Schuster Inc.).

—— (1994a) *Amurita*, Tokyo: Fukutake. Kadokawa bunko (1997). English translation *Amrita* (1997), trans. Russell F. Wasden, London: faber and faber.

—— (1994b) *Banana no Banana* (*Banana's Banana*), Tokyo: Metarōgu.

—— (1994c) *Hachi-kō no saigo no koibito* (*Hachi's Last Girlfriend*), Tokyo: Metarōgu. Chūkō bunko (1998).

—— (1994d) *Marika no nagai yoru* (*Marika's Long Night*)/*Bari yume nikki* (*Bali, Dream Diary*), Tokyo: Gentōsha. Gentōsha bunko (1997).

—— (1996) *SLY*, Tokyo: Gentōsha. Gentōsha bunko (1999).

—— (1997) *Honeymoon*, Tokyo: Chūōkōronsha. Chūkō bunko (2000).

—— (1999) *Hard-boiled, Hard-luck*, Tokyo: Rockin'On. Gentōsha bunko (2001).

—— (2000a) *Furin to nanbei* (*Adultery and South America*), Tokyo: Gentōsha.

—— (2000b) *Karada wa zenbu shitteiru* (*The Body Knows Everything*), Tokyo: Bungei shunjūsha.

—— (2002a) *Yoshimotobanana.com*, Tokyo: Gentōsha.

—— (2002b) *Niji* (*Rainbow*), Tokyo: Gentōsha.

—— (2002c) *Ōkoku: Sono 1* (*Kingdom: volume 1*), Tokyo: Shinchōsha.

—— (2003a) *Hagoromo* (*The Robe of Feathers*), Tokyo: Shinchōsha.

—— (2003b) *Deddoendo no omoide* (*Memories of Dead-End*), Tokyo: Bungei shunjūsha.

—— (2004) *Ōkoku: Sono 2* (*Kingdom: volume 2*), Tokyo: Shinchōsha.

Yoshimoto Banana and Kawai Hayao (2002) *Naruhodo no taiwa* (*Dialogue of 'I See'*), Tokyo: NHK shuppan.

Yoshimoto Takaaki (1968–1975) *Yoshimoto Takaaki zen chosaku shū* (*Complete Works of Yoshimoto Takaaki*), 15 vols, Tokyo: Keisō shobō.

—— (1968–1975) *Yoshimoto Takaaki zen chosaku shū (Zoku)* (*Complete Works of Yoshimoto Takaaki: Continued*), 15 vols, Tokyo: Keisō shobō.

—— (1980–1981) 'Ajia-teki to iu koto 1–4' ('Things Asiatic') in Yoshimoto Takaaki et al. (2002) *Dokyumento Yoshimoto Takaaki: <Ajia-teki> to iu koto* (*Document Yoshimoto Takaaki: Things Asiatic*), Tokyo: Yudachisha. Originally published in a Journal *Shikō*, numbers 54–57 (May 1980 to October 1981).

—— (1981) *Shomotsu no kaitaigaku* (*Anatomy of Books*), Tokyo: Chūkō bunko.

—— (1982a) *Kaitei shinpan: Gengo ni totte bi towa nani ka* (*What is Beauty for Language?: A Revised New Edition*), 2 vols, Tokyo: Kadokawa bunko.

—— (1982b) *Kaitei shinpan: Kyōdō gensō ron* (*A Theory of Collective Fantasy: A Revised New Edition*), Tokyo: Kadokawa bunko.

—— (1982c) *Kaitei Shinpan: Shin-teki genshō ron josetsu* (*An Introduction to the Theory of Mental Phenomena: A Revised New Edition*), Tokyo: Kadokawa bunko.

—— (1983–1993) *<Shin> no kōzō* (*The Structure of <Belief>*), 4 vols, Tokyo: Shunjūsha.

—— (1984) *Sekai ninshiki no hōhō* (*The Way of Recognising the World*), Tokyo: Chūkō bunko.

—— (1986–1988) *Yoshimoto Takaaki zenshū sen* (*Selected Complete Works of Yoshimoto Takaaki*), 8 vols, Tokyo: Yamato shobō.

—— (1987) *Yoshimoto Takaaki taidanshū: Yorokobashii kaikō* (*Collection of Table Discussion of Yoshimoto Takaaki: A Joyful Encounter*), Tokyo: Seidosha.

—— (1990) *Hai edipusu ron – Kotai gensō no yukue –* (*On the High Oedipus: The Future of Self-fantasy*), Tokyo: Gensōsha.

—— (1995) *Ten Poems For Transposition* (*Ten'i no tameno 10 pen*), trans. Miyagi Ken, Tokyo: Sunakoya shobō.

—— (1996a) *Miyazawa Kenji*, Tokyo: Chikuma gakugei bunko, originally published by Chikuma shobō in 1989.

—— (1996b) *Yoshimoto Takaaki no bunkagaku: Pure-Ajiateki to iu koto* (*A Cultural Studies of Yoshimoto Takaaki: On the Pre-Asian Pratique*), Tokyo: Bunka kagaku kōtō kenkyūin.

—— (1998a) *Isho* (*Testament*), Tokyo: Kadokawa.

—— (1998b) *Afuricateki dankai ni tsuite* (*On the African Stage*), Tokyo: Shunjūsha.

Yoshimoto Takaaki et al. (2002) *Dokyumento Yoshimoto Takaaki: <Ajia-teki> to iu koto* (*Document Yoshimoto Takaaki: Things Asiatic*), Tokyo: Yudachisha.

Yoshimoto Takaaki and Baudrillard, Jean (1995) *Seikimatsu o kataru* (*Talk on the End of the Century*), Tokyo: Kinokuniya.

Yoshimoto Takaaki and Foucault, Michel (1984) 'Sekai ninshiki no hōhō' ('The Way of Recognising the World') in Yoshimoto *Sekai ninshiki no hōhō* (*The Way of Recognising the World*), Tokyo: Chūkō bunko.

Yoshimoto Takaaki and Yoshimoto Banana (1997) *Yoshimoto Takaaki x Yoshimoto Banana*, Tokyo: Rockin'On.

Young, Robert (1990) *White Mythologies: Writing History and the West*, London and New York: Routledge.

Žižek, Slavoj (1989) *The Sublime Object of Ideology*, London and New York: Verso.

—— (1994) *The Metastases of Enjoyment: Six Essays on Woman and Causality*, London and New York: Verso.

Index